SONGS OF TRUE ACCOMPLISHMENT

Commentaries on Naropa and Jamgön Kongtrül's Songs

Rangjung Yeshe Books • *www.rangjung.com*

Padmasambhava: *Treasures from Juniper Ridge* • *Advice from the Lotus-Born* • *Dakini Teachings* • *Following in Your Footsteps: The Lotus-Born Guru in Nepal* • *Following in Your Footsteps: The Lotus-Born Guru in India*

Padmasambhava and Jamgön Kongtrül: *The Light of Wisdom, Vol. 1, Vol. 2, Vol. 3, Secret, Vol. 4 & Vol. 5*

Padmasambhava, Chokgyur Lingpa, Jamyang Khyentse Wangpo, Tulku Urgyen Rinpoche, Orgyen Tobgyal Rinpoche, & others

Dispeller of Obstacles • *The Tara Compendium* • *Powerful Transformation* • *Dakini Activity*

Yeshe Tsogyal: *The Lotus-Born*

Dakpo Tashi Namgyal: *Clarifying the Natural State*

Tsele Natsok Rangdröl: *Mirror of Mindfulness* • *Heart Lamp* • *Empowerment and Samaya*

Chokgyur Lingpa: *Ocean of Amrita* • *The Great Gate* • *Skillful Grace* • *Great Accomplishment* • *Guru Heart Practices*

Traktung Dudjom Lingpa: *A Clear Mirror*

Jamgön Mipham Rinpoche: *Gateway to Knowledge, Vol. 1, Vol. 2, Vol. 3 & Vol. 4*

Tulku Urgyen Rinpoche: *Blazing Splendor* • *Rainbow Painting* • *As It Is, Vol. 1 & Vol. 2* • *Vajra Speech* • *Repeating the Words of the Buddha* • *Dzogchen Deity Practice* • *Vajra Heart Revisited*

Adeu Rinpoche: *Freedom in Bondage*

Khenchen Thrangu Rinpoche: *Crystal Clear* • *Songs of True Accomplishment*

Chökyi Nyima Rinpoche: *Bardo Guidebook* • *Collected Works of Chökyi Nyima Rinpoche, Vol. 1 & Vol. 2*

Tulku Thondup: *Enlightened Living*

Orgyen Tobgyal Rinpoche: *Life & Teachings of Chokgyur Lingpa* • *Straight Talk* • *Sublime Lady of Immortality*

Dzigar Kongtrül Rinpoche: *Uncommon Happiness*

Tsoknyi Rinpoche: *Fearless Simplicity* • *Carefree Dignity*

Marcia dechen wangmo: *Dzogchen Primer* • *Dzogchen Essentials* • *Quintessential Dzogchen* • *Confessions of a Gypsy Yogini* • *Precious Songs of Awakening Compilation*

Erik Pema Kunsang: *Wellsprings of the Great Perfection* • *A Tibetan Buddhist Companion* • *The Rangjung Yeshe Tibetan-English Dictionary of Buddhist Culture & Perfect Clarity*

chokgyur lingpa, jamgön kongtrül, jamyang khyentse wangpo, adeu rinpoche, and orgyen topgyal rinpoche • *The Tara Compendium Feminine Principles Discovered*

SONGS OF TRUE ACCOMPLISHMENT

Commentaries on Naropa and Jamgön Kongtrül's Songs

Khenchen Thrangu Rinpoche

Foreword by Chökyi Nyima Rinpoche

Translated by Erik Pema Kunsang

Edited by Marcia Binder Schmidt

Rangjung Yeshe PUBLICATIONS

Boudhanath, Hong Kong & Esby

2006

Rangjung Yeshe Publications
526 Entrada Drive, Apt. 201
Novato, CA 94949 USA

Address emails to:
Rangjung Yeshe Publications
C/O Above
www.rangjung.com
www.lotustreasure.com

First paperback edition published in 2025

Printed in the United States of America

Distributed to the book trade by:
Publishers Group West/Ingram

ISBN13: 978-1-7328717-4-5 (pbk)

Title: *Songs of True Accomplishment*
Sub. Commentaries on Naropa and Jamgön Kongtrül's Songs

Thrangu Rinpoche, Khenchen (b. 1933-2023). Translated from the Tibetan by Erik Pema Kunsang (Erik Hein Schmidt). Edited by Marcia Binder Schmidt.

1. Vajrayana—Tradition of Pith Instructions
2. Buddhism—Tibet

Photo on opposite page by Karma Jangchub

Thrangru Rinpoche

DEDICATION

May this collection of Songs of True Accomplishment *from two great masters bring about the swift rebirth of the Great Lion of Speech, Khenchen Thrangu Rinpoche.*

by Gloria Jones

CONTENTS

FOREWORD

The main practice in the Kagyü teaching system is Mahamudra. The lineage of Mahamudra chiefly comes through Marpa Lotsawa's two root gurus, Naropa and Maitripa. The texts explained here — A Summary of Mahamudra and The View, Concisely Put — were spoken by Naropa.

Naropa's songs are very important for practitioners of Mahamudra, pithy words, rich with meaning. This is why I chose to teach them during my courses. The songs and my explanations are now translated by lotsawa Erik. These teachings are about essential meditation training. I consider them very important for future students to pay attention to and study. Doing so will greatly benefit one's understanding of the key points of Mahamudra.

—Khenchen Thrangu Rinpoche

PREFACE

Khenchen Thrangu Rinpoche was born with an exceptionally high intelligence as the result of former training. He was a sublime being whose eminent character never departed from loving kindness and compassion. More specifically, he was a great Buddhist teacher possessing the three qualities of learning, pure conduct and noble-mindedness. He is also an expert in exposition, debate, and composition. He has ascended within the Karma Kagyü school to the lofty position of a Khenchen, a great pandita whose mastery encompasses both the scriptures and the traditional sciences.

Given in the style of pith instructions, these profound lectures on the key points of two songs by Naropa, are accompanied by an explanation of the lord of the Dharma, Jamgön Lodrö Thaye's song of experience in Mahamudra. It is, therefore, my request that all Dharma practitioners take the meaning of these extremely precious teachings to heart and make it a personal experience through correct practice. Please treasure this Dharma book with great care and appreciation.

—Chökyi Nyima Rinpoche

The View, Concisely Put

In Sanskrit: Adhi Siddhi Sama Nama.
In Tibetan: *lta ba mdor bsdus pa zhes bya ba*, [Tawa Dordüpa].
In English: The View, Concisely Put.

Homage to the Vajra Dakini!

To the omniscient lord of refuge,
The protector of beings, I pay homage!

After pursuing statements and reasoning
I have condensed and established the true meaning.

All these apparent and existing phenomena
Are nowhere apart from mind, your own awareness.
Since it perceives and is cognizant,
It is like experience that is self-known.

If this mind was not like that,
There would be no link and therefore no experience.
This is how I have established the relative:
"Understand that all phenomena are based on mind," as it is said.

The very basis of phenomena, which is mind essence,
Can be analyzed, dissected with reasoning, and so forth,
But this naturally luminous mind
And the momentary defilement of thought, these two,
Whether they are one or different
Is a topic of extreme profundity.
Because of this depth, scholars analyze.
Though they explain, I shall not write about it here.

This mind that knows emptiness
Is itself the awakened mind, bodhichitta.
The buddha potential is just this.
The sugata essence is just this.

Because of tasting what is,
It is also the great bliss.
The understanding of Secret Mantra is just this.
Means and knowledge is just this.

The vast and profound is just this.
Samantabhadra with consort is just this.
This space and wisdom, perceiving while being empty,
Is what is called 'knowing original enlightenment.'

This self-knowing, while one is still defiled,
Does not depend on other things,
So self-existing wakefulness is just this.

Being aware, it is cognizance.
A natural knowing that is free of thought.
This self-knowing cannot possibly form thoughts.

Without conceptualizing a 'mind,'
Since it is not something to be conceived,
This original wakefulness, cognizant yet thought-free,
Is like the wisdom of the Tathagata.

Therefore, it is taught, "Realize that luminous mind
Is the mind of original wakefulness,
And don't seek an enlightenment separate from that."

Nevertheless, this mind does become disturbed
By the defilement of momentary thoughts.
Like water, like gold, like the sky,
It may be either pure or impure.

But the naturally luminous mind
Is free from even a hair-tip of concrete substance,
Like the analogy of a sky flower.

It does not exist as it seems to be,
Therefore, it cannot be established to be nonexistent.
As everything is mutually dependent,
When one side is invalid, the other side also does not exist.

Mind is neither existent nor nonexistent,
Since each of these [constructs] is negated.
It is also not both,
Since existing and not existing are a contradiction.
It is not a living being
Nor other than living beings.

Therefore, it is free from all constructs.
This is how I have established the ultimate:
"Mind is based on space," as it is said.

This unconstructed self-knowing
Perceives while empty, and while empty it perceives.
Experience and emptiness are therefore indivisible,
Like the analogy of the moon in water.
This is how I have established nonduality:
"Space is not based on anything," as it is said.

This unconstructed self-knowing
Is itself the very basis of samsara.
Nirvana as well is also just this.
The Great Middle Way is also just this.
That to be seen is also just this.
That to train in is also just this.
That to attain is also just this.
The valid truth is also just this.

The renowned threefold tantras
Of basic cause, method, and result,
And what is known as ground, path, and fruition,
Are just different situations of this.

The basic consciousness, the all-ground,
And all possible aggregates in samsara,
Are known as the 'dependent,' and so forth.

Emaho!
The creations of this mind essence, while one is still defiled,
The six classes of beings, and so forth,

Extending to the bounds of space,
Are the magical machinery of suffering, which surpasses the grasp of thought.

This unconstructed self-knowing itself
Which is free from the defilement of thought,
Is the nondwelling nirvana.
The Vajra Being is also just this.
The Sixth Buddha is also just this.
The six families are also just this.
Manjushri Kumara is just this.
Vairochana is just this.

Dharmakaya, the great bliss,
And the state of unity are also just this.
This itself is the fourth empowerment.
Innate joy is also just this.
Natural purity is also just this.

All these and other different indicators
Known from the sutras and the tantras,
Are for the most part based on this;
Simply combined with this in whichever way is suitable.

Emaho!
The creations of this undefiled mind essence,
What comprises the kayas of form:
The buddhafields of utter purity,
The magically created mandalas, and so forth —
All these creations of great wonder —
Appear, extending to the bounds of space.

The non-Buddhist Tirthikas,
In their ignorance of mind itself,
Are submerged in an ocean of erroneous philosophy
Involving a self, a supreme godhead, and the like.

The schools of Buddhism, such as the shravakas,
The pratyekabuddhas, and the followers of Mind Only,

Maintain the duality of perceiver and perceived,
And conceptualize nonduality as being the true.
Moreover, they get caught in the web of concepts
Such as whether the perceived is real or false.

By not mistaking the view in this way,
You attain enlightenment through the meditation training and conduct,
That are in harmony with the real,
Just like a well-trained race horse.

Unless you are in harmony with the real view,
Your meditation training and conduct will be mistaken
And you will not attain fruition,
Like a blind man without a guide.

How can my conceptual mind, [limited in its perceptions] like a frog in a well,
Discover the profundity by stirring up
The ocean-like depth of the true meaning!
May all learned masters forgive my errors!

Through whatever goodness there is from writing this
May the stain of delusion be fully cleared away
In fortunate and worthy beings,
And may the knowledge of realization grow forth!

This completes The View, Concisely Put by Naropa.

In the presence of the pandita Jnana Siddhi, this was translated and corrected by the lotsawa Marpa Chökyi Lodrö.

I

I am very happy for this opportunity to teach the Dharma, and especially to explain two of Naropa's songs of realization: *the Song of Naropa* and *the Summary of Mahamudra.* It is both important and necessary to study and reflect upon such extraordinary teachings on the view of Mahamudra. When put into practice these instructions are incredibly effective. However, please remember that together with a high view, it is the responsibility of each practitioner to maintain an accordingly conscientious conduct. Be very careful about your behavior. Please don't profess to maintain a very high view and at the same time only pretend to have a 'high' way of behaving. You may certainly keep a high view, but be very careful about how you conduct yourselves.

At the beginning of Dharma studies, traditionally the masters of the past would encourage students to form the resolve towards enlightenment, to engender bodhichitta. This is not merely a custom. Requesting and receiving teachings with this attitude of a bodhisattva will definitely cause our training to become true Dharma practice. Without bodhichitta, our practice may of course still be spiritual, but it will not be nearly as effective as it could be. Therefore, please motivate yourself with the proper enlightened attitude.

The attitude of bodhichitta encompasses both compassion and discriminating knowledge. It involves forming the determination to attain supreme enlightenment for the benefit of all beings. Just think: every single one of the infinite number of sentient beings, a multitude as infinite as the sky is vast, have all been our own mothers and fathers in past lives. Every single one of them wishes to be happy and avoid suffering. But in going through the different states of samsaric existence they suffer incredibly. They don't know how to avoid the causes of suffering; nor do they know how to produce the causes of happiness. In cultivating bodhichitta, we make up our minds to remove their suffering and establish them in a state of permanent happiness. At present, being ordinary sentient beings ourselves, we don't have the ability to eradicate the suffering of others. We are not able to give them protection or refuge, and we are unable to ensure their happiness. To remedy that, we should first study and reflect upon the sacred Dharma, then put it into practice, so that we will be able to bring immense benefit to all sentient beings.

Thus, compassion is the attitude of wanting to understand and practice the Dharma as a necessary prerequisite to establishing each and every being in the state of complete enlightenment. Discriminating knowledge, prajña, means to aim at accomplishing the lasting benefit of beings — their liberation from samsara and the attainment of the omniscient state of enlightenment. These states are not transitory, but permanent; thus, they are of the highest value. In that kind of bodhichitta, both compassion and discriminating knowledge are combined.

This topic is very important, and I would like to expand upon it a little further. Ordinary beings in samsara have one single predominant thought: "What is best for me?" The attitude of wanting to help others is neither well-developed nor vast. We as individuals are not unique in being somewhat selfish. Virtually all sentient beings are equally self-seeking. We have wandered about in samsaric existence for such a long time that we have a deeply ingrained habit of treating ourselves as the most significant person in the world. We really aren't that concerned about the welfare of others. Paradoxically, however, considering ourselves paramount has not been that comforting. We haven't attained infinite happiness with all our preferential self-treatment, have we? To complicate matters, not only are we not able to help ourselves and others — we actually slip into harming them. The habit of treasuring ourselves gives rise to all sorts of disturbing emotions. We feel attached, angry, dull, proud, jealous ... the list is endless. All these negative emotions disturb our state of mind. They are expressed in actions that hurt others and make it even more difficult for ourselves. It's all so unpleasant, isn't it!

The Buddha taught us how to deal with this selfish pattern. He explained that we should try our best to replace it with the attitude of bodhichitta. The frame of mind of a bodhisattva will also reduce disturbing emotions by reducing the selfish attitude. It won't immediately uproot egotism — that is difficult to do in the beginning. However, cultivating relative bodhichitta will reduce excessive self-indulgence and disturbing emotions. Using relative bodhichitta as a basis, the Buddha imparted a method to totally eliminate the very root of selfishness — namely, how to cultivate ultimate bodhichitta. Through practicing relative and ultimate bodhichitta, we are able to create the causes for bringing an end to suffering, and for benefiting both ourselves and others.

Whether we are receiving teachings or trying to apply them, we may have the feeling that we can gain personally from this — an attitude of "this is for my sake." This is an ingrown habit, reinforced since beginningless samsaric existence. It is necessary now to try to change that attitude. Of course, these teachings will benefit us, but instead of being exclusively self-centered, think: "I will receive and put the teachings into practice for the benefit of all sentient beings." It's all right for that attitude to be a little artificial at present. Don't expect that it will immediately arise naturally. In the beginning we have to apply effort to change our normal habit into a broader, more altruistic frame of mind. So temporarily our compassionate attitude is artificial, a little contrived. But slowly, as we train and become more accustomed to thinking in a bodhisattva's way, this attitude becomes natural and spontaneous.

Every day we should try our best to form the resolve towards supreme enlightenment. Instead of continuing the tendency to think selfishly, endeavor to bring benefit to all beings. All the different practices start out with taking refuge and generating bodhichitta. There's a reason for this. Every time we apply a practice, we gradually shift our attitude. By doing this, we will eventually transform our nature into that of a bodhisattva.

Please understand that ultimate bodhichitta is not a temporary shift in attitude. It is not an artificial fabrication of a frame of mind, but a permanent change. Ultimate bodhichitta cuts disturbing emotions at their very root. We need to train in ultimate as well as relative bodhichitta. Ultimate bodhichitta is the very heart, the essence, of Buddhist practice. By beginning with relative bodhichitta, we are able to improve our minds and uplift our attitudes. Through ultimate bodhichitta we are able to thoroughly eliminate disturbing emotions.

Acting out of great kindness, the Buddha revealed to us the way things truly are. He encouraged us to question our concept of ourselves. We begin to get glimpses of this basic state when we look for that thing we call 'I' and discover that there is no such entity to mind. 'I' does not have any reality to it; it does not possess any real existence.

We can come to this understanding through intellectual reasoning — we figure it out and become convinced. We can also reach this understanding through meditation practice. Whichever way we experience egolessness so that it becomes an actuality is fine. The bottom line is that we need to gain certainty about egolessness, then grow accustomed to that truth through our training.

It is not only the individual self that does not exist: all phenomena have no real existence. This is explained in the famous *Heart Sutra, the Heart of Transcendent Knowledge,* in particular the line: "No eye, no ear, no nose, no tongue, no body, no mind…" What this tells us is that no knowable things can be established to truly exist anywhere.

In the Vajrayana context, the emphasis is placed on personal experience rather than intellectual reasoning. We are taught to look directly into our mind to see whether it is some concrete entity that can be taken hold of that can be identified. We begin by listening to descriptions of how the nature of mind is. This gives us an idea through inference. Based on what we are told, we begin to comprehend that "This is probably how it is." We approach realization of the mind as devoid of any concrete self-nature. Then, when we personally look into our minds and recognize, we obtain direct experience. We finally know "This is how it really is!" Now we have a conviction about the true nature of mind.

The sequence of methods is thus first, to discover the absence of the individual self, egolessness; next, to ascertain that all things are emptiness; and finally, to be introduced to the natural state of mind. The great masters of India and Tibet applied these exact methods to reach realization.

Mistakes are inevitable when one begins Vajrayana practice. Here are two common ways of going wrong. The first one is called 'deluded meditation' — literally, 'the meditation of a fool.' This happens when we proceed without any clarity as to what we are supposed to train in. We may stubbornly and even diligently practice our own form of meditation, without knowing what needs to be transcended, and what experience and realization needs to be brought forth. We do it ignorantly, not knowing how, why or what; but simply persevering in our misconceptions of what practice is. Of course, such meditation practice won't produce any profound result.

Another mistake is to pursue only the intellectual understanding of what meditation is. We read through many texts and listen to many teachings, and at some point, we decide that we now possess a very distinct picture of what meditation practice is. This mental picture can become very clear; we can be thoroughly convinced. We may even be able to easily talk about it and explain meditation to others! We are pretending to understand, but we lack any actual personal experience. This is the mistaken path of an intellectual, whose words about meditation practice are merely empty talk. Please try your best to avoid both of these mistakes: either involvement in deluded meditation or involvement in platitudes.

How did great masters like Vairochana, Marpa, and Longchen Rabjam instruct others to avoid these two mistakes? They told their followers to begin by studying according to the Sutra tradition. They led them to understand the absence of the individual self and the emptiness of all phenomena. Their students gained certainty in these essential aspects of reality, and only then engaged in the Vajrayana practices of the development and completion stages. Finally, the master imparted real guidance in the meditation trainings of Mahamudra and Dzogchen. This type of training allows us to avoid the two mistakes discussed above.

So, by studying and reflecting upon the Sutra teachings, we avoid falling into the trap of deluded meditation. And by undergoing genuine Vajrayana training, we avoid the trap of becoming a mere intellectual. These instructions, which have been personally practiced and taught by great masters through the centuries, are still available. The lineages and the realization for these teachings remain unbroken. At the present time there are masters who are learned as well as accomplished in the truth.

Now, some people may argue it's possible for us to figure the ultimate truth out for ourselves. We can read books and ponder the meaning; we can gain an intellectual understanding of how to practice. That may very well be true. But the profound nature of emptiness, the true natural state, is seldom the object of our thoughts. Indeed, it's not within the reach of ordinary thinking. For this reason, it's extremely important to receive proper guidance and pith instructions in Mahamudra and Dzogchen from a living lineage master.

There are many other extraordinary teachings in Vajrayana, including the Six Doctrines of Naropa and the instructions on how to train in darkness and daylight. All these teachings can be received from the great masters of our times. A receptive student can meet with a qualified master, achieve a correct understanding of practice, and gain certainty. Without this, we are bound to encounter difficulties in practice.

Teachings like Mahamudra, also known as the path of liberation, as explained by Naropa in this book, have the complete, true view. A beginner can embark on this training in a very gentle and relaxed way. It is not necessary to grapple with too many difficulties. For present day students, I feel it is a very good idea to first study, then understand, and finally put into practice a teaching like this.

When beginning Dharma practice, some people experience tremendous interest and devotion, to such an extent that it becomes difficult for them to continue their normal work and life. Wanting to engage in intensive practice, we may neglect our careers; while pursuing our careers, our practice is neglected. This can become a very frustrating situation! A teaching like Mahamudra, however, is something that we can practice while working. The solution for the apparent dilemma is simple: 'work some, practice some.' Doing this, there is no real contradiction between daily life and Dharma practice.

A good example of this harmony between work and practice is provided by the lives of the Eighty-four Mahasiddhas of India. Look at thangkas of them and read their life stories. One was a weaver; another a farmer; Tilopa is depicted as grinding sesame seeds. Then of course there was Nagarjuna, who was an incredibly great scholar, and Indrabodhi, a powerful king. So, you see it doesn't matter whether you have a significant or trivial job; whether you are an important person or a nobody in society. These masters exemplify the possibility of training and attaining accomplishment in Mahamudra in any walk of life. They show how it is possible to practice and work at the same time.

Mahamudra is incredibly beneficial for anybody's mind. It always has been, of course, but this is especially true in modern times. In the past, people seemed to have had more perseverance, like Milarepa, and applied themselves whole-heartedly to practice. Due to better circumstances, you could be a full-time practitioner and not worry about survival. Nowadays things are not like that. Practically speaking, we cannot abandon everything and say, "Now I only want to practice." It doesn't help if the teacher says, "Now give up everything, forsake the world and focus one-pointedly on meditation." It is just not practical. We need to be responsible for our own living situation. On the other hand, it certainly doesn't help to think "Well, times have changed, I can't practice like they did in the old days." To attain accomplishment, we have to practice and personally apply the teachings. Given the constraints of modern life, I feel that Mahamudra is a very convenient and suitable practice, one that is always applicable.

Mahamudra is the type of teaching we can keep in mind in our daily lives. Whenever we have a free moment, we can think about the meaning of Naropa's words, paying attention to and bringing those profound teachings into our lives. Being mindful and attentive and applying the teachings whenever we have the opportunity will definitely be of great benefit.

The View Concisely Put and *the Summary of Mahamudra* are very succinct texts that explain the view, meditation, conduct, and fruition of Mahamudra in simple terms. They don't cover much eyond that: we don't find details on how to sit, for example, or how to place our attention while meditating, because these are not necessary for the advanced practitioner. However, this is not so for a beginner. Someone new to Mahamudra cannot simply jump into the text abruptly. Therefore, first I will briefly discuss physical posture to be used when practicing Mahamudra.

When teaching Mahamudra, our basic state, usually called the nature of mind, is pointed out and is supposed to be recognized. The nature of mind, the nature of Mahamudra, may be recognized, or it may not. Sometimes the student is not so clear or confident about recognizing. Sometimes even though the student may have recognized the nature of mind, he or she is still overcome by disturbing emotions. Perhaps these disturbing emotions don't subside to the extent they should, or perhaps we still get carried away in one way or another. Whatever the particular problem may be, the qualities of wakefulness don't seem to increase. Even though the vipashyana aspect, the insight, may be all right in itself, to support or to stabilize it we need shamatha. If our minds are stabilized by shamatha, our practice of Mahamudra will also be stable. In practicing shamatha, posture is very helpful in obtaining calmness and steadiness of mind.

The posture used here is called the 'seven-fold posture of Vairochana.' The literal meaning of the name Vairochana is 'manifest clarity.' By applying the seven points of posture, clarity is brought forth in one's experience. The first point is the cross-legged vajra position. Sitting in the full vajra posture for someone unaccustomed to it can be painful, however, and this can make meditation practice difficult. If this is the case, it's sufficient to sit in the ordinary cross-legged position. The instruction specifies one should sit, not stand up or lie down. The reason for sitting is if we stand up or lie down it's harder to be stable-minded. Our attention is more easily distracted, or we may fall asleep.

The second point is to keep a straight back. The backbone is the center of the body, so, if it is kept straight, we can be sure the body is in alignment. Inside our body are subtle channels. When the body is straight, these channels are aligned, and the energy currents circulate freely inside them. Our normal state of mind is influenced or literally supported by these energy currents. When the flow of energy is free and unhindered, our state of mind is at ease. We feel calm and stable, which is good for practice.

Third, place your hands in the posture of equanimity or composure. Generally, this means to put the right hand on top of the left and rest them both palm-side up in your lap. Another way to explain this is that you should arrange your hands in a balanced way — don't place one hand on the ground and the other on your lap. It is also acceptable to rest the hands palm up on the knees.

The fourth point is to hold the elbows straight. They should be neither rigid nor bent. Once again, we are maintaining balance with the arms. The fourth point is sometimes described as 'keeping your arms like a vulture.'

Point five is to bend your neck slightly. Do not let the head hang down, which squeezes the throat. The head should not lean backwards either, as this makes it difficult to be at ease. To bend the head or the neck slightly forward creates the support for keeping correct attention.

Sixth, lightly touch the tongue to the palate. This reduces the flow of saliva, which means we don't have to deal with thoughts about whether we should swallow or not.

The seventh point is to leave your gaze in mid-air, in the direction of your nose. Occasionally this is misunderstood. Some people think they have to stare into mid-air and try to see space in front of themselves. This is obviously very hard! They think, "I have to see something. How can one simply look at space? I usually only look at things, and fix my mind on them. This looking at nothing seems really difficult. What should I actually do?" Thinking like this is not necessary. We don't have to sit and look at something. To leave your gaze in mid-air in the direction of the nose simply means to not look at anything in particular. When our attention is not occupied with any visual object, our mind is freer to look into itself. Remember, the real goal here is for the attention to look into itself. We don't have to sit and stare into the space in front of us. Some people do this so rigidly that their eyes get irritated and water! That is not necessary. It's more important to suspend the focus, to not hold a focus on any visual object.

2

In past years I have taught other texts on Mahamudra*: Moonlight of Mahamudra* by Dakpo Tashi Namgyal, *Pointing Directly at Dharmakaya* by the Ninth Karmapa Wangchuk Dorje, and *River Ganges of Mahamudra, the Gangama,* by Tilopa. This year's text is *The View, Concisely Put* by Naropa. It is a song about the view, which is a truly extraordinary teaching.

You may already be familiar with the life story of Naropa, but I will summarize it. Naropa was born as the son of a king. Growing up, however, he had no inclination to become the ruler of a country. Instead, he renounced his kingdom and took ordination as a monk. He studied and became extremely learned. Later, he stayed at the great monastic university of Nalanda in eastern India. It was the custom of that time to appoint panditas or great scholars to safeguard the Dharma at the four gates of the monastery in the four directions— north, south, east, and west — with an additional one in the center. After a certain master passed away, Naropa replaced him at the northern gate.

Naropa received blessings from Vajra Yogini, possibly due to some past karmic connection with her. The opening line in the song says, "Homage to the Vajra Dakini!" This refers to Vajra Yogini, about whom there is the following story. One day Naropa was sitting outside the temple reading a scripture. Suddenly a shadow fell upon the page. He looked up and saw a very old woman standing before him. She asked him, "What you are reading? Tell me, is it the words you understand, or do you understand the meaning?"

Naropa answered, "It's the words I understand. I am learned in the words." When the old woman heard this, she was overjoyed. She smiled and laughed; she danced around; she clapped her hands and sang. As she showed such great delight and carried on so jubilantly, Naropa wondered, "Why is she so happy to hear that I know the words? 'Knowing the words' simply means to be clear about the idea through intellectual reasoning." He then thought: "If that is the case, she will be even more happy when I say that I know the meaning."

Naropa then told her, "I understand not only the words but also the meaning." Her reaction was exactly the opposite. She stopped smiling.

She stopped dancing. She looked incredibly sad and created quite a scene by crying and wailing. He of course wondered, "Why would she be really happy when I say, 'I understand the words,' but miserable when I say, 'I understand the meaning'?" Naropa asked her "Why are you acting like that?"

The old lady replied, "You say that you understand the words, and that is true. You are a learned pandita who guards the northern gate to Nalanda. But when you say that you understand the meaning, that is not true; you are lying. It made me very sad. You have not yet achieved the totality of experience and realization. That is why I appeared upset."

Naropa asked, "What can I do to understand the meaning? Who is learned in the meaning?" The old lady replied, "Find my brother Tilopa. If you meet him, you will be able to understand the meaning as well." Merely hearing Tilopa's name, Naropa was overjoyed. From the core of his heart, he experienced a strong conviction that "I must meet him!" He prayed fervently to be able to do so, and then began the sadhana of Hevajra. While he was practicing, a voice from the sky said, "In order to meet Tilopa, it is better if you practice the Chakrasamvara sadhana." So, he did that, reciting the mantra of Chakrasamvara seven hundred thousand times. After this he received another prediction that indicated he would be able to meet Tilopa if he journeyed to the east.

Naropa underwent twelve minor and twelve major trials in search of this master, but due to his pride he missed several opportunities to meet Tilopa. For instance, during his journey he encountered several deformed or disgusting beggars. Naropa behaved quite arrogantly towards them, and after he passed by, they would say, "If you behave like that you will never meet Tilopa." The beggar would then instantly disappear, and Naropa would realize that they were emanations of Tilopa. Another time a beggar stood in the middle of the road blocking his way. Naropa asked him to please move so he could get by. He retorted, "I'm not moving. You can either walk around me or you can jump over me, whichever you please. But there is no way I'm going to move from this spot." Naropa proceeded to jump over him. The beggar said, "If you are that arrogant, you will never meet Tilopa." Once again, the man vanished into mid-air and Naropa was left behind feeling deep regret.

On another occasion Naropa heard that Tilopa would go begging for alms that day. He thought, "If I go to the nearest temple, where the beggars usually line up, I will probably meet Tilopa." When he arrived, he asked if anyone knew the Mahasiddha Tilopa. They answered, "We don't know the Mahasiddha Tilopa who you are looking for, but there's one beggar by the name of Tilopa around here somewhere." When he first met this beggar, Naropa bowed respectfully to him, walked around him and requested teachings. Putting his hand inside his shirt, the beggar brought out a clump of lice, and said, "Throw these in the fire." Naropa thought, "I'm a monk! I'm a pure Buddhist! I can't do anything like that. It would be terrible if I were to kill sentient beings." Being attached to his self-image, he couldn't do what the beggar said. The beggar then snapped, "If you have that kind of attachment, you will never meet Tilopa." And again, he vanished.

At the end of his twelve minor trials, Naropa was at the brink of complete despair. He thought, "I will never meet Tilopa. There is nothing I can do. I just don't have the fortune, so I might as well kill myself." He took a knife and was about to cut his throat. Suddenly he heard a voice saying, "If you do that, it is of no benefit, even if you meet Tilopa." He looked around, and Tilopa was standing right there. At last, they had met. Those were the twelve minor trials of Naropa. Later, I will explain the twelve major ones.

In Sanskrit: Adhi Siddhi Sama Nama
In Tibetan: *lta ba mdor bsdus pa zhes bya ba*
In English: *The View, Concisely Put*

The text I am about to explain opens with the Sanskrit title and follows with the corresponding title in Tibetan, which is *Tawa Dordüpa,* or *The View, Concisely Put.* In Mahamudra there are four aspects: view, meditation training, conduct, and fruition. This teaching is about the view. While it is possible to explain the view in great detail, that is not the case here. This song is a condensed explanation of the view; hence, *concisely put.*

Homage to the Vajra Dakini!

There is a direct connection between Mahamudra and Vajra Yogini, who is Naropa's personal deity or yidam. In the Sutra system this deity, as the female buddha Prajnaparamita, symbolizes the mother of all buddhas and bodhisattvas. Prajnaparamita, transcendent knowledge, is the innate natural state. The realization of this gives birth to the fruition of the path of shravakas, pratyekabuddhas, bodhisattvas, and the complete enlightenment of the buddhas. This realization, being the mother or source of all awakened ones, is depicted in the form of a female. Ordinarily the natural state is called *Chagya Chenpo,* Mahamudra, but sometimes it is called *Chagya Chenmo*, in which the 'mo' at the end is a female derivative. The connotation is that which gives birth, the mother or source of realization.

Paying homage is a gesture of respect and devotion. Out of sincere interest, appreciation and delight we are able to understand and realize the nature of what it is we respect. Paying homage towards that which represents the state of Mahamudra with openness, pure respect, devotion, and appreciation acts as a conduit to being able to experience and realize Mahamudra. That is the meaning of the line, "Homage to the Vajra Dakini!".

> To the omniscient lord of refuge,
> The protector of beings, I pay homage!

Next is an homage to the Buddha. There is a particular reason to pay homage to the Buddha at this point. In ancient India certain teachings predominated in different periods: First the shravaka teachings were eminent; then the Mahayana teachings became widespread; later the Vajrayana teachings prevailed. This has caused certain scholars to make conclusions concerning the importance of the different teachings. For instance, some declare that the shravaka teachings, now embodied in the Theravada tradition, are the authentic teachings of the Buddha. They don't consider Mahayana and Vajrayana to be the Buddha's teachings. Other scholars have determined that most shravaka teachings and Mahayana teachings are the authentic words of the Buddha, whereas the Vajrayana is not. In order to alleviate any doubt or hesitation people may have in studying a teaching like this, Naropa put in "Homage to the Buddha" at the very beginning. He wanted to show that the Mahamudra view is in complete harmony with the words of the Buddha.

The three main qualities of the Buddha are knowledge, compassion, and capability. When paying homage to the Buddha, the great master Naropa starts out, "To the omniscient...". 'Omniscient' here refers to the characteristic of perfect knowledge. This perfect knowledge sees the nature of all things as they are and perceives all that can possibly exist. In addition to perfect knowledge, kindness is needed. If the kindness that is directed towards helping other beings is missing, a person's wisdom doesn't help anybody else. Compassion is equally important. This is illustrated by the term "lord of refuge," meaning the one who safeguards or acts for the welfare of others. In doing so he wants to protect, guard, or give refuge to all beings.

It's not enough merely to want to help others. One has to have the ability to do it as well. The third quality of an awakened one is the capability that is expressed in the words "the protector of beings." Those who possess these three qualities are the ones who truly protect and act for the welfare of all sentient beings.

> After pursuing statements and reasoning
> I have condensed and established the true meaning.

The next two lines contain the traditional declaration of intention to make this composition. 'Statements' refers to both the words of the Buddha and the teachings given by all noble beings. Naropa's understanding is in accordance with what enlightened beings have taught. He is indicating that his teaching is not something invented by himself. It is in full harmony with the words of the Buddha and with the statements of enlightened beings. Moreover, this is not simply an exercise in blind faith: Naropa thoroughly investigated the meaning of what was said, intelligently analyzing it and presenting it in a manner that is logical and reasonable. With regard to both statements and reasoning, Naropa is saying, "I have condensed and established the true meaning." He offers this in a clear, short, direct way.

Generally speaking, the system of Mahamudra points out the nature of mind itself. The disciple with sincere interest and devotion who is confident in the recognition will then practice it diligently. However, unless something is reasonable, it is hard to have true interest and appreciation regarding it. Making sense is dependent upon intelligent analysis. What we understand should be in accordance with the statements of the awakened ones — their teachings. So, "After pursuing statements and reasoning" also refers to the student.

In Mahamudra there are often four steps. The first is showing that the perceived — meaning what we experience — is mind. Next is the realization that mind is empty. Third is the understanding that this emptiness is spontaneously present, and fourth, the knowledge that this spontaneous presence is self-liberated. This is called the 'four-fold pointing-out instruction.' The starting point is to show that what is experienced, what we perceive, is actually mind. This is contrary to our normal attitude that what we experience is outside and apart from ourselves. When what we experience is pleasant, we are attracted. If it is unpleasant, we are repulsed. We feel attachment and desire towards something that is attractive, and aversion and anger towards disgusting objects or people. Through this attachment and aversion, we create negative karma.

To counteract this pattern, the Mahamudra teachings first introduce us to the fact that the perceived — that which seems to be outside and external to ourselves — is actually created by the perceiving mind. Perceptions are mentally created, like a dream. The inner, perceiving mind is empty. Understanding this naturally reduces the clinging and attraction. When clinging and attraction lessen, liking and disliking also weaken. When likes and dislikes decrease, joy and sorrow diminish. When joy and sorrow diminish, aversion and attachment naturally fall away. That is the purpose of the first instruction in Mahamudra.

> All these apparent and existing phenomena
> Are nowhere apart from mind, your own awareness.
> Since it perceives and is cognizant,
> It is like experience that is self-known.

Let's look at the first line. 'Apparent' refers to the objects of the five senses: all that is perceived. 'Existing' refers to the perceiving mind within, that which apprehends and perceives phenomena. 'All phenomena' means anything that can possibly exist. We should understand that whatever takes place, all phenomena, are not really outside us, but are actually inside our minds. In other words, nothing exists apart from our mind. There are four schools of Buddhist philosophy, the Vaibhashika, the Sautrantika, the Chittamatra or Mind Only, and the Madhyamika or Middle Way. This song sounds very much like the Mind Only philosophy, which established that whatever is experienced is mind. The great master Dharmakirti presented a proof through which we can establish that all phenomena are actually mind. The proof is that no thing is separate from the mind that experiences it. It cannot be demonstrated or conceived that any possible thing exists apart from being experienced by a mind. All sights, all visible forms, are never separate from visual cognition, the seeing that takes place through our eyes. Audible sounds do not take place anywhere apart from sound cognition or hearing. Similarly, all memories and thought forms do not take place separate from mental cognition, the mind consciousness. The text here says, "Since it perceives and is cognizant…" That means that no phenomenon is separate from that perception or cognizance.

Emotions and thoughts are what we feel and think. We experience them, and when we do it is none other than our mind that experiences. When we perceive something as being outside of ourselves, as an external object, it is actually we ourselves who have externalized the content of our experiences. Everything is in truth our own experience.

Experiencing is exactly what mind does, as pointed out by the line that says, "Since it perceives and is cognizant." The next line provides an example of this when it says, "It is like experience that is self-known." We know when we experience, because we possess the abilities of perception and cognizance. If what was experienced was not already mind, there could be no link between external things and mind. If what we encountered was separate from and outside the mind, it would be impossible to experience it. The inescapable conclusion is thus that whatever is perceived is mind.

> If this mind was not like that
> There would be no link and therefore no experience.

> This is how I have established the relative:
> "Understand that all phenomena are based on mind," as it is said.

External phenomena, inner phenomena, the perceiver and perceived — all are within the mind. Mahamudra practitioners don't spend too much time analyzing the emptiness of external phenomena. Rather, the practitioner is directly introduced to the natural state, the nature of his or her mind. That all things, whatever is experienced, is mind can be established either through reasoning or through meditation training. In this teaching I have presented the general intellectual idea, so that you can become convinced that it is reasonably so. Once you understand the point, you will have the trust necessary to begin training so that you can fully realize that this is so.

According to the Sutra system of Buddhism, to arrive at complete enlightenment we need to perfect the accumulation of merit for either three or seven incalculable eons. According to the extraordinary teachings of Vajrayana, it is possible to arrive at the unified level of a vajra holder in this same body and lifetime. Which is true? Both are! The difference lies in whether or not the practitioner is introduced to the very heart of the training, the natural state of mind. After being introduced to the natural state we can, by means of fully training in it, gain complete enlightenment in this very lifetime. If we do not engage in this training and instead focus on outer objects in a way that is meritorious or virtuous, enlightenment will take three incalculable eons. The determining factor is whether or not the nature of mind has been pointed out, and whether or not one has recognized it.

It's interesting to note that the accomplished great masters of Tibet had a slightly different approach to study and practice. When studying the Dharma, they would place more emphasis on examining the Sutra system of Madhyamika, Abhidharma, the Prajnaparamita and so forth. But when engaging in meditation training, however, they would focus on the vajra vehicle of Secret Mantra, Vajrayana.

Within Vajrayana itself there are many different ways of training, such as the development stage of visualizing deities and mandalas, reciting mantras and so forth. However, the key to attaining true and complete enlightenment in one lifetime lies in being introduced to, recognizing, and training in the natural state of mind. All the great siddhas attained accomplishment based on this.

Through Madhyamika we can establish how all phenomena are devoid of true existence, of any self-entity. It is a very convenient, very practical approach through which we can intellectually understand that all things are emptiness. When it comes to actually experiencing this emptiness for ourselves, however, the Madhyamika system seems to be a very roundabout method. Personal application involves looking into our own mind. The practice of the accomplished masters of India and Tibet was not to look outward by analyzing external phenomena, but rather to look into that which thinks — our own mind. In the moment of looking towards the thinker, you don't have to really establish emptiness or articulate any particular philosophical position. In the very moment of looking into that which thinks, it is seen as already empty, all by itself. The emptiness doesn't have to be proven in any way whatsoever. This very direct approach is the tradition of the siddhas, and it starts with looking into the nature of mind.

Now I have covered the first point: that everything you perceive, all appearances, are mind. Next, I will discuss the second point: that mind is empty.

3

You always hear the Buddhist teachers say that we should study the Dharma with a pure motivation. Being ordinary people, it does happen sometimes that we don't exactly have pure motivation. The definition of an ordinary person is someone who doesn't have pure motivation. Let's check ourselves every so often: "Exactly what is my motivation for studying these teachings?" If we find that our motivation is selfish, we should gradually try to change that into having a pure motivation. On the other hand, if we already have a pure motivation, it may be that it is not so expansive, yet. It may be limited to only our group. We should try to our best to gradually enlarge it and make our unselfish motivation all-encompassing. That kind of training is very beneficial. Training now in having pure motivation, will help in the future. Then the true and authentic awakened attitude of bodhichitta will come quite naturally.

To continue the story of Naropa, the author of this text, I already covered the twelve minor trials he underwent while searching for Tilopa. After meeting Tilopa he underwent even more hardship. I will continue by telling how he received the ripening empowerments and the liberating instructions.

When bestowing the ripening empowerments, Tilopa showed Naropa twelve symbolic signs. Tilopa would show Naropa one gesture or one sign at a time. After Naropa again begged him to teach more, he would show one more sign, but without any explanation. Finally, having shown Naropa twelve different gestures of symbolic meaning, Tilopa sang a song in which he explained the meaning of these twelve signs.

The first sign Tilopa showed Naropa was a piece of cloth that he set on fire. After it burned and turned to ashes, the cloth looked exactly like the same as before, in that it still maintained its original shape. As Tilopa explained later in the song, our disturbing emotions are like the cloth, and the oral instruction of a qualified master is like the fire that burns the cloth. The training in the pith instructions sets our disturbing emotions on fire and burns them to cinders. What we finally end up with in our minds is something that resembles disturbing emotions, but which doesn't really have the fiber or texture of genuine disturbing emotions. Although we appear to be an ordinary human being, our nature, the continuum of buddha nature, is originally pure and clear, like a crystal ball.

For the next instruction Tilopa tied a knot in a piece of rope and told Naropa to untie it. Our attachment to the aims and entanglement within the struggles of this life are like a knot tied in a rope, which needs to be released. Next, Tilopa placed a jewel on the crown of Naropa's head. This means that although our stream of being is originally and utterly pure, we are fettered by temporary mistaken, impure perceptions that need to be released. In order to do so, we need to depend on a qualified master who is like a precious jewel to be revered at the crown of our head. In the next symbolic sign, Tilopa merely looked at the jewel very carefully for a long time. The implication here is that once you meet a qualified master, you should follow him very mindfully and attentively for a long time.

Then Tilopa took out a large basin and filled it with water. He ordered Naropa to drink all of it, which Naropa succeeded in doing. The meaning here is having connected with a qualified master, you need to absorb or assimilate all the pith instructions in their entirety. After Naropa begged repeatedly for the next instruction, Tilopa simply showed a design known as the 'source of dharmas.' This showed that all phenomena have never come into being; they are non-arising.

When Naropa again supplicated Tilopa to instruct him, he showed him a circle. The meaning of that is once you realize that phenomena are empty, the nature of emptiness is the unchanging single sphere of dharmakaya. Then Tilopa pointed his finger towards his own heart, meaning that the single sphere of dharmakaya is not somewhere else; it is in oneself. Next, Tilopa tied a knot in a snake and placed it in front of Naropa. Without doing anything to the snake the knot was untied by itself. The meaning of this is that once we realize the natural state, samsara doesn't have to be unraveled — it is liberated by itself. When Naropa requested Tilopa to give the next instruction, Tilopa simply remained silent like a mute, not uttering a single word. This signified that the ultimate pith instruction is too profound to be expressed in words. It is inexpressible; we need to experience it ourselves. When requested again, Tilopa showed a piece of fruit, his way of symbolically indicating, "If you train in this instruction that I have given you, you will accomplish an excellent result." Lastly, Tilopa sang a song explaining the meaning of all twelve symbolic indications. He concluded by telling Naropa: "You have understood all these signs correctly. Your nature has been ripened, and you are now qualified to receive the pith instructions."

This was from the life story; now, back to the song. I have described how all phenomena, whatever is experienced, is mind. I will start on the next point; that this mind is empty.

> The very basis of phenomena, which is mind essence,
> Can be analyzed, dissected with reasoning, and so forth,
> But this naturally luminous mind
> And the momentary defilement of thought, these two,
> Whether or not they are one or different
> Is a topic of extreme profundity.

'Basis' means that the root or the basic nature of all phenomena is mind. When we scrutinize this mind, we discover that it is empty. In the general system of the Dharma there are two approaches to this end. One is to take inference as path: the student tries to deduce how the mind is by analyzing through reason. He asks, "Does the mind come from anywhere? Does mind remain anywhere? When it disappears, where does it disappear to?" Through such intellectual deduction, we can gain an understanding of how the mind is and will eventually come to the conclusion that mind is empty. The 'but' that starts the third line means that although we can analyze and arrive at the conclusion that mind is empty, we can also use the approach of direct perception, and simply see in actuality that mind is empty.

The analytical approach proceeds step by step. First, we scrutinize this thinking mind, how it is and what it looks like. We have a vague feeling that mind is something very strong, powerful, and solid. We determine it to be an entity that concretely exists, somewhere. We haven't looked for it, though, so we don't really know. Somehow it must be there. Later, we receive instructions on looking for our mind. We search for it and try to define what it looks like, but we fail to find a concrete thing that has a particular shape, color, or form. Did we fail because we didn't know how to look? Or is it because somehow, we made a mistake, missed the point and weren't able to find this mind? Neither case applies. It is simply because mind is not a real "thing" that can be seen in any concrete or material way.

So, inference can be used to examine external things. Reasoning intellectually in this way, we conclude that all things are empty. However, when it comes to looking into our own mind to find out how it is, it is not necessary to deduce or infer. We can also see directly, in actuality, that our mind is empty. The third Karmapa, Rangjung Dorje, expressed this in a song, declaring, "You cannot say that mind exists, because even the buddhas do not see it." Mind is not a concrete thing that even a buddha can find as something to behold.

Mind is empty, but does this mean it is a complete nothing? No, it is not. Let's continue with the text. "But this naturally luminous mind and the momentary defilement of thought, these two..." What these lines mean is that mind is empty of any entity whatsoever. Yet although the essence is empty, at the same time it is not utterly non-existent. It is not comparable to a physical void or vacant space. Mind is not like the horns on the head of a rabbit— a traditional Tibetan example for something that doesn't exist at all. There is a luminous or cognizant capacity to mind that is naturally present. Even though mind is not a concrete entity, still there exists an unobstructed ability to cognize, to experience. That is why the third Karmapa continued, "It is also not non-existent, because it is the basis for samsara and nirvana." This cognizant quality of the empty mind is the very basis that makes possible the existence of samsara. It is also the basis for the possibility of attaining nirvana.

By this point, we may well comprehend that mind is empty of any tangible entity and yet is naturally cognizant. The next question that arises is: Why do we have thoughts? Some are good thoughts, loving and compassionate, full of devotion and sincere appreciation. We also have bad thoughts — attachment, anger, jealousy, pride, dullness, and so forth. Whichever is the case, whether the thoughts or emotions we experience are positive or negative, they are all only momentary. They appear suddenly and vanish just as quickly because they have no substance, they don't last in any permanent way.

We hear that the nature of mind is luminous, clear light, meaning that it possesses the ability to cognize. We also hear that we obscure our own nature by involvement with thoughts — that we somehow fool ourselves or distract ourselves from our essential nature with momentary thoughts. Now, here is the next important question: Is this luminous nature the same as or different from the momentary defilement of thought involvement? If our nature is essentially empty and cognizant, and we are continuously fooled by our own thinking, how does this thinking equate with the natural luminosity?

You cannot claim that the thinking is a separate entity, because it is impossible for any thought to occur apart from the natural luminosity. On the other hand, you cannot say that this luminous nature is identical with the defilement of momentary thinking, because they are related to one another in a causal fashion. The innate luminosity becomes obscured by the defilement of momentary thinking. Hence the next line, "Whether or not they are one or different."

> Because of this depth, scholars analyze.
> Though they explain, I shall not write about it here.

This is an incredibly profound point. Everything stands or falls with this point: Do we know the very identity of momentary thoughts to be the empty and luminously cognizant mind, or not? That is what makes the entire difference. If we know that the nature of any momentary thought or emotion is empty cognizance, we are no longer fooled by it. Because this is so crucial, scholars investigate and analyze this in great detail, carefully elucidating upon it, quoting from scriptures, and using intelligent reasoning, proofs and counter-proofs. It doesn't seem that Naropa deemed it necessary to write about all these details, however. His main concern is for us to truly experience the nature of mind, not simply talk about it.

> This mind that knows emptiness
> Is itself the awakened mind, bodhichitta.

When mind knows this emptiness, its natural state, that itself is bodhichitta, awakened mind. Normally the word bodhichitta is explained as the resolve towards true and complete enlightenment: "I will attain enlightenment for all beings." That extraordinary and special frame of mind, which is compassionate, loving, and has tremendous fortitude is called conventional bodhichitta. There is also ultimate bodhichitta, which I briefly touched upon earlier. The bodhi in bodhichitta means enlightenment. The Tibetan equivalent, *jangchub,* refers to the state of an awakened one, which is the perfection of both abandonment and realization. That kind of awakened state of mind in itself is ultimate bodhichitta. This is the meaning here.

> The buddha potential is just this.
> The sugata essence is just this.

It is important first to comprehend exactly how the natural state of mind is. After comprehension comes meditation, which means to train in experiencing the natural state of mind. By doing this, we will eventually fully realize it. We all have the potential for the realization of enlightenment, which is called 'buddha potential'.

People are of different types. Certain people, very pure types, are hardly obscured at all. Then there are those who are somewhat obscured by disturbing emotions, and those who are incredibly obscured. No matter which type we are, we all have the possibility for understanding and realizing buddhahood if we train in the nature of mind. Furthermore, our nature of mind doesn't differ in quality. The *Uttaratantra* calls our nature of mind 'sugata essence' and 'buddha nature.' This buddha nature is the nature of every sentient being's mind. It is our original basic state that is empty of any entity whatsoever, yet at the same time is naturally cognizant. This empty cognizance has never and will never change. It doesn't increase or decrease in quality or size in any way. It is the unchanging, original basic nature of our minds.

> Because of tasting what is,
> It is also the great bliss.

This empty cognizance is something that we can 'taste' — that is, experience exactly as it is — in meditation practice or in samadhi.

When tasting what is exactly as it is, this originally empty and naturally cognizant essence at that moment cannot be harmed or disturbed by any external enemy, be it an evil spirit, a disease, or any other kind of impairment. The buddha nature is invincible. It cannot be destroyed or lost; indeed, nothing can destroy this innate empty cognizance. The knowledge of this essence is thus accompanied by a fearlessness that is totally free from the threat of suffering in any form whatsoever. This state of being free of all dread, free of all worry, free of all pain is therefore called 'great bliss.'

> The understanding of Secret Mantra is just this.

'Secret Mantra' is a synonym for Vajrayana. There are many different skillful means for Vajrayana practices, in terms of visualizing the forms of deities and mandalas, training in controlling the channels, the energies, and essences, and so forth. These skillful means are all utilized to realize the main point of Vajrayana, which is the view of Mahamudra. Therefore, "Understanding of Secret Mantra is just this."

> Means and knowledge is just this.

In Vajrayana there are the two aspects of means and knowledge, prajña and upaya. Prajña, meaning insight and knowledge, is considered to be of primary importance. The means — here implying 'skillful means' — is what is used to bring about this knowledge. Sometimes it is said that practicing development stage and visualizing a male form emphasizes skillful means, while visualizing the deity in a female form puts more emphasis on the knowledge aspect. Other times the development stage is described as the aspect of skillful means, while the completion stage is equated with the knowledge aspect. There are many ways of describing means and knowledge in Vajrayana, but basically, what means and knowledge is all about is to realize the very basic, innate nature of mind. Therefore, "Means and knowledge is just this."

> The vast and profound is just this.

'Profound' refers to the state of emptiness, the mind of all buddhas. 'Vast' refers to the extensive actions undertaken to benefit all sentient beings, called bodhisattva conduct. Sometimes the vast and the profound refer to the different types of Buddhist scriptures, the different levels and so forth. Whatever the categories may be, the very essence, the very heart of these teachings that are profound and extensive is nothing other than the nature of mind. "The vast and the profound is just this."

> Samantabhadra with consort is just this.

According to the teachings of the Great Perfection, *Dzogpa Chenpo*, the originally awakened state is depicted as Samantabhadra in union with his consort Samantabhadri, emphasizing the knowledge aspect. Samantabhadra is known as the Primordially Awakened One who never fell into samsara and thus never had to be enlightened at some point afterwards. He is considered the original state of enlightenment itself. What is this buddha Samantabhadra in actuality? It is the nature of our own mind.

> This space and wisdom, perceiving while being empty,
> Is what is called 'knowing original enlightenment.'

This unity of basic space and wisdom, of emptiness and original wakefulness, is the knowledge of original enlightenment. In other words, the heart of the matter is to truly realize what originally is — the primordially awakened state. The nature of our minds and the nature of the fully enlightened buddhas' mind are both primordially empty and naturally cognizant. This nature is not a thing that we make enlightened by creating an empty or cognizant entity that didn't previously exist. If we don't practice, our nature will not lose being empty and cognizant. If we do practice it is not that we achieve an empty-cognizant state. The 'space and wisdom' described here is our basic nature, the original unity of empty cognizance, which has always existed and will continue to exist. What is necessary is to realize it, to know it — described here as 'knowing original enlightenment.'

4

Whether we study the Dharma or apply it in practice, all the mahasiddhas or accomplished masters and all the spiritual teachers of the past have taught that it is important to have correct motivation. Adopting pure motivation ensures that our Dharma practice will be pure. Conversely, if we have an impure, ego-oriented motivation when studying and practicing, it is impossible to reach perfection through practice. Sometimes it may seem difficult to really have pure motivation, but if we try our best, it is possible. This is a key instruction: we should try our best to transform our motivation into something really pure.

Now I will continue with the life story of Naropa. I have covered how Naropa was given the ripening empowerments through thirteen symbolic indications. After that, Tilopa imparted the liberating instructions, also known as the oral instructions in the path of liberation. Tilopa put Naropa through twelve major trials, giving one pith instruction at the end of each. The first instruction is called 'the universally wish-fulfilling jewel.'

At one point Tilopa remained in samadhi for an entire year. Although Naropa circumambulated him, prostrated, and made supplications, Tilopa did not say a single thing. At the end of the year, Tilopa opened his eyes and looked at Naropa. When Naropa asked for the liberating instruction, Tilopa stood up and said, "If you want a liberating instruction, follow me." They went up onto the roof of the monastery of Odantapuri, and Tilopa said, "If a worthy disciple were here, he would jump." Naropa looked around and thought, "It seems like there is no one else except me to whom he could be talking!" Naropa then simply jumped off the roof. He landed quite painfully in the dirt, having broken many bones. Tilopa came by and said, "What's up? What are you doing?" Naropa replied, "Well, I'm lying in the dirt because my bones are broken. It's very difficult." Tilopa replied, "To cling to this body as being yourself is difficult. Actually, it is like a clay pot — it doesn't really matter that much if it breaks." Tilopa then touched him gently, and Naropa's pain disappeared.

This was the first of Naropa's twelve major trials, Tilopa then said, "Now I'll give you the pith instruction known as the universally wish-fulfilling jewel." This teaching is mainly about the various visualizations of the deity Chakrasamvara and his consort Vajra Yogini. Depending on the classification, there are either three or six forms of Chakrasamvara. In a condensed form, when one emphasizes skillful means, Chakrasamvara is practiced as a single form. When one emphasizes the knowledge aspect, he is visualized with his consort Vajra Yogini. In a more extensive way, there is the mandala of Chakrasamvara with sixty-two deities, and the mandala of Vajra Yogini with fifteen deities. There are also medium versions of these practices, in which Chakrasamvara has thirteen deities and Vajra Yogini has seven goddesses. Tilopa gave Naropa the instructions on how to practice all these different ways.

After that, Tilopa again remained for one year in the state of samadhi. After a year when he opened his eyes and looked at Naropa, Naropa again requested, "Please bestow the pith instructions." Tilopa got up and said, "If you want them, follow me." They came to a large plain where a huge fire was burning. Tilopa told him, "If you are my disciple, jump into that fire." Naropa immediately did as he was told. He got quite badly burned, of course, and suffered terribly. When Tilopa asked him, "How are you doing?" Naropa answered, "This body of mine, the result of karmic ripening, didn't fare well from its encounter with the element of fire. That is why I'm suffering." Tilopa responded, "To cling to this transient body as being yourself is what's actually painful. It doesn't matter that much if it's burned a bit. Now I'll give you an instruction in what does matter." He then gave the instruction on equal taste: mingling pain with equal taste, mingling disturbing emotions with equal taste, and mingling pleasure with equal taste. In other words, whatever the content of one's experience is, it is possible to train in equal taste. Once again Tilopa touched Naropa gently and all his pain vanished.

After having given the teachings on equal taste, Tilopa went to stay in the jungle and remain in samadhi. He told Naropa, "Serve me. Go beg for alms and get us food." So Naropa did that every day, returning with food for Tilopa. Usually Tilopa didn't seem to appreciate the food at all; he just ate it. However, one day Tilopa expressed great pleasure when eating the rice; remarking how nice the taste was. Naropa thought, "Usually, he isn't so enthusiastic, but today I have the chance to please him. Maybe I should go ask for more." Tilopa said again, "Very good!

This food has an excellent taste." So Naropa went off, carrying with him a pot of water. He requested more rice, but the benefactor refused to give any. Naropa waited until he thought the man wasn't looking, then dipped his bowl into the food, stole it and ran off. Unfortunately, somebody did see him doing this. Now, according to Indian custom, putting one's bowl into a central container of food contaminates everything. The benefactor and his companions got very upset and chased after Naropa, who took flight with them in hot pursuit. At one point he poured his vase of water all around him, and it transformed itself into a lake. His pursuers couldn't reach him because he was in an island in the center, so they all got into a boat in order to catch him. When they got close, Naropa took his sword in hand and waved it around in the air above his head, creating an iron dome-like shelter. The benefactor's people set a fire outside it. The dome became so hot inside that Naropa eventually couldn't bear it and had to come out. The benefactor and his followers then beat him severely and tried to strangle him. Naropa again suffered miserably.

When he Finally returned, Tilopa asked, "What happened?" Naropa told the story about how he was beaten and strangled, and moaned about how much pain he was in. Tilopa said, "In samsaric existence, it doesn't really matter if you get ruffed up a bit. What is really important is the samaya." This was the instruction in the wish-fulfilling jewel of samaya, looking into the mirror of one's mind. Tilopa then gave him the instruction on how to keep a pure link between master and disciple. After that he gently touched him once more, and Naropa's pain vanished.

A few days later, Tilopa told him, "If you want a pith instruction, follow me." They came to a steep cliff below which a river raged in great turmoil. Tilopa said, "I want to go to the other side. Please arrange yourself as a bridge so that I can walk on top of you and arrive at the other shore." Naropa did so. When Tilopa was halfway across, standing on the middle of Naropa's back, he stepped extra-hard. Naropa fell in the freezing water, which also happened to be full of leeches. Eventually Naropa crawled out of the river and dragged himself soaking wet back to Tilopa. Tilopa asked, "What happened?" Naropa answered, "It was so cold. I really suffered, and on top of that these horrible leeches sucked my blood." Tilopa said, "Actually, to get cold and be attacked by leeches is not such a big deal. What is important is an instruction called tummo." Tilopa then gave him the fourth pith instruction on how to practice tummo.

On another occasion, Tilopa said, "Bring me a piece of bamboo." Tilopa split it up into thin pieces and stuck them into Naropa's body. Naropa sat there in great pain. Tilopa asked him, "How are you doing?," and Naropa replied, "It really hurts." Tilopa responded, "I think you need a pith instruction in the illusory body," and he imparted it to Naropa.

Next, they went out onto a vast plain. In the distance they could just see a man carrying a big load. Tilopa said, "That man is going to hurt us! Go chase him away!" Naropa started to run after the man, but no matter how fast or how long he ran, he could never catch him. The man appeared to be even farther away. Finally, he reached the point of complete exhaustion and collapsed on the ground. Tilopa came by and inquired, "How are you doing?" Naropa said, "I am so exhausted, I cannot possibly move." Tilopa told him, "You have been roaming about in samsara for so long that this little amount of exertion should be no big deal. Here, I'll give you an instruction in dream practice."

So, you see the pattern: first Naropa would undergo a major trial, then Tilopa would give him an important pith instruction. Out of the twelve major trials, we have covered six so far. I'll tell you about the other six later. Right now, I'd like to get back to discussing the song.

> This self-knowing, while one is still defiled,
> Does not depend on other things,
> So self-existing wakefulness is just this.

I have already covered the topic on the innate emptiness of mind. I have more to say on this point, because it's really necessary to understand it thoroughly. Although we possess buddha nature, we are not utterly pure and perfect like a buddha. We still have disturbing emotions, and are covered by karma and obscurations. Although we are veiled by these defilements, our empty essence remains unchanged, untainted by these obscurations. Because it is not dependent upon anything else, it is simply called self-existing wakefulness — *rangjung yeshe*.

Being aware, it is cognizance.

The nature of our mind is empty of any entity whatsoever. It is not a concrete thing. When we search for our mind, where is it? What is this mind? What does it look like? No matter how much we analyze, we never find an actual object that we can feel comfortable pointing at and saying, "This thing is my mind." This is proof that the mind is empty, like space. But the emptiness of mind is not exactly the same as space, which is merely a physical emptiness. While space is a complete nothing, a void without wakefulness, empty mind is able to cognize while being empty. Clarity exists in the sense of being aware, being conscious. That is why Naropa said, "Being aware, it is cognizance."

A natural knowing that is free of thought.
This self-knowing cannot possibly form thoughts.

This empty essence is rigpa, knowing. This knowing quality has two options. It can face away from itself towards external objects, making thoughts that grasp in delusion. Here I am speaking of being aware in a deluded fashion, of being mistaken in the sense that there is no knowing what the nature of mind is. The other possibility is that this knowing quality looks towards itself and sees how the empty nature of mind actually is. This is a recognizing of the nature of mind itself. At this point there is no thought. You see in actuality. When there is this kind of direct seeing, it is not possible to form any concepts. Self-knowing is free of all thoughts.

So, our minds have two aspects: crude or coarse thinking, which is deluded, and the nature of mind. In thinking, the mind faces away from itself towards objects, which is mistaken. Yet, if while thinking of something, we look the opposite way into what thinks, we see there is no thinker of the thought at all. This is because the thinker is empty and inconcrete, not some thing that thinks. This is why Naropa said that the essence of mind is nonconceptual.

One of Milarepa's students, called Nyama Paltabum, once asked him, "I can train in natural mind, but what do I do when a thought arises?" Milarepa answered, "When you train in natural mind, you should see thoughts as the magical display of mind. Then work to further establish the natural state of mind." What Milarepa was saying was that thoughts are merely an expression of the mind, like waves moving on the surface of water. Realizing this, we should continue to train further, and establish that the movements of thoughts are simply the magical display of mind. "When you more deeply explore the natural state of mind," Milarepa continued, "you will eventually realize that it is nonconceptual," meaning free of any thought whatsoever.

> Without conceptualizing a 'mind,'
> Since it is not something to be conceived,
> This original wakefulness, cognizant yet thought-free,
> Is like the wisdom of the Tathagata.

This empty nature of mind is also cognizant. It is cognizant yet thought-free. Empty mind is able to know whatever takes place. It is a fact that we do perceive; we do experience; we do cognize. This basic quality of being cognizant is not momentary; it is always there. Our sense of knowing, our original wakefulness is cognizant, yet thought-free. This basic quality of being awake does not fluctuate. It is not something that occurs all of a sudden. It is primordial.

However, all the various thought movements, along with emotions like anger or attachment, are momentary. It is important to distinguish between temporary thought movements and the primordial cognizance that is the nature of mind.

When Naropa writes, 'Like the wisdom of the Tathagata,' he refers to the way a buddha, a fully enlightened one, perceives. That kind of wisdom is original wakefulness, which sees the nature of all things as they are. It is ultimate truth, in actuality. At the same time wisdom perceives the superficial or relative reality of all existing things. One may wonder if a tathagatha's experience of perceiving relative truth is somehow mixed with thoughts and emotions of pleasure and pain, like and dislike. The answer is no, it isn't. A tathagata's way of perceiving is totally free of that.

Therefore, it is taught, "Realize that luminous mind
Is the mind of original wakefulness,
And don't seek an enlightenment separate from that."

'Luminous mind' means that the nature of mind itself is an awake brightness that is original wakefulness. Our basic nature is in itself the state of realization of all buddhas. To fully awaken to this natural state, it is not necessary to go to some other place to reach enlightenment. The state of enlightenment is not extrinsic to ourselves. Buddhahood is not something that will appear suddenly in the future. It is really nothing other than a matter of first recognizing, then fully training in, and realizing in actuality, the nature of our own mind. That is why Naropa said, "Don't seek an enlightenment separate from that." The awakened state of enlightenment, the real buddha, is not something we should seek separate from the nature of our own mind.

Nevertheless, this mind does become disturbed
By the defilement of momentary thoughts.

Nevertheless, having not fully realized that this is so, we do get involved in thoughts of this and that, in the temporary movements of mind. We get attached; we become angry; we feel competitive. While involved in these disturbing emotions, we lose the realization that the nature of our mind is original empty cognizance. We are obscured by ignorance and disturbing emotions, and at that moment we cannot really claim to be a buddha. Although our real nature is empty cognizance, identical with that of the awakened ones, while we are involved in disturbing emotions, while we are ignorant, it doesn't help much to say that we are the buddha.

Like water, like gold, like the sky,
It may be either pure or impure.

This is a statement of profound truth: though our essence is utterly pure, we are at the same time temporarily obscured, temporarily defiled. There seems to be a contradiction here at first glance. It is very hard to grasp how something can simultaneously be both pure and defiled. *The Uttaratantra* describes this state with eight analogies, while Naropa here uses the three examples of water, gold, and the sky. Water is in itself always water. It is pure in being water; but it can appear to be muddy. When there is dirt in the water, at that moment it doesn't appear to be clean. The water itself is unchanged, whatever its condition. If you let muddy water settle, the water will again be seen in its original state. Another example is of gold. A nugget of gold in its natural state remains pure in terms of its basic characteristic of being gold. Even though it may be covered by dirt or other foreign elements and may not look like pure gold, in essence the gold is unchanged. It is the same way with the sky: The sky is inherently empty, yet it's possible for it to be covered by clouds. At other times when there are no clouds, a clear sky appears — yet the sky itself has not changed.

These analogies illustrate how something can be at once pure and impure. Water can be clear or muddy, gold can be pure or encrusted in dirt, and the sky can either be clear or covered by clouds. Likewise, although our original nature is unchanging and empty in itself, it can be either impure — when it's covered by thought involvement — or pure — when conceptual thinking is absent.

> But the naturally luminous mind
> Is free from even a hair-tip of concrete substance,
> Like the analogy of a sky flower.
>
> It does not exist as it seems to be,
> Therefore, it cannot be established to be nonexistent.
> Being mutually dependent,
> When one side is invalid, the other side also does not exist.

This naturally luminous mind, the basic condition or the nature of mind itself, does not possess any concrete existence whatsoever, not even as much as a hair tip. It is like the example of a flower made out of air. The existence of such a flower cannot be established. Likewise, we cannot say that the mind exists in a concrete way, because it is not made out of anything whatsoever. At the same time, we cannot establish that it is non-existent, because non-existence is dependent upon something being existent. We use the word non-existent to negate something that was already thought to exist. If the nature of mind cannot be established as existent to begin with, there is also nothing necessary to negate as being non-existent. Isn't it true, then, that the two concepts of existing and not existing are mutually dependent? One depends upon the other, just like 'this side' depends on 'that side.' Thus, we cannot say that mind either exists or does not exist.

Terms like 'this side' or 'that side' can only be used in relation to each other. If there wasn't another side to compare it to, 'this side' wouldn't make any sense. The two constructs are mutually dependent. If the first term doesn't exist, the validity of the second naturally collapses.

> Mind is neither existent nor nonexistent,
> Since each of these [constructs] is negated.
> It is also not both,
> Since existing and not existing are a contradiction.

You cannot say that the nature of mind both exists and does not exist at the same time, because that is a contradiction. You cannot have something that both is and is not. Since each of them is negated, individually, then having either one or the other, or both at the same time, or neither one or the other — all of these statements collapse under the weight of their own internal contradictions.

5

Once again, I would like to repeat the importance of forming the resolve towards complete and true enlightenment. Develop the bodhichitta attitude, and purify your motivation. This pure motivation ensures that we will progress in our intended direction and thereby progress in our practice.

I have been explaining parts of the life story of Naropa, because I believe that by knowing more about who Naropa was and what he did, you will have more faith when you study his teachings. When our minds are filled with the openness of devotion, we are better able to taste the meaning of his words, to really savor them. Devotion arises naturally when we understand the kind of person Naropa was, the master he followed, and the many hardships he gladly undertook in order to receive the pith instructions. Understanding the depth of Naropa's devotion to the teachings will naturally inspire our own.

I mentioned earlier that Naropa received teachings in two sets or two aspects: the path of ripening and the path of liberation. I also explained how he underwent twelve major trials in order to receive twelve teachings. I've already described six of these, the last being the instruction in dream practice. Now we come to the seventh instruction, which was on luminosity, in Tibetan known as ösel.

Once again, Tilopa arose from his samadhi and told Naropa, "Follow me!" They went off, and after a while came across a marriage procession. The chieftain of the land was escorting his bride, who rode on top of an elephant. Casually Tilopa said, "If I had a worthy disciple, he would jump up on that elephant, grab hold of the bride and drag her across the ground." Naropa took that comment personally. He jumped up on the elephant, grabbed hold of the bride, dragged her down and pulled her across the ground. Immediately, of course, the minister's people jumped on him and gave him a severe thrashing, beating him almost to a pulp. Later, Tilopa asked him, "How are you doing?" and Naropa replied, "Well, I was beaten mercilessly by the chieftain's people. I feel awful." Tilopa said, "When this body that you perceive as being yourself gets a thrashing, it's not such a big deal. What you need is the instruction in luminosity" — in ösel, which he then gave to him.

The eighth instruction Naropa received was on phowa, the ejection of consciousness. Tilopa took Naropa for a walk once more, and they came to a place where the king, his queens, ministers, and retinue were traveling. Tilopa rather off -handedly remarked, "You know, if I had a worthy disciple, he would leap up, seize that queen there and give her a good slap." Without hesitation Naropa did just that. And again, he got beaten, not just severely, but this time almost to death. Later on, when Tilopa came and asked, "What happened to you?" Naropa replied, "Well, the king was like a bow and I was like an arrow that was shot here and there until finally my mind left my body." Tilopa said, "Leaving this illusory body behind is not such a big deal. What is necessary is to know how to eject consciousness." Naropa then received the teaching on phowa, the ejection of consciousness.

The next teaching, the ninth, concerns the transference of consciousness, *drong-jug* in Tibetan. Again, a dramatic story precedes the teaching. Tilopa once more took Naropa for a walk. This time they came upon a prince riding in a chariot. The prince was beautifully ornamented with an elaborate crown, rich jewelry and splendid clothing. Tilopa remarked, "If I had a worthy disciple, he would leap up onto the chariot, snatch all the jewelry off the prince and kick him off the chariot." Naropa proceeded to do exactly that. All the prince's bodyguards tried to seize him, but this time Naropa fled. He managed to escape back to Tilopa, shouting said, "Protect me! Protect me!" When the soldiers arrived, Tilopa asked them, "What do you want?" They said, "We want this bandit who tried to steal the prince's jewelry and kick him off his chariot. Let us have that one!", they raged, pointing at Naropa. Tilopa said, "Well, if he did that it's his own fault; you can have him." They beat Naropa nearly to death. When Tilopa asked him "How are you doing?," Naropa groaned, "I'm almost dead." Tilopa responded, "To leave behind this body is not such a big deal. What you need is the teaching in transference of consciousness," which he then gave.

Now we will leave the biography and return to the song. Up until this point I have discussed how the nature of mind is empty in essence. It is not a void blank, however. The nature of mind, while unconstructed, is able to cognize and experience. This empty cognizance cannot be established as an existing thing. At the same time, it is not something that can be established as being nothing, totally nonexistent. It's not both of these, and it's not neither of these. In other words, it totally defies any theory we may formulate about it.

> It is not something material,
> Nor is it apart from what is experienced as material.
> Therefore, it is free from all constructs.
> This is how I have established the ultimate:
> "Mind is based on space," as it is said.
>
> This unconstructed self-knowing
> Perceives while empty, and while empty it perceives.

It is not necessary to establish the nature of mind as something that remains after suppressing all relative experience. Mind nature is not only relative experience, of course. That's why the text says "It is not something material". However, it is not apart from what is experienced as material — and "therefore, it is free from all constructs," or devoid of all mental concepts.

"This is how I have established the ultimate," the real meaning. "Mind is based on space." Space is empty by itself. In the same way that space is naturally empty, mind is naturally empty. This unconstructed self-knowing is both empty and cognizant. It is unconstructed in the sense that it cannot be conceptualized as being either existent or nonexistent, both or neither. Still, while remaining nothing whatsoever that can be established, it experiences whatever takes place.

> Experience and emptiness are therefore indivisible,

You often hear the statement that appearances and emptiness are a unity — that perception and emptiness are indivisible. Usually, we assume that the perceived is not empty, because we understand emptiness of experience to be no experience. Thinking that emptiness and experience are contradictory and mutually exclusive is a mistake. In reality, all the accomplished masters of the past have realized that experience and emptiness are an indivisible unity. That which experiences is definitely empty, yet at the same time, this very emptiness allows any experience to unfold. Thus, mind nature is empty while experiencing, and it experiences while being empty.

> Like the analogy of the moon in water.

This indivisibility of experience and emptiness appears to be contradictory from an ordinary point of view. When we try to understand it through reason, it is still difficult to grasp exactly how experience and emptiness are indivisible. And when we try to bring this into our own experience in actuality, it is still difficult! That is why Naropa uses a comparison to illustrate this point — "Like the analogy of the moon in water." The moon can be reflected on the surface of water, can't it? While it looks like there is a moon in the water, the moon is not actually in the water. Nonetheless, while there never was and never will be any moon in the water, we still see the moon right there on the surface. We see it — but it isn't really there. That is a very good analogy for how experience and emptiness are indivisible. When looking at external things, we do find that something appears, something is perceived, but while appearing, it does not really exist. In this way, perception and emptiness are indivisible.

That was about perceived objects. In meditation training, we should look towards the perceiving mind. If we look into that which perceives directly, and not as an act of reasoning, we can discover the unity of perception and emptiness in a very immediate and actual fashion. We don't have to infer that this is so. We can actually see that, by looking for the mind that perceives and failing to find any real thing that is the mind. Mind is empty of any identity whatsoever; yet we still experience whatever takes place. Experience is not blocked or suppressed. To sum up: while being empty, there is experience; while experiencing, mind is still empty.

In the tradition of the pith instructions, the lineage masters speak of present, naked, ordinary mind. This present ordinary mind is the very nature of superficial experience. Any common situation in which we think of something or experience something is known as relative truth. At that very moment, leave that which experiences uncontrived. Don't try to alter or correct its nature in any way whatsoever. Simply allow the natural state of experience to continue. That itself is the ultimate truth, the nature of mind. When we don't do anything to our nature, the very essence of relative experience is the ultimate. To reiterate: first, we become aware of the fact that our minds have a cognizant aspect, that we experience. By simply allowing this cognizant quality to be, without trying to modify it or improve upon it, it becomes obvious that this mind is not made out of anything — that it is empty. In addition, it becomes perfectly clear that being empty and being cognizant are an indivisible unity.

> This is how I have established nonduality:
> "Space is not based on anything," as it is said.

Space is by nature empty; mind too is by nature empty. This mind is self-knowing, unconstructed. It is not made out of anything: it does not exist as something, and neither does it not exist. Any idea we can possibly have about it is superficial.

> This unconstructed self-knowing
> Is itself the very basis of samsara.

Every experience that takes place, whether pleasant or unpleasant, is only possible because of the cognizant quality of the nature of mind. If we are in one of the higher realms, experiencing the pleasure or happiness of being a god or a human being, our experience only takes place because of the cognizant nature of mind. Equally, if we find ourselves in the hell realms being tormented by unceasing suffering and pain, that also takes place because of the cognizant nature of mind. Thus, mind's natural cognizance is the very basis of samsara. The reason why samsaric experiences do take place is because this cognizant nature of mind is ignorant and deluded. This state of deluded experience is called 'samsara'.

> Nirvana as well is also just this.

Undeluded experience is called 'nirvana'. When leaving behind so-called samsara and attaining nirvana, mind does not go to some other location. The essential nature of mind remains totally unchanged. It's not like the mind travels to another land called nirvana.

> The Great Middle Way is also just this.

This nature of mind has been established as being natural emptiness by means of the great reasoning propagated by Nagarjuna, Shantideva, Chandrakirti and other great masters.

> That to be seen is also just this.
> That to train in is also just this.

When speaking of path, there are two aspects: the path of ordinary beings and the path of noble beings. The path of noble beings has three divisions: the path of seeing, the path of cultivation, and the path of no more learning. In the first division, what is it exactly that is being seen? It is the innate nature of things, the innate truth. Seeing the innate truth is thus the starting point of the path of seeing. That is why Naropa states, "That to be seen is also just this." The path of cultivation involves growing more accustomed to seeing the innate nature of things. The practitioner trains again and again, cultivating his or her insights further and further. Thus, Naropa says "That to train in is also just this."

> That to attain is also just this.
> The valid truth is also just this.

So, the first thing we should do is to see the innate nature; next is to train in that. In other words, having seen what should be seen through the path of seeing and trained what should be trained in through the path of cultivation; the outcome of these actions is the attainment of fruition, which is called the path of no more learning. "That to attain is also just this," which is no other than the basic state of the mind itself. "The valid truth is also just this." When distinguishing between what is true and false, we see that there is something that is really true — the basic state, the basic nature. Therefore, the valid truth is also just this.

The renowned threefold tantras
Of basic cause, method, and result,
And what is known as ground, path, and fruition,
Are just different situations of this.

The vajra vehicles of Secret Mantra mention the three-fold tantras or continuity of cause, method, and result. The tantra of cause is simply the buddha nature present as the essence of mind of an ordinary being. The tantra of method refers to the skillful means of the development and completion stages that belong to the path. The tantra of result is the fruition; the outcome of having practiced the path and realized one's potential. While these three differ in name, in actuality, the very basis for practice — the cause tantra — is simply buddha nature, the basic nature of mind. The principle of development and completion is also nothing other than that, and what is realized as the result is this very nature itself.

It is exactly the same with ground, path, and fruition: the difference between these is merely a variance in terminology. The terms cause, method, and result belong primarily to Vajrayana, while ground, path, and fruition could be used either in the Sutra system or in the Vajrayana context. In the *Uttaratantra* there is a clear explanation of the meaning of ground, path, and fruition in terms of these being impure, semi-pure and utterly pure. Impure refers to the starting point, the ground of being an ordinary sentient being. Semi-pure means one is already established on the path, and utterly pure refers to the time of fruition, when one has attained the ultimate result of buddhahood. All these "are just different situations of this." In different Dharma teachings, other words are used.

The basic consciousness, the all-ground,
All possible aggregates in samsara,
Are known as the 'dependent,' and so forth.

One example is the basic consciousness, the all-ground. As long as a person is involved in samsaric existence, this basic state is known as 'the dependent'. The Mind Only school, the Yogachara philosophy, explains three characteristics or three natures, called 'the imagined,' 'the dependent' and 'the absolute.' In this context, the word 'dependent' refers to the dependent as being indivisible from the nature of mind itself.

So, up until now we have established that mind is empty. Next, Naropa will introduce that this emptiness of mind is spontaneously present. If you have any doubts or uncertainty at this point, feel free to clear them up now.

STUDENT: I have a question about the expression 'luminous mind.' What does the word luminous mean? Is it a symbol for something you can't explain in words, or is it like visible light that we can see?

RINPOCHE: The word ösalwa, often translated as luminous, is related to the word light in that it expresses some kind of brightness or clarity. However, the real meaning of this is not a light that is visible to the eye. Luminosity refers more to the capacity to know. This ability is present within us at any point in that we always can understand; we always have a readiness to perceive and cognize. So, luminosity is the capacity to know. Hearing that mind is emptiness may lead us to believe that there is no mind. It sounds like we are a mindless piece of matter, which we are not. We are able to experience. Our natural cognizance is available at any moment. That is luminosity, which is not made out of anything whatsoever.

STUDENT: Who experiences the taste of empty luminosity?

RINPOCHE: This is something you should try to discover in your meditation training! (students laugh.) You should look into what is it actually that experiences. (Rinpoche laughs.)

STUDENT: How beneficial is it when I sit in these teachings, since I don't understand much of this at all? I like it anyway, but my meditation practice is not very good, not very deep.

RINPOCHE: It's very nice that you want to attend the seminar, because, as we repeat daily in the chanting, "devotion is the head of meditation, as is taught." Devotion can be equated with sincere interest. Being interested makes it possible to understand the teachings. Remember, though, the teachings are about your own mind, which is not something that is that far away from you (students laugh). If you can be a little more diligent in your meditation practice, I feel the point of this will slowly dawn upon you. In reality, what Naropa speaks about is not impossible to understand, nor to realize.

Same student (holding up the Tibetan text): But this is really crazy …

Translator: You are holding the text upside down (students laugh).

Same student: Sorry, I just feel a little bit sick about all these words about empty mind and luminosity. I feel like a Dharma junkie — I need these teachings, but I can't stand them. How can I deal with this? I comprehend what you're saying intellectually, but it doesn't reach my heart. Is it better for me to go practice than to sit in these teachings?

Rinpoche: I would like to give a direct and frank reply now (students laugh). What I'm going to say is true. You are a little proud. You hold the thought, "Listening to this teaching about emptiness again and again doesn't do much for me." Holding onto that thought is a form of pride. Try to reduce that pride, and replace that rigidity with interest. Think, "These words come from a great accomplished master. Maybe there is something I can learn from them." Then lend your ear and sincerely listen. I feel that you will be able to understand something then. (Rinpoche laughs).

Another student: Rinpoche, earlier you quoted Naropa as saying, "Self-knowing cannot possibly conceive itself." Does he mean it can't form concepts about itself, or that it doesn't have experience of itself?

Rinpoche: The term 'self-knowing' refers to the Tibetan *rang-rig.* This is a synonym for the nature of mind, which is naturally aware, cognizant by itself. "Cannot possibly conceive itself," means that while you can experience the nature of mind, what our nature is, you cannot conceive of it as an object of thought. The nature of mind is not something that can be conceived of or thought of. In logic there are two different ways of perceiving: conceptual and non-conceptual. You cannot make your own nature an object of conceptual thought. It can only be experienced while one is free of concepts.

STUDENT: I think, Rinpoche, you are speaking to us through a microphone, and the microphone is being recorded by a tape recorder. Most of us arrived in Nepal by jet plane, and you have a car that takes you to Namo Buddha. These things actually provide some merit. They allow Dharma to be spread and more people to understand the Dharma. Nevertheless, they are in our world because minds have gone out in thought as opposed to in, as in the teachings and meditation. I'm wondering how do we balance these two things in our lives: How much time and effort should we devote to *progress*, or thoughts which create objects that benefit spreading the Dharma, and how much should we spend on the actual practice itself?

RINPOCHE: You may be familiar with the distinction between relative truth and ultimate truth. The Buddha gave teachings to enable sentient beings to reach permanent happiness and enlightenment. He told them that the true way to do so was to turn the attention towards the ultimate nature of mind and train in that. While doing so, while practicing to reach enlightenment, we still live within relative circumstances, don't we? It's important to remember that these circumstances are relative truth, not relative falsehood. There is some genuineness in them, although it is relative. This was exemplified very nicely by the eighty mahasiddhas. As I mentioned before, they all had different occupations. A few herded cattle while training in Mahamudra. Tilopa pounded sesame seeds into oil while training in Mahamudra. Another ruled his country while training in Mahamudra; and another, Nagarjuna, composed precious treatises on the Dharma while training in Mahamudra. Isn't it quite wonderful that this kind of simultaneous activity is possible?

STUDENT: You mentioned three natures: the imputed or imagined nature, the dependent nature, and the absolute nature. What is the difference between these?

RINPOCHE: The Tibetan words for the dependent and the absolute are *shen wang* and *yong drub*. Shenwang refers to the perceiving quality, and yongdrub to the empty quality. Any given thing has a perceived as well as an empty quality to it. Perceiving is dependent, in that it is not something that is stable in itself. Perceiving takes place in conjunction with various factors, whereas emptiness is independent. It could stand alone, so to say, and is therefore called absolute. These two aspects are not utterly separate, however. Let's take the example of the moon in water. When the moon is reflected on the surface of water, the fact that there is no real moon, or the emptiness of moon in that reflection is something that is absolute. That emptiness is unshakable. Nobody can change the ultimate fact that there is no real moon in the water. However, the appearance of the moon is dependent. Because of the conjunction of the moon in the sky and the surface of the water, the reflection has to appear. It has no choice. That is why it is called dependent.

6

I have already described nine of the twelve major trials Naropa underwent, and how Naropa received one very important, profound instruction at the end of each of these. In the tenth trial, Tilopa said to Naropa, "At this time, you must accept a consort, a dakini." Naropa did so, but the dakini he found was a very tough one who put him through a lot of pain and misery. After a few encounters with her, he met Tilopa, who asked, "How are you doing?" Naropa said, "I feel terrible — I am really suffering!" Tilopa told him: "Both samsara and nirvana do not really exist. What you need is the instruction in how to sustain the state of samadhi while engaging with a dakini." He imparted to Naropa the instructions known as the great bliss of the lower gate.

After this Tilopa said, "Well, you'd better become a monk, since having a consort didn't seem to help you very much. At the same time you should punish yourself for how you have been behaving. Since all your trouble is caused by your secret chakra, you should take a stone and give it a battering!" Naropa did that, and he of course suffered immensely. Tilopa came by and asked, "How are you doing?" Naropa said, "Well, I feel just terrible." Tilopa replied, "What you need is the instruction on equal taste." For the eleventh instruction, he gave him the instruction called Nine Cycles of Equal Taste. Sometimes we feel pleasure; sometimes we feel pain; sometimes joy; sometimes sorrow. The instruction Naropa received was on equalizing the state of all these.

The last instruction, the twelfth, is the instruction in Mahamudra. Tilopa said to Naropa, "You should offer me your consort." Naropa did so. When Tilopa received Naropa's consort, he slapped her. He asked Naropa, "How do you feel now when I beat up your consort?" Naropa replied, "I feel fine. I had the great fortune to be able to offer my consort to my teacher, so I experience great bliss because of that." Within that state Tilopa instructed him in Mahamudra.

After this, Tilopa imparted some further vital instructions. In order to receive these significant instructions, Naropa offered his body, which was the greatest offering. The story is as follows: Tilopa said, "Come! Follow me." They went out onto a vast open plain and Tilopa said, "I'll give you the teaching, but first prepare the site; make a mandala offering." To make the area clean, Naropa had to sprinkle water to settle the dust. But there was no water available, and Naropa wondered what to do. Tilopa said to him, "Well, if you punch holes in your body, liquid will come out, and you can use that." So Naropa used his own blood to make the dust settle. When he was about to make the mandala offering there was nothing to give. Tilopa said, "Why don't you use your own fingers and limbs?" Naropa cut them off and offered them as a mandala offering. At this point Tilopa asked, "Are you well? Are you feeling all right?" Naropa said, "I feel great because I have the incredible fortune to make an offering of my flesh and blood." Tilopa said, "The conditioned aggregates of samsara are futile, insubstantial and painful. It is a very fortunate disciple who is able to perceive parting with these as being a cause of great joy. You are a fortunate person." Then he gave Naropa the teaching on bardo.

Now let's leave the biography and return to the Song of Naropa: *the View Concisely Put.* The first key point put across in this song was that all phenomena are mind — that whatever is perceived is mind. Next it was explained that this mind is empty. Now we will discuss how this emptiness is spontaneously present. Spontaneous presence in this context refers to the fact that anything can arise in our mind; anything can be experienced. All possible experiences unfold, both pure and impure; the impure experiences of samsara and the pure experiences of nirvana. That this great potential is spontaneously present in empty mind is indeed marvelous and wondrous. Therefore, Naropa begins with Emaho! an exclamation of wonder and amazement.

> Emaho!
> The creations of this mind essence, while one is still defiled,
> The six classes of beings, and so forth,
> Extending to the bounds of space,
> Are the magical machinery of suffering, which surpasses the
> grasp of thought.

When this spontaneously present empty mind is defiled, the impure experiences of samsara take place. When this mind is undefiled — not covered by coarse conceptual thinking or disturbing emotions — the pure experiences of nirvana unfold. At the time this mind essence is defiled, its creations take place as the six classes of sentient beings. Now, when we speak of the six classes of sentient beings, we must mention misdeeds and obscurations. Misdeeds refer to negative karma created through either thought, wrd or deed. Obscurations refers to the habitual tendencies for disturbing emotions. The disturbing emotions that we are ready to feel at any point and inevitably become engaged in can be either coarse, subtle or latent. Disturbing emotions reoccur because of the ingrained habits created through our involvement with them. Although disturbing emotions may be subtle, because of these tendencies they can easily manifest on a coarser level as well.

For instance, when we get irritated and angry, we should apply some remedy against ill-will, rather than nurturing it. The remedy is based on seeing that anger is unwholesome and negative. Once we see that anger is a flaw and we apply a remedy to reduce it, it lessens. If we do not apply an antidote against anger, it proliferates. It can become expressed in thoughts of wanting to kill or beat up others, of wanting to inflict injury. The fully manifested state of anger is what is called the hell realms, where one perceives everything as a battleground, a realm of murder and violence.

Likewise, if we use an antidote to reduce the disturbing emotion of stinginess or avarice, it diminishes. But if we allow greed to take over and run wild, we entertain thoughts like, "I don't have enough, my wealth and enjoyments are going to run out. What am I going to do! I'll be poor! I'll be hungry! It's so terrible!" When this mental pattern is allowed to fully manifest, that is what is called the preta realm, the world of the hungry ghost filled with incredibly agonizing hunger and thirst.

The different phenomena for each of the remaining realms of the six classes of beings arises similarly. Each occurs when the defilement of the different disturbing emotions is permitted to run wild without applying any antidote. We go further and further astray into the painful realms of samsara. Earlier I mentioned that the essence of mind, the natural state, is utterly pure. The problem comes from the fact that our minds are temporarily obscured. The fact the mind is utterly pure does not exclude the existence of suffering when it is obscured. Although the essence is pure, sentient beings covered by obscurations undergo innumerable painful experiences.

While we are enmeshed in this magical machinery of suffering, it is necessary to train in the sacred Dharma, particularly in the state of profound samadhi. Otherwise, this momentary obscuration of samsaric states will never end. Even if we want to accomplish only our own welfare, we still need to clear up and purify these temporary defilements. Yet honestly, it is not enough to do practice simply for ourselves. Just as our nature of mind is originally pure and empty, so is the nature of mind of all other sentient beings. The essential purity of our natures doesn't help us much if we do not realize that. We will simply continue in samsara, experiencing tremendous, inconceivable and overwhelming suffering.

These four lines describe how the spontaneously present quality of empty mind allows the impure experiences of samsara to unfold, out of the defiled thinking. It is also possible for the pure experiences to unfold out of the spontaneously present quality of empty mind when it is free from the defilement of thought. When looking into that which thinks, we discover that although a thought appears as some entity that exists by itself, it is not independent. It is like the movement of a wave on the surface of water. As the wave is not separate from the ocean, likewise the thought is not separate from the thinker. Milarepa stated, "Thoughts are the magical display of mind. Resolve this magical display. Resolve the nature of mind." What is necessary is to recognize the essence of thought, which is unconstructed self-knowing.

> This unconstructed self-knowing itself
> Which is free from the defilement of thought,
> Is the nondwelling nirvana.

In the *Dorje Chang Chenma prayer* we recite daily at these teachings, there is one sentence that says, "The essence of thought is dharmakaya, as is taught." Even though thought involvement is a defilement, the very essence of this thinking — indeed, of any thought — is not different from the nature of mind itself. Therefore, the essence of mind is dharmakaya. Thoughts are not something that concretely exist. A thought does not have any substantial existence. When looking into the very essence of that which thinks, we meet the natural and unconstructed awareness. That, itself, is what is called nondwelling nirvana. In ordinary usage the word nirvana simply refers to escape from samsaric existence. In the context of Vajrayana, however, it is the basic state, the nature of mind.

> The Vajra Being is also just this.
> The Sixth Buddha is also just this.
> The six families are also just this.
> Manjushri Kumara is just this.
> Vairochana is just this.

Here the nature of mind is expressed in the form of the buddha Vajrasattva, called 'Vajra Being,' the all-encompassing lord who pervades all other buddha families. He is also known as 'the Sixth Buddha,' Vajradhara, the dharmakaya buddha who is counted as sixth in addition to the five buddha families. In the next line, "The six families are also just this," means that the five buddha families and Vajradhara are essentially nothing other than the nature of mind itself.

In the next sentence Naropa says, "Manjushri Kumara is just this." As I mentioned earlier, the awakened state has three main qualities: wisdom, compassion, and capability. These three qualities are personified by the Lords of the Three Families. Thus, the natural form of wisdom knowledge is pictured as Manjushri. In his bodhisattva form, he is called Manjushri Kumara, which literally means 'youthful, gentle splendor.' In the development stage Manjushri is depicted as orange-golden in color, holding a sword in his right hand and a blue lotus flower with a scripture in the left hand. Essentially, Manjushri represents nothing other than the nature of mind itself.

"Vairochana is also just this." The buddha Vairochana is the natural form of dharmadhatu wisdom, one of the five wisdoms. Wisdom, literally 'original wakefulness,' is often described in two aspects: one is called "the original wakefulness that cognizes the ultimate," and the other, "the original wakefulness that perceives the relative." There are other attributes to wisdom as well, such as the empty and perceiving qualities of original wakefulness. Buddha Vairochana embodies dharmadhatu wisdom — the original wakefulness that sees the ultimate state of the dhatu, the sphere of all dharmas, all phenomena, exactly as it is. This wisdom has been personified as Vairochana, the central figure of the mandala of the five Buddhas. Essentially, he represents the unmistaken view, the nature of mind.

> Dharmakaya, the great bliss,
> And the state of unity, are also just this.
> This itself is the fourth empowerment.
> Innate joy is also just this.
> Natural purity is also just this.

Dharmakaya is the nature of mind. "Great bliss" in this context refers to sambhogakaya, that manifests out of the realized nature of mind. "And the state of unity is also just this" means that the unity of basic space and original wakefulness, the unity of experience and emptiness, is likewise nothing other than the nature of mind. Vajradhara, the six families, Manjushri, Vairochana, and so forth, all refer more to the development stage; whereas dharmakaya and sambhogakaya, as great bliss, refer to the ultimate fruition.

Next Naropa says, "This itself is the fourth empowerment." The four empowerments are usually called the four ripening empowerments. The first of these is the outer abhisheka, the vase empowerment. It is given for the purpose of realizing the natural purity of the aggregates and elements. Next is the inner secret empowerment that is given in order to realize the natural purity of the channels, energies, and essences. The third, the innermost or wisdom-knowledge empowerment, allows one by means of samadhi to realize the example wisdom, the great bliss of emptiness. The fourth is the ultimate or most supreme empowerment, and is often given by means of a symbolic gesture or the display of a symbolic implement. For example, the vajra master may hold up a crystal, to indicate how the nature of mind actually is. Sometimes he will show a mirror, or allow a reflection to appear in the mirror. Because this fourth empowerment, often known as the word empowerment, directly introduces us to the nature of mind itself, it is called the most supreme.

The next sentence is, "Innate joy is also just this", referring to the coemergent joy experienced through tummo practice. When beginning to train in tummo, we sustain a sense of inner bliss. When stabilized and intensified, this bliss has four degrees, the fourth of which is called innate joy. Innate refers to that which is unproduced. It is not some new thing that suddenly dawns, but is a discovering of the natural state of mind itself as innate joy. "Natural purity" means the utterly pure nature of mind "is also just this."

All these and other different indicators
Known from the sutras and the tantras,
Are for the most part based on this;
Simply combined with this in whichever way is suitable.

The first line refers to the different terminologies used in the sutras and tantras. Mainly these words used are based on the realization of the nature of mind. These names and terms may vary to suit different individuals' inclinations. The last line indicates that all these different teachings and phrases can be used to link the individual with the nature of mind in whichever way is most suitable. The important point is to realize the nature of mind.

7

These Vajrayana teachings being presented here are words spoken by great masters like Tilopa and Naropa, and are extraordinary and extremely profound. After studying the sacred teachings, we are able to put them into practice and to eventually attain fruition. Remember that in any of these steps, it is the bodhichitta resolve that enables us to perfect the path and reach the ultimate destination. Therefore, at whatever time, either studying or putting the teachings into practice, motivate yourself with the precious resolve towards true and complete enlightenment.

We have arrived at the point where Naropa has undergone the twelve minor and twelve major trials and has received the pith instructions concerning the paths of ripening and liberation. Tilopa then tells him, "Just remaining like this will not be so beneficial. It is like a blind person who cannot see, a deaf person who cannot hear, an idiot who can't understand. Something more is necessary." Naropa thought, "What is it I need? Maybe I should embark on the action," meaning the courageous yogic disciplines. Tilopa responded, "Until you have untied the knot of ego-clinging, it won't help to 'enter the action'. What you need is the instruction in how to bring forth enhancement."

After Naropa received the instructions on bringing forth enhancement, he commenced those practices. One day, he and Tilopa went to the Vikramashila monastery, where Naropa engaged in some Dharma discussions. Later he returned to Tilopa who looked quite displeased. Tilopa said, "That was not very useful. There was not much benefit in that." Naropa asked, "Well, then, what should I do? Should I go and practice in the charnel grounds? Should I become a Dharma teacher? What should I do?" Tilopa said, "I think the best results will come from relying on the blessings of a qualified master." "What do you mean?" Naropa implored Tilopa didn't say a word. He took out his kapala, or skull cup, and heaped it with all sorts of disgusting substances of different kinds inside. He assembling a whole pile of foul-smelling stuff, he commanded Naropa, "Eat this. You have to." Since Naropa didn't have any choice, he began to eat it. Much to his surprise, he discovered not only did it have a fantastic aroma, its taste was amazing.

After this experience, Naropa thought, "If one doesn't train in meditation, then one's emotions become the direct cause for furthering samsaric existence. If one does train in meditation, the emotions are naturally purified, and the fruition will become the benefit for both self and others." He didn't say anything, but Tilopa understood immediately and said, "Yes! It's exactly as what you just thought." After that they both took on the attire of mahasiddhas and began what is called entering the action, wandering about living off alms with no fixed aims.

Naropa would walk around begging, calling out, "Benduria!," which means, "Whatever you give, I will eat and digest!" Some kids heard that and wanted to tease him. One of them gave him a knife, gesturing that he should eat it. Much to their surprise, Naropa swallowed the knife — tip first. The children were amazed and the word went around the country that Naropa was somebody truly amazing. Finally, the king of that area heard the talk, and wanted to check Naropa out for himself. Mounting his elephant, he rode out in search of him.

The elephant arrived in great majesty right in front of Naropa. Quite dignified, Naropa held up his right hand in the menacing mudra, and the elephant simply dropped dead right there. The king was quite distressed, because it was a very expensive elephant. The villagers of that area were also upset, because a dead elephant is quite difficult to get rid of, and once it starts to rot it becomes almost unbearable to live in the area. The king asked, "Who told me to come here to begin with?" The reply was "Your ministers." "Where did they hear it from?" Finally, the rumor was traced back to the children. The king said, "Well, the children will have to pay for a new elephant." Since it was a very rare and expensive type of animal, the children's parents were now also very upset. There was no way that they could afford to reimburse the king for his dead elephant. Everybody went on agonizing about this affair, until one old lady said, "You don't have to solve this by yourselves. Why don't you ask the siddha himself? Maybe he will help you." They beseeched Naropa and he agreed to lend a hand. First, he practiced the transference of consciousness, transferring himself into the elephant and moving it away from the village. All the villagers were quite happy that they didn't have a rotting elephant right next to their homes. Next, he summoned back the consciousness of the elephant and revived it so that it could be given back to the king, who was also happy. In this way they were all very pleased, and Naropa was invited to return to the king's palace. He accepted and stayed on as the object of everyone's veneration.

However, Naropa didn't quite behave as one should in a royal court. He acted like a siddha, meaning his behavior was both shocking and outrageous. The ministers, the queens, and the other members of the royal family all slowly became quite distressed. The other priests living at the court were especially infuriated. They supplicated the king, saying, "In the past, Your Majesty has been very wise, but now you are housing this crazy person. His behavior is a disgrace to the dignity of the royal court." The king didn't do anything, so the priests decided to kill Naropa themselves, in secret. They lured him out to a narrow gorge, where they confronted him, saying, "The way you speak is obnoxious. Your behavior is offensive. Now you must die!" Then they tied him up with ropes and chains, cut him into pieces and cremated his remains in a big fire until there was nothing left. Yet, the next morning they found Naropa sitting right there in samadhi in the middle of the fire.

Incredibly regretful, the priests all apologized. Naropa simply replied, "Don't worry about this at all. Actually, it's all been just perfect. All the abuse you heaped upon me helped me to train in further patience. Cutting up my body helped to interrupt the stream of samsaric existence; and burning my body in the fire helped to burn away disturbing emotions."

Naropa then engaged in the 'child-like conduct,' the behavior that is like a child. He would go to the villages and live with the children. Sometimes he would cry with them. Sometimes he would laugh. Sometimes he would just play around. One time, Tilopa happened by and said to him, "To engage in the action [meaning yogic discipline] without the permission of your guru or the dakini is not appropriate. You shouldn't do that." Naropa asked, "What should I do instead? Should I request more teachings?" Tilopa said, "To request teaching after teaching is like drinking water from the ocean — the more you drink, the thirstier you get. You'll never end this craving." Naropa again asked, "What should I do? Should I just try to reflect on the teachings?" Tilopa answered, "The more you think about the teachings, the more you envelop yourself in the web of concepts." "Well, should I practice more meditation?" Naropa asked. Tilopa replied, "What is the use of meditation practice if you haven't left attachment behind?" At his wit's end, Naropa begged, "What should I do?"

In reply, Tilopa sang a song that said something like this: "All that you experience is dependent origination. Dependent origination is non-arising. It is emptiness. Until you realize the unity of dependent origination and emptiness, don't ever separate yourself from gathering the accumulations of merit and wisdom. Non-attachment is most important. Attachment to even the tiniest thing is like a fly stuck on glue. Whatever you do, be totally free from attachment."

Tilopa then told Naropa, "You must go to Pullahari and reside there. In the future, you will have a disciple called Mati. Accept him as your student and dispel his darkness." In this way Tilopa predicted the coming of the Tibetan translator Marpa, one of whose names is Lodrö, the Tibetan for 'Mati'.

Now we return to the song. We have now reached the fourth of the song's four topics, which shows that this spontaneous presence is self-liberated. In the former chapters I have explained how mind is essentially empty, and how this empty mind facilitates the unfolding of all experience, both pure and impure. I have explained how defiled mind gives rise to impure experience, such as unceasing samsara and the different unbearable sufferings of the six classes of sentient beings. Undefiled mind gives rise to nirvana, buddhahood, with all its qualities. This unfolding of pure experience happens automatically, in that it spontaneously manifests. When we have fully realized this spontaneous presence of the nature of mind, it is self-liberated. To express the wondrous quality of this, Naropa again starts with "Emaho!"

> Emaho!
> The creations of this undefiled mind essence,
> What comprises the kayas of form:
> The buddhafields of utter purity,
> The magically created mandalas, and so forth —
> All these creations of great wonder —
> Appear, extending to the bounds of space.

"This undefiled mind essence" means the mind essence that is, in itself, free of any stain. Defilement does not have to be deliberately cast away to recognize that the nature of mind is originally empty. In the very moment of recognizing the nature of mind, defilement is self-liberated; it simply vanishes. This is also called realizing the nature of dharmakaya.

The recognition of the empty essence, the ability to experience the nature of mind exactly as it is, is called dharmadhatu wisdom. It is knowing the sphere of the innate nature of things. Through realizing the nature of mind to be empty in itself, we automatically arrive at the understanding that all phenomena are devoid of any self-nature whatsoever. This seeing the nature of both mind and phenomena exactly as it is, is called dharmadhatu wisdom, one of the five wisdoms.

Is this state of dharmadhatu wisdom, the basic space of all things, an empty, blank voidness? No, it isn't. It is a basic space in which any form of experience can unfold unobstructedly. Whatever takes place, whatever is perceived, is seen as being indivisible from basic space itself. Therefore, no experience is conceptualized of as being 'good' and preferable, nor is anything seen as 'bad' and rejectable. Everything is seen as being of equal nature. This is what is called the wisdom of equality.

If both the ultimate and relative are experienced as being of equal nature, does this mean that everything is somehow mixed together and indistinguishable? No, it is not. Everything that is perceived arises clearly and exactly as it is, as unblurred and as distinct as an exact reflection in a mirror. This is what is called the mirror-like wisdom.

These first three aspects — dharmadhatu wisdom, the wisdom of equality, and the mirror-like wisdom — are predominantly aspects of seeing the ultimate. This doesn't mean that a buddha who arrives at the sphere of the innate nature is totally blind to what takes place on the relative level. A further aspect of the clarity described by the mirror-like wisdom is to see every single thing unmixed and individually, exactly as it is. This is discriminating wisdom, or literally, the wakefulness that differentiates things individually.

There is one final aspect: an unobstructed activity that works for the benefit of beings in a manner that is always timely and perfectly appropriate. This perfect knowing of what needs to be carried out for the benefit of others is called the all-accomplishing wisdom. The awakened state of the buddhas is endowed with all five of these aspects of wisdom.

Looking further into this subject, can one benefit beings by simply knowing what they need? No, one can't. Activity must also manifest for the welfare of others. This activity takes form as the magical creations comprised of the kayas of form, the rupakayas, which for pure beings manifest as the sambhogakayas and for impure beings manifest as the nirmanakayas. These manifestations are what carry out the four activities [of pacifying, increasing, magnetizing, and subjugating].

Briefly described, the sambhogakayas are the buddhafields of utter purity and the magically created mandalas. All these manifest out of the awakened state of dharmakaya. These sambhogakaya realms of utter purity are traditionally described in terms of the five certainties. The certainty of place is a pure sambhogakaya buddhafield. The certainty of retinue covers the entourages of a buddha, which is made up of bodhisattvas at the level of the tenth bhumi. The certainty of the teacher expresses the extraordinary form of the sambhogakaya. The certainty of teaching means that these teachings are unlike those given by a nirmanakaya buddha in this world of impure beings. Normally, these contain teachings on both the expedient and the definitive meaning. But the retinues that receive teaching in the sambhogakaya realms are exclusively bodhisattvas on the ten bhumis who perceive the innate nature of suchness. The teachings given to them thus deal exclusively with the definitive meaning. finally, there is the certainty of time. In our world, a supreme nirmanakaya appears only occasionally, but in the sambhogakaya realm, there is a continuous expounding of the definitive meaning of the Dharma.

In addition to these sambhogakaya manifestations, there are many other wondrous magical creations of the awakened state. These include the supreme nirmanakaya, like Buddha Shakyamuni, who appeared in this world and turned the three consecutive wheels of the Dharma. They also encompass other types of nirmanakaya called incarnated and variegated nirmanakayas. All these marvelous creations manifest to the furthest reaches of space, connecting an infinite number of sentient beings with the Dharma, who become established within it and are led to the state of liberation. Next, Naropa brings up what happens when we fail to realize the correct view. He explains what it is to be in error, and to have only a partial understanding of the correct view.

> The non-Buddhist Tirthikas,
> In their ignorance of mind itself,
> Are submerged in an ocean of erroneous philosophy
> Involving a self, a supreme godhead, and the like.

When we don't understand the correct view, we are deluded. 'View' here means knowing the actual, true nature of this empty, cognizant mind. When we are deluded, we give rise to all kinds of erroneous conceptions about what really is. For instance, Naropa mentions the non-Buddhist philosophers who he describes as being ignorant of mind itself. They are, he says, submerged in an ocean of erroneous philosophy of a self. They attach existence to a spirit or a self, to that which is conscious and aware. They believe it to be a concrete, real thing. They may posit that the individual identity is a material substance or assert that there is a mind to be identified.

As another example, take the non-Buddhist philosophy called the Samkhya. Its followers do not understand that all experience is a magical creation of the empty cognizant mind. Instead, they assert that there is a supreme godhead characterized by five attributes. The godhead is the source or projector of the experiences of sentient beings. This system lacks any comprehension of the nature of samsaric existence and the possibility of transcending it. As Naropa says, its followers are adrift in an ocean of erroneous philosophy.

> The schools of ours, such as the shravakas,
> The pratyekabuddhas, and the followers of Mind Only,
> Maintain the duality of perceiver and perceived,
> And conceptualize nonduality as being the true.

Shravakas and pratyekabuddhas, both Hinayana schools, maintain that both the perceiver (the perceiving mind) and the perceived — the perceived objects — both have ultimate existence in some form. Followers of the Mind-Only school understand that both the perceiver and the perceived are insubstantial, yet they still hold onto the concept of the wisdom that is a non-dual state of knowing as a true, ultimate entity.

> Moreover, they get caught in the web of concepts
> Such as whether the perceived is real or false.

Here Naropa is further discussing the view of the Mind-Only school. There is some difference within this school with regard to the reality of objects, meaning the content of experience. Some hold that the perceived is real in that it is experienced. Another group asserts that whatever is perceived is utterly empty and is thus false and unreal. After all, whether one regards the content of experience to be real or unreal, one may still fail to see that which experiences as being totally empty of a self-nature. The Mind-Only school apprehends the perceiving mind as having some substantial existence. It's this clinging to a concept of non-dual knowing that prevents Mind-Only followers from reaching the ultimate destination of the path. Due to this subtle conceptual attachment, they are unable to attain true and complete enlightenment within this very same body and life.

8

Now I will finish the life story of Naropa. After he received Tilopa's prophecy regarding his future disciples, including the Tibetan translator Marpa Lotsawa, Naropa felt extremely fortunate. He had met a qualified master and received the authentic instructions. True realization had sprung forth within his stream of being. He had such confidence that even if he met with the thousand buddhas of this aeon, he felt there would be nothing he needed to ask or clear up. After this he was extremely delighted! He left Tilopa to go wander aimlessly, without any fixed abode. Two other disciples of Tilopa, Riripa, and Kasoripa, went to pay their respects to Tilopa and Naropa. Finding Naropa nowhere to be found, they asked Tilopa, "Where has Naropa gone?" Tilopa answered, "He has reached accomplishment in Mahamudra and has left for unknown places." These two disciples were themselves accomplished masters. They said to Tilopa, "The two of us are Dharma friends with Naropa. Naropa is like a second Buddha, totally unrivaled by anyone. If he disappears and does not vigorously work for the benefit of beings, the activity of the Buddha will be interrupted." Tilopa said, "Well, if that is so, you can call him back." So, the pair set out to search for him, and after a long journey they finally found him sitting in meditation in an empty valley. They told him, "Tilopa told us to call you." Naropa said, "If Tilopa commands me to do so, I will come," and he got up from his meditation and returned with them.

Meeting Tilopa again, Naropa was told, "Since you have realized the natural state of nonarising awareness, the time has come for you to shower the rain of the Dharma on fortunate disciples by bringing them to maturation." His friend Riripa added, "If you remain alone in solitude, you will look like a shravaka." And Kasoripa said, "The time has come for you to dispense the medicine of the sacred Dharma to beings who are afflicted by the illness of suffering."

Naropa prostrated to Tilopa and said, "I accept what the vajra master and my vajra brothers ask me to do. I will teach all sentient beings without any prejudice whatsoever." Naropa went and stayed at Pullahari, where he had a vision of Chakrasamvara. In it he received a prediction that he would soon meet with a destined and worthy disciple, who would come from Tibet to eastern India. Naropa sent out one of his disciples, called Getsül Sherab, to find this disciple and bring him back. And this is how Marpa met Naropa.

That concludes the life story of Naropa. Now let's return to Naropa's song. I have offered the fourth point, on how the spontaneously present quality is self-liberated. Unless we realize that, we are in delusion. Whether we follow a non-Buddhist philosophy or a Buddhist system, until we truly recognize the natural state as it is, we will still be caught in the web of concepts. If we understand the natural state of mind exactly as it is, both the meditation training and the conduct will be correct.

> By not mistaking the view in this way,
> You attain enlightenment through the meditation training and
> conduct,
> That are in harmony with the real,
> Just like a well-trained race horse.

The first line means to not be like a non-Buddhist philosopher, or like the shravakas, the pratyekabuddhas, and the Mind Only followers. A mistaken view prevents us from reaching the level of Vajradhara in one body and lifetime. It is necessary to ascertain the correct view, as explained previously.

In Buddhism there are two approaches to a correct view: one makes use of inference, while the other uses direct perception, or 'seeing in actuality.' The view of Mahamudra uses the second approach, the seeing in actuality. In the Sutra system, one arrives at a correct view by means of inference, using intelligent reasoning. This is also true of several Mahayana schools. For instance, the Middle-Way school called *Rangtong* establishes the emptiness of all things by exposing their lack of self-nature, first, by intellectual comprehension and then by attaining complete certainty. Since things are in fact devoid of a self-nature, the Rangtong understanding is a correct view. The other Madhyamika school, the *Shentong* system, uses inference to establish certainty in how the natural state of all things is the nondual wisdom of emptiness and cognizance. This is also a correct view.

Despite their philosophical correctness, these Middle Way schools are not especially practical for training in Mahamudra because their views are intellectual assumptions, the products of inference. In the Sutra system before reaching true and complete enlightenment one must perfect the accumulations of merit and wisdom for an incredibly long time. The reason why it is a longer path is because the Sutra system takes inference as the path. Sooner or later, we must all proceed to 'seeing in actuality.'

Mahamudra training involves embracing direct perception. We do start out with scrutinizing the nature of mind, but not as a conceptual idea or an object of philosophical speculation. Rather, we look into the mind to see how it is in actuality, and we see that its nature is an original wakefulness in which emptiness and cognizance are indivisible. Because we are seeing directly rather than inferring, Mahamudra is superior. It is truly an unerring and extraordinary view. The meditation training that comes from applying this true and correct view will also be profound and extraordinary, unlike meditation based on inferior views.

When a view is unmistaken, the training in that will be unmistaken as well. And our conduct, our acting upon that view, will be equally unmistaken. When we train in the correct view of Mahamudra, the disturbing emotions and other flaws present within our stream of being will automatically subside. In addition, the good qualities present, the intrinsic qualities of original wakefulness — like offering kindness and compassion — will spontaneously increase. All this is possible only when the training is unmistaken, and unmistaken training is possible only when the view is unmistaken. What is an unmistaken view? It is in harmony with the real, meaning with the natural state. When the view is correct, the training and behavior will also be correct or in harmony with the real.

By keeping a view, meditation training and conduct that is in harmony with the real, we will definitely arrive at enlightenment. Naropa shows us the necessity of applying the correct view with the analogy of a fully trained race horse. A well-trained and well-bred horse will take an experienced rider to wherever he or she intends to go. There will not be any sidetracks or stumbles at any point on the way. The rider will safely and easily arrive at the desired destination. Arriving at enlightenment through a correct view, meditation, and conduct is like riding a well-trained horse.

A great number of practitioners in the past attained accomplishment by training in this unmistaken view. Many of them departed from this life to celestial realms without leaving an ordinary corpse behind. There have been a great number of practitioners who left in the rainbow body. How is such mastery achieved? Again, true accomplishment is based on the unmistaken, correct view, which is exactly what Naropa presents in this song.

> Unless you are in harmony with the real view,
> Your meditation training and conduct will be mistaken
> And you will not attain fruition,
> Like a blind man without a guide.

On the other hand, to practice a view that is not in harmony with what is real will result in mistaken training and behavior. The outcome will not be what we intended. Take the example of the non-Buddhist philosophers who impute the erroneous existence of an independent self or a supreme godhead. Practice based on this kind of assertion does not facilitate the realization of what is real — egolessness and emptiness. It is certainly possible to accumulate some merit based on the false ideas of self and a godhead. However, that merit only ripens as a rebirth with the pleasures of the higher realms within samsara. Realizing egolessness is the only actual remedy against disturbing emotions. Without realizing emptiness, we are unable to cut the root of disturbing emotions. Without cutting the root of disturbing emotions, true liberation is a "Mission: Impossible". So let me repeat again: if the view is not correct and true, our meditation training, conduct and fruition are also mistaken.

Among the Buddhist schools, the views of shravakas and pratyekabuddhas are said to be partially correct or incomplete, in the sense that they do not fully see emptiness, nor realize the natural state to be empty cognizance. For instance, the shravaka view of emptiness is limited to an understanding of egolessness, the non-existence of the individual self. Lacking the complete view, the shravakas' meditation training is also incomplete, as is the conduct and fruition. By following the shravaka path, one can eliminate the obscuration of disturbing emotions, but the cognitive obscuration remains. The end result achieved by training in egolessness and emphasizing impermanence is called the shravaka arhat level.

The pratyekabuddhas, on the other hand, understand the non-existence of the self-entity of phenomena to some extent, in that they understand that perceived objects have no ultimate existence. Based on this view, they achieve the pratyekabuddha arhat level, but they are unable to attain the ultimate fruition of complete enlightenment.

Among the Mahayana schools, followers of the Mind-Only and the Middle Way realize the correct view, but this realization is also incomplete. Mind-Only followers comprehend that all experience is mind. However, they still hold that this mind truly exists. The Middle Way view, though correct, is arrived at based on an inferred idea of emptiness. And it is not possible to attain complete enlightenment in a single body and lifetime by training in an idea that is created through inference.

To reiterate, non-Buddhist philosophers with mistaken views are incapable of accomplishing fruition through their training because their view is not in harmony with what is real. The shravakas and pratyekabuddhas do attain liberation from samsara, but because their view is only partially true, they cannot attain complete enlightenment. Followers of the Mahayana schools of Mind-Only and Middle Way can attain complete enlightenment because their view is basically correct, but because it is an inference, they cannot attain this state very quickly.

The crucial point that everything depends upon is whether or not the view is perfect and complete. No matter how much effort you might make by training in an incorrect view, a false assumption will never be in harmony with reality. The outcome of one's training cannot be anything other than what has been trained in. In other words, if the view is not truly and fully in accordance with the natural state of all things, the result of training in it will also be imperfect. The analogy used for the wrong view here is that of a blind person left alone on a vast plain. Unable to see clearly, he will inevitably take the wrong track and will not reach his desired destination.

How can my conceptual mind, [limited in its perceptions] like a
frog in a well,
Discover the profundity by stirring up
The ocean-like depth of the true meaning!
May all learned masters forgive my errors!

Now we are nearing the end of the text. Here Naropa apologizes for any faults he might have made in writing this. 'The true meaning' mentioned here is the truth of what is real, the nature of all things. This is the state of Mahamudra, which is extremely vast and profound. The realization of that, the fruition, is equally vast and profound, like an ocean. Naropa humbly compares his intellect, his conceptual mind, with that of a frog living in a well. The frog, with its narrow perspective and confined horizon, knows the size of the well and the depth of its water. However, it is unable to fully fathom the depth and the vastness of the ocean.

When he writes 'Stirring up the ocean-like depth of true meaning' Naropa means that a narrow little mind like his own is incapable of measuring the true depth of Mahamudra, the nature of all things. Naropa apologizes for any faults that may have occurred in attempting to express it. He indicates here that his conceptual understanding of the nature of Mahamudra doesn't approach the true reality of how Mahamudra actually is. Even his actual, direct understanding of Mahamudra may not be complete. And even if he does possess a complete understanding of Mahamudra he acknowledges he may lack the clarity to express it fully. Thus, he begs forgiveness from all learned masters for any shortcoming he may have committed.

These four lines sound like a simple apology by Naropa. Indirectly, though, they contain advice and instruction for us. We want to train in Mahamudra and are interested in receiving teachings on it. But we should be cautious because we are ordinary people with a weakness for becoming conceited at the slightest sign of progress. We enthusiastically congratulate ourselves at the tiniest attainment, and when we become even a little stable in our meditation state, we immediately feel, "Now I've really gotten somewhere! I've reached some accomplishment!" That kind of conceit automatically puts development on hold. It is just like pushing the pause button on a tape recorder. If we check closely, we can discover for ourselves how such pride hampers progress. Naropa teaches us by example that we should consider ourselves to be like frogs in a well. There is no reason to be proud about minor progress in practice. Much better to understand that we have not yet completed the path and still have a long way to go. Use slight advances in practice to inspire you to work harder, cultivating the attitude, "I must meditate! I must train further, because I have not reached complete enlightenment!" By doing this, we can advance further.

It is of course very beneficial to be interested in Mahamudra. It is an extremely great blessing to be able to receive the instructions and to practice. There are indeed extraordinary results and signs of the path but experiencing small indications of progress doesn't mean that we should stop there and feel satisfied with ourselves. On the contrary, we should understand that they are just signs. Remind yourself, "The instructions are profound and effective, but I will persevere with fortitude until reaching complete and true enlightenment. Not only will I train in Mahamudra but also in devotion and compassion. The time has not arrived to stop the practice. I shouldn't feel proud." Heed the inner advice in these four lines.

> Through whatever goodness there is from writing this
> May the stain of delusion be fully cleared away
> In fortunate and worthy beings,
> And may the knowledge of realization grow forth!

In these last four lines, Naropa dedicates the merit generated by the writing of this song and makes aspirations. *The View, Concisely Put* is, exactly as the title implies, a concise expression of the view of Mahamudra. Merit is created not only by writing this but by studying it, by trying to understand and put this text into practice. Because this song has survived and has been handed down to the present day, teachings can be given and individuals can increase their understanding and progress in training. An inconceivable amount of beneficial activity can unfold, based on Naropa having written this song. He makes the wish that all that goodness be dedicated so that fortunate and worthy beings will be able to receive, understand, and put these teachings into practice. It is through the accumulation of vast merit that we come into contact with the words of the Victorious Ones. Most especially, among the expedient and the definitive meaning, only extremely fortunate people are able to connect with, receive and understand teachings on the definitive meaning such as *The View, Concisely Put.* In addition to receiving it, if we are practitioners who are willing to persevere and train with fortitude, we can truly be called worthy people.

Naropa continues to wish that the stain of delusion, which is the exact opposite of understanding the true view, may be cleared away. May the defilement of not being able to train correctly in meditation, and the shortcoming of not truly being able to enact the correct view, both be cleared away! Naropa makes the aspiration that, having cleansed the stain of delusion, the knowledge of realization may grow forth. How incredibly wonderful and auspicious to meet a teaching like this! Naropa adds to these blessings by sealing it with the aspiration that whoever connects with it will attain realization.

This completes *The View, Concisely Put* by Naropa.

In the presence of the pandita Jnana Siddhi, this was translated and corrected by the Lotsawa Marpa Chökyi Lodrö.

The text ends with the remark that in the presence of the Pandita Jnana Siddhi, one of Naropa's names, this teaching was translated into Tibetan and then corrected by the Tibetan translator Marpa Chökyi Lodrö.

To conclude, let me say that I am very pleased by your interest in this teaching. Having received it, please put it into practice by applying it in your meditation training. Be aware also that there could be some negative effect from the profundity of this song, in that the emphasis on the view may seem to preclude the importance of proper conduct in daily life. The view of Mahamudra is a high one, and there is always the danger that we may neglect the importance of appropriate behavior and act in a crude way. That is not what is truly meant. Follow what

Tilopa advised, in the quotation I mentioned earlier: "Until you fully realize the dependent origination of all experience, do not separate yourself from the chariot of the two accumulations." While training in a high view, please conduct yourself in accordance with the Dharma, gathering the accumulations and purifying the obscurations.

Let's dedicate whatever merit we accumulated from studying, teaching and practicing *The View, Concisely Put* to the purpose of all sentient beings fully comprehending the view of Mahamudra. May we realize the view of Mahamudra, perfect the training in it and attain true and complete enlightenment!

The Summary of Mahamudra

In the Indian language: *Mahamudra Padametha.*
In Tibetan: *phyag rgya chen po tshig bsdus pa,* [*Chagya Chenpo Tsig Düpa*].
In English: *The Summary of Mahamudra.*

Homage to the state of great bliss!

First, stating the nature of Mahamudra of perception:

Concerning what is called Mahamudra:
All things are your own mind.
Seeing objects as external is a mistaken concept;
Like a dream, they are empty of concreteness.

Second, stating the nature of Mahamudra of awareness:

This mind, as well, is a mere movement of attention
That has no self-nature, being merely like a gust of wind.
Empty of identity, like space,
All things, like space, are equal.

Third, stating the nature of the Mahamudra of union:

When speaking of 'Mahamudra,'
It is not an identity that can be shown.
Therefore, the mind's suchness
Is itself the state of Mahamudra.

Thus, he taught the Mahamudra of the view through the threefold perception, awareness, and union. Next, among the three points on the Mahamudra of meditation, first stating the nature of Mahamudra of the basic state:

It is neither something to be corrected nor transformed,
But when anyone sees and realizes its nature,

All that appears and exists is Mahamudra,
The great and all-encompassing dharmakaya.

Second, stating the nature of the Mahamudra of realization:

Naturally and without contriving, allowed to simply be,
This unimagined dharmakaya,
Letting it be without seeking is the meditation training.
But to meditate while seeking is deluded mind.

Third, stating the nature of Mahamudra of indivisibility:

Just as with space, just as with a magical display,
While neither cultivating nor not cultivating
How can you be separate or not separate!
This is a yogi's understanding.

Once more, for the three points about the Mahamudra of conduct, first, stating the nature of Mahamudra of self-liberation:

All the good deeds and harmful actions
Dissolve by simply knowing this nature.
The emotions are the great wisdom;
Like a jungle fire, they are the yogi's helpers.

Second, stating the nature of Mahamudra of equal taste:

How can there be staying or going?
What meditation is there by fleeing to a hermitage?
Without understanding this, all possible means
Never bring more than temporary liberation.

Third, stating the nature of the Mahamudra of indivisibility:

When understanding this nature, what is there to bind you?
While being undistracted from its continuity,

There is neither a composed nor an uncomposed state
To be cultivated or corrected with a remedy.

Once more, for the three points about the Mahamudra of fruition, first, stating the nature of Mahamudra of what appears and exists:

It is not made out of anything.
Experience self-liberated is dharmadhatu.
Thinking self-liberated is great wisdom.
Nondual equality is dharmakaya.

Second, stating the nature of Mahamudra of samsara and nirvana:

Like the continuous flow of a great river,
Whatever you do is meaningful.
This is the eternal awakened state,
The great bliss, leaving no place for samsara.

Third, stating the nature of Mahamudra of ultimate perfection:

All things are empty of their own identities.
The concept fixed on emptiness has dissolved in itself.
Free of concept, holding nothing in mind;
Is in itself the path of all buddhas.

To conclude, instructing and stating the dedication:

For the most fortunate ones,
I have made these concise words of heartfelt advice.
Through this, may every single sentient being
Be established in Mahamudra.

This was given orally by the great pandita Naropa, to Marpa Chökyi Lodrö at Pullahari.

These thirteen verses that concisely show Mahamudra in completeness were divided up in accordance with their meaning. The details should be known from oral teachings. Do not fix your mind on other variations; since this is copied from the old manuscripts, I feel it should not be changed.

(This note was added by Shamar Kachö Wangpo. There is a saying that "The pith instructions in Mahamudra should be known from an instruction in concise words." It is the opinion of all past sublime masters who upheld the Practice Lineage that this teaching summarizes all the key points of Mahamudra instruction.)

9

The next text by Naropa is called *The Summary of Mahamudra.* It is very short and thus not difficult to learn by heart. Nor is it difficult to practice, understand, and apply. As a matter of fact, this is exactly how it was meant to be. Naropa wrote this with the thought of future generations in mind, offering it with the aspiration that they would understand, memorize and apply this teaching. This brief text is truly profound, for it contains all the key points of the view, meditation, conduct and fruition of Mahamudra.

To repeat a bit about the life of Naropa: before Naropa met Tilopa he was already a great pandita. Although he was incredibly learned, he was not satisfied with his intellectual knowledge. He set out to search for a master who could give him the profound pith instructions. Naropa suffered tremendous hardships in trying to find Tilopa, and even after he encountered Tilopa and was accepted as his disciple, he underwent unimaginable trials trying to receive instructions. Finally, he succeeded in obtaining the pith teachings from Tilopa. Among these extraordinary instructions were the teachings on Mahamudra, which he put into practice. He trained in them and attained complete realization of Mahamudra. Later on, he taught Mahamudra, often by using *The Summary of Mahamudra.*

Lord Buddha taught the Dharma in a way that was adapted to the mental capacity of his listeners. He taught beginners how to practice in a gradual fashion so that they could start at whatever level they happened to be at and progress step by step. When the Buddha turned the wheel of the first set of teachings, he focused on the Four Noble Truths. The first Noble Truth is the truth of suffering, which we should all be able to easily understand. The second is that suffering has a cause, which is karmic actions and disturbing emotions. The third Noble Truth is that suffering can be brought to an end, and the fourth describes the way that leads to the cessation of suffering, called the path. In order to help beginners actually applying the teachings, the Lord Buddha began by introducing egolessness, the absence of the individual self.

It is a fact that ordinary sentient beings do suffer. They have problems and troubles, hardships and grief. Most of this suffering takes place in the realm of thought. The most difficult and troublesome thoughts are disturbing emotions. One of the main disturbing emotions is anger, or a hostile frame of mind. Out of this anger, we may use harsh words or act out physically, throwing or breaking something or hitting someone. Sometimes our negative actions are motivated by attachment or greed. Other times they come from ignorance, indecision, or being unclear, stupid or deluded. Sometimes we feel conceited or proud, sometimes jealous or competitive. So, do you understand the sequence of events? First, disturbing emotions occupy our minds, making us unsettled. Next, we express them through words, complicating matters. The worst situation is when we physically act out these unhealthy thought patterns. Disturbing emotions create a tremendous amount of problems, for ourselves and others. All of these disturbing emotions are based on ego-clinging — the feeling "Me, I am the most important." Once we understand this point clearly, we may decide to consciously do the opposite, saying to ourselves: "I will no longer consider myself important." Unfortunately, this doesn't solve the problem. Merely thinking, "I shouldn't behave like that" is not in itself a direct remedy against ego-clinging. A thought cannot eliminate the concept of self.

Previously I mentioned relative bodhichitta as a way to reduce disturbing emotions. By shifting our attitude away from selfishness and aspiring to help others, disturbing emotions can be reduced. This type of training diminishes their strength, but it doesn't totally uproot them. That is why that type of bodhichitta is called 'relative' or superficial. It only decreases disturbing emotions, but does not bring them to an end.

Ultimate bodhichitta, on the other hand, brings disturbing emotions to a permanent end. If we are introduced to and become certain about the nature of our mind, we can fully understand that there is no such thing as a self. Without carefully investigating, however, we tend to believe in the existence of a self. We're not very clear on exactly what constitutes 'myself,' assigning that term to all sorts of different things — our body, our consciousness, or some unclear mixture of these factors. We must practice to the point that we become clear on the fact that whatever the word 'me' refers to, this object is not to be found anywhere at all. First, we must learn to look for this 'me.' Next, we need to become completely certain that there is no such thing as an I or a self.

At that point, the very basis for disturbing emotions and selfishness is totally eliminated from the very root.

This is why the Buddha taught in his very first set of teachings how we can cultivate insight into egolessness. In the second set of teachings, the Buddha went even further. He taught that it is not only the individual self that is non-existent. Everything, all phenomena, all objects, as well as consciousness itself, is devoid of any true identity. All things have the nature of emptiness. Discovering this for ourselves changes our perspective. When we fully actualize emptiness, we are no longer obstructed by anything. Our minds are able to remain at great peace, at total ease. This is a wider or more expansive insight than that of simply realizing egolessness.

The understanding that all things are emptiness is entirely correct. However, we might misconstrue the meaning of emptiness to mean nothingness, a complete voidness. This misunderstanding fixates on the thought that all things are a blank, nothing whatsoever, which is not correct. To remedy this, the Buddha taught that not only is the identity of all things utterly empty; it is emptiness itself. This emptiness, by nature, has the capacity to know, to experience, to cognize. That is the wakeful wisdom quality that is indivisible from emptiness itself. This is the intent of the third set of teachings, the final turning of the Wheel of Dharma.

The great master Naropa expresses the view of Mahamudra under three headings. The first is called stating the nature of Mahamudra of perception. The second is stating the nature of Mahamudra of awareness. The third is stating the nature of Mahamudra of union.

First, stating the nature of Mahamudra of perception:

> Concerning what is called Mahamudra:
> All things are your own mind.
> Seeing objects as external is a mistaken concept;
> Like a dream, they are empty of concreteness.

What does it mean when we use the word Mahamudra? What is it that we are talking about? What does this term refer to? What is Mahamudra about? This verse introduces the nature of the Mahamudra of perception. Actually, what is it that we as sentient beings perceive? I discussed this topic briefly when explaining the first song and will now go into it in more detail. Through what is called the eye consciousness, we perceive visual objects and see sights. Because we have the capacity to hear through our ears, the ear consciousness, we hear sounds. We have the capacity to taste with our tongues, which is called the tongue consciousness. Through our nose consciousness, we can experience smell, and through our body consciousness we can touch. In general Buddhist terminology these are labeled the five sense consciousnesses, or the five sense cognitions. The mind experiences the world through these five senses. However, our mind consciousness itself does not experience sights, smells, sounds, tastes or textures directly. What is being perceived is a mental impression of these experiences. Based on that mental image, we create secondary thoughts about past, present, and future. We determine what we like and don't like, what should be accepted or rejected. That activity is named the sixth consciousness. Sometimes it is called the ideational consciousness; other times simply mind consciousness. Thus, there are six consciousnesses altogether.

The term "all things" refers not only to mental objects but to the objects of all six consciousnesses — sights, sounds, smell, taste, and textures, as well as mental objects. What is normally being experienced is an impression or an image that takes place in the mind. Not knowing this, we tend to believe, for example, that when the object of the eye consciousness is presented to the mind, that this perceived object is somewhere outside. It is apprehended as being outside of ourselves, while the perceiver, the mind, is considered to be somewhere inside. Likewise, whatever quality we attach to these perceived objects as being either pleasant or unpleasant, good or bad, is similarly apprehended as a 'real' entity that exists outside of ourselves.

This is how it seems to be, in that this is how we normally perceive. But is this the real state of things? No, it isn't, because it only seems like what we see is outside. Actually, what we experience is an impression that arises in or exists in our own mind. Whether it's something that is seen, heard, smelled, tasted or felt physically, all these impressions or perceptions take place within our mind. All perceptions, be they the objects of the six consciousnesses or all the different thoughts and emotional reactions that might arise, — are not external to ourselves; they are mental occurrences that take place in our own mind. Therefore, all things are your own mind. Believing objects to be external is a mistaken concept. To believe that what is being experienced is other than our own perception, some object that exists by itself, apart from and separate from our experience of it, is a deluded idea.

The great masters give all sorts of different teachings to help us understand how things actually are. They may ask us to use our own intelligence to figure out whether the normal way of experiencing is true or not. For example, look at a pillar in a room. The pillar appears to us through our seeing, our visual cognition, and in our minds the image of the pillar is perceived. Based on that we form the thought "There is a pillar in the room." The real proof of whether this is or isn't true is our own experience. The great Buddhist logicians Chandrakirti and Dignaga explained that we use our personal impressions as the final authentication of reality. They state that the sole evidence beings have that things are perceived as being outside is because we say, "I see them, therefore they exist." There is no other way to validate a perception. That is called the proof of clearly knowing. Based on this reasoning, there is no reason to believe that things exist outside our own experience or are separate from their being known.

Mahamudra is the catalyst that changes our normal comprehension. The starting point in the tradition is proof through experience. The belief that things are outside of ourselves is nothing other than a mental perception. When examined, it becomes apparent that this mere presence has no reality to it. It is likewise with the perceiving mind in that it does not possess any concrete existence. When mind is pointed out and recognized, it is possible to realize that both perceptions and the perceiver are nonexistent.

We can discover this through intellectual reasoning or through direct experience. The end result is the same. The Buddha and many great masters used the analogy of a dream to facilitate the understanding of the essential unreality of all things. Whatever we perceive during the daytime, we also can experience at night in dreams. We can see and vividly experience mountains, houses, people and all sorts of different things. Do they really exist because we see them in our dreams? Are there actually mountains and houses while we dream? No, it only seems like there are. While they don't really exist, still, for the dreamer it feels as if they do. That is why it is said that all things are like a dream — because, just as in a dream, all impressions of external objects in our waking experience appear only in the mind. Therefore, they're empty of concreteness. This point covered the nature of Mahamudra of perception.

Second, stating the nature of Mahamudra of awareness:

> This mind, as well, is a mere movement of attention
> That has no self-nature, being merely like a gust of wind.
> Empty of identity, like space,
> All things, like space, are equal.

The first verse was about what is perceived. The second verse is called stating the nature of Mahamudra of awareness. In this context, you can simply call awareness the mind, the perceiver. When talking about mind, we get the impression that there is a doer, the instigator or someone in charge. We feel that mind is very forceful, very powerful. We need to look at exactly what this mind is. We must ask: "What is it that thinks; where are the thoughts?" At that moment it is very hard to pinpoint anything. However, simultaneously, there is a presence of thought that is similar to a reflection in a mirror. Look into a mirror very closely. Find exactly where the reflection is; where it comes from; where it goes to afterwards. If you turn the mirror around and the reflection disappears, you are at a complete loss to find a fixed place to assign the reflection to. It is the same with the images we experience in a dream. First, we dream of one thing, then another. During the second dream, where exactly did those first images go? It is invariably impossible to find a place that they went to, because there is no such place. In the same way, what we call mind, the knower, is only a seeming presence. There's no reality to it. It's a mere movement of attention: the attention moves as a thought, as a feeling, as a memory, but there is no substance to it.

Let's investigate anger. When we are extremely angry, it feels like the anger has a power of its own. It overtakes us so that we lose control. We can't handle it; instead, it seems to handle us. It is so strong that we have to shout nasty words and contort our faces with rage. This is how it seems to be at that moment while our attention is directed outward towards the target of our anger. Instead of doing that, why not let our attention face itself, and turn inward. Look at what the anger is. Who feels angry? Where does this anger rise from? Is there a place where this anger is now? Is there someone who is angry, since we feel so strongly "I am angry"? Is there a real substance, a force? Questioning in this way, it's absolutely impossible to find such a thing. There is neither a place to find, nor a substance, nor any entity. It's simply a seeming presence, a mere movement of the attention that has no reality to it whatsoever. It is like a bubble on the surface of water. Anger arises from the empty essence; and it is nonexistent. We believe the anger is real. When we look into its essence, we find that it is not.

Sometimes our aversion towards a thing or a person manifests as anger. Other times it's not as strong, but lingers as a more subtle form of aggression. We keep our hostility in mind and hold a grudge. We don't want to let go of the negativity. It is just ready to be provoked There's another shade of anger called ill-will, in which we wait for the opportunity to retaliate, to cause harm; we simply want that person to suffer. There is an additional type called spitefulness, when we wait for the opportunity to say nasty words that can hurt another's feelings. All these are different flavors of anger. In any of these situations, if we look into that emotion, or into the one who feels this emotion, we fail to find any concrete thing.

Anger, resentment, ill-will, spitefulness — all are nothing more than a mere movement of the attention. They are a seeming presence that is not made out of anything. The moment we look into an emotion, we find 'no thing'. The emotion has no self-nature. The analogy given describes feelings as 'being merely like a gust of wind.' When you feel a gust of wind on your skin, is there anything to take hold of? No, because it is not substantial in the normal sense. You don't have to think of the analogy as referring only to external wind. You can also think of it as the wind that moves within the channels of the body, which causes our attention to flutter. Yet it is a mere movement, a seeming presence of thought, of cognition, of disturbing emotion. The moment we look into this movement, there is no thing. It is said that it is empty of identity, possessing no core to it, like space.

"All things", meaning all things perceived as being outside, "are equal;" they are "like space." Whatever is perceived has no real identity. There is no substance to it — it is empty, so in that sense perceived things are like space, or equal to it. Space is used as an example because space has no color or concrete substance. This verse also implies that both outer and inner things, meaning both perceived objects and the perceiving mind, are equal in that they have no identity to them. They are all equal, like space, in being empty.

If you have doubts about anything, here's your chance to ask.

STUDENT: During meditation practice I try to look directly at a disturbing emotion like anger. When I investigate the emotion, questioning, "What is it? Where is it? Where does it exist?" it seems like the harder I try, the more vivid it becomes, and it becomes more difficult to actually find the emotion itself. Somehow looking into the emptiness heightens the vividness of it. I was wondering if Rinpoche would discuss that. There's another aspect to that, too, which is that it's somewhat paralyzing, the simultaneity of it. It leaves me feeling dumbfounded, completely perplexed.

RINPOCHE: There are two common mistakes in dealing with disturbing emotions in practice. One is to intellectualize the emotion. We think, "It must be empty because this is what I've heard; therefore, this emotion is empty." We plaster over the naked emotion with the idea of emptiness. While the intellectual understanding is quite forceful in this case, it is not actual meditation experience. The actual practice is rather to face the disturbing emotion directly, without holding onto some idea about what a disturbing emotion is. Look in a naked way and ascertain what the real identity of the emotion is. Discover there is no 'thing' to it; that it's empty. In this way, the disturbing emotion has no foothold upon which it can remain. It dissolves. However, if we only have the idea of it being empty, the experience of its emptiness is pressed into the background. That's one way that we could be mistaken.

The other is when we experience emptiness in actuality, but only for a fraction of a second. We look towards the emotion, and see that it's empty. Then we let it slide, thinking that is sufficient. Actually, the direct experience of the emptiness of any emotion needs to be sustained, in order to totally uproot any basis for further continuation of the disturbing emotion. This is called 'straying into the remedy' or going astray as to what concerns the remedy. Whenever we feel a disturbing emotion, we immediately use the idea of its emptiness as a hammer to knock the emotion on the head, so to speak. We then think that is sufficient. And we immediately become distracted again, until we remember to give the emotion another whack. That is not the correct way either.

STUDENT: Do all these things have to do with relaxing, in a way?

RINPOCHE: The remedy is not to figure out intellectually that the identity of an emotion is empty. It is to directly see this emptiness, and to sustain the continuity of this insight. By sustaining the continuity of the insight into emptiness, it becomes possible for all disturbing emotions to dissolve. That is the remedy.

Sometimes when we are angry, we do really try to look into the empty essence of this anger. We look and we look, but at the same time in the corner of our mind we feel: "I should retaliate because what he or she did was really not right. Something has to be done about that. It's my responsibility to make sure that justice gets served." As long as we retain fondness for resentment and manage to justify it, it is very hard to penetrate to the core of the emptiness of the emotion.

10

In this text, *The Summary of Mahamudra*, Naropa explains the view under three headings: the Mahamudra of the perceived, the Mahamudra of awareness, and the Mahamudra of union. There are different traditions of teaching Mahamudra. Sometimes it is emphasized that one realizes the nature of the perceived, and after that the Mahamudra of awareness, which is mind. Another style maintains it doesn't matter much whether one understands that the objects perceived are, in fact, mind. That conviction is not as important as understanding and realizing the nature of the Mahamudra of awareness. However, in this text, the great pandita Naropa teaches first the Mahamudra of the perceived, then the Mahamudra of awareness in a gradual way.

The beginning verses on Mahamudra of the perceived introduce us to the fact that what we perceive does not really exist, by nature. Moreover, it cannot be established as truly existing. It is emptiness. In the second verse we find that the perceiver, awareness, is likewise devoid of true existence by nature and is emptiness. In both of these cases, the empty quality rather than the cognizant quality is emphasized.

The third point, under the view of Mahamudra, is called the nature of the Mahamudra of union. The nature of mind is not only empty, but cognizant as well. These two qualities of being empty and cognizant are an indivisible unity. First, we are introduced to what we perceive and the perceiver as being empty and devoid of true existence. Understanding the emptiness of mind is not necessarily understanding the true nature of mind. Not only is the mind empty; it has the capacity to know, to cognize.

Third, stating the nature of the Mahamudra of union:

When speaking of 'Mahamudra,'
It is not an identity that can be shown.
Therefore, the mind's suchness
Is itself the state of Mahamudra.

Now in this third verse about the Mahamudra of union, the first line states: "When speaking of Mahamudra." What is referred to as being Mahamudra? What do we take as the object of our meditation? What are we supposed to realize through our practice? Is Mahamudra a certain thing that can be pointed out and shown? No, Mahamudra is not an entity that we can hold in mind. It is not an object of our perception. It is not seen through the eyes, heard through the ears, smelled through our nose, tasted through the tongue, or felt through the body.

Mahamudra is not a thing that can be shown, and yet it is the very nature or suchness of our mind. Mind is explained as the six groups of cognitions or as the eight groups of cognitions. These six were mentioned previously as the consciousnesses of sight, sound, smelling, tasting, touch, and the mind consciousness. 'Mind' implies a sense of clarity, an ability to be conscious, to cognize. Looking into what that actually is, it is impossible to find a place where that clarity or conscious quality abides. Mind is not made out of anything. This actuality of how the mind really is, is called the 'suchness', and that itself is the state of Mahamudra.

What do we think of when we hear a statement like: "Emptiness not made out of anything whatsoever."? Since we are ordinary people we think of something that is utterly void, like space. Space is empty, totally empty. There is no concrete substance that we call space. However, this is not the same as the empty essence of Mahamudra. Empty space is empty of any capacities, any properties. There is nothing wrong with space, nothing negative about it. It is merely the dimension that is empty of matter. When the question is raised, "Is the Mahamudra nature of mind identical with space?", the answer is no, because space doesn't have any positive qualities. There is no basis for the capacity of wisdom, knowledge, great bliss, and all the other enlightened attributes. Even though there are no negative characteristics about space, there are no positive ones either. The total absence of good or evil characteristics is not the same as the Mahamudra nature of mind. The Mahamudra nature of mind, while being empty, does possess a nature of cognizance.

Our traditional guidance manuals explain that when seeking to understand the essence of Mahamudra, we should begin by investigating the arising, dwelling, and disappearance of the thinking mind, the flow of thought. We usually feel that there is some 'thing' that experiences. That feeling is precisely what we should look into when a thought moves. We should question in these ways: "Where does a thought come from? What is the source of the thinker? From where does a cognition take place? Can we find a thought anywhere?" We should try not only to find the location of a thought, but also to determine how a thought is formed, and whether there is some substance to it. Looking into this very closely, we will sooner or later discover that there is neither a place of origin nor any thoughts to find anywhere, no matter how hard we search. Moreover, there is no 'thing' called mind that thinks or comes about from somewhere. After some investigation, we discover that the nature of mind is nonarising, which means that there is no origination of mind. Next, we look into where mind abides. Finally, we examine where mind, the thinking, goes when it disappears. When mind vanishes, what is it that vanishes, and into which place or location does this vanishing happen? We likewise fail to find any 'thing' that dwells anywhere, or that disappears. All this is because mind is not made out of any concrete substance whatsoever.

When we looked for this knowing entity called mind, and we failed to find any thing, is it because we somehow failed to look well enough? No, that's not so. Mind is not some thing that is out of reach. We are the ones who think and perceive, so our minds are something very close at hand that can be looked for. When we fail to find anything, the reason is none other than that there is no thing to find. Mind is not a concrete thing lying and waiting to be discovered. It is not that we needed to continue a little longer and eventually would have found it. Mind is unfindable. This is what the Third Karmapa stated in The Aspiration of Mahamudra: "It cannot be said to exist, since even the buddhas do not see it." What exactly does that mean? A buddha with perfect wisdom, should be capable of seeing the mind, if such a thing existed. But if even a buddha cannot see a thing called mind, then definitely we as ordinary sentient beings will not be able to do so. Why is this? Again, it is because mind is not made out of anything whatsoever.

The Buddha described the nature of mind exactly when he said: "Transcendent knowledge, prajnaparamita, is beyond thought, word and description." We cannot adequately find words that describe exactly how the nature of mind is. It is not possible to use thoughts to figure out, reason, and come up with a mental picture of how the nature of mind is, because this nature, this 'transcendent knowledge', lies beyond both words and thoughts. It is inconceivable, beyond the grasp of normal intellect. When we searched and didn't find the mind, did that mean there was no thing at all? Is mind void like physical space? No, it's not like that either. The next line in the Karmapa Rangjung Dorje's composition is: "You cannot say it is nonexistent, because it is the basis for both samsara and nirvana." Even though mind is not made out of anything, it's not totally non-existent. It is the basis for both samsara and nirvana. Our ignorance of this empty cognizance is the basis for the whole of samsaric existence. Seeing this empty cognizance clearly, exactly as it is, becomes the basis for progressing through the paths and bhumis towards complete enlightenment.

When an ordinary person hears about something that both exists and doesn't at the same time, it sounds like nonsense. If a thing exists, it is not non-existent. Conversely, if there isn't anything, you cannot say concurrently that it exists. For any other entity in this world, to be and not to be are a contradiction; it's either one or the other. However, mind doesn't really fall into either one of these two categories of existence or nonexistence. It is not our job to invent an adequate philosophical way of describing that which both exists and doesn't simultaneously. What we as practitioners need to do is simply experience how this nature of mind is — not merely figure it out intellectually. In the next line from the same verse, the Third Karmapa describes it thusly: "These two are not a contradiction, but the middle way of unity." There is no conflict between the essence of mind being empty and its nature being cognizant. While mind in essence is non-existent or empty, its nature is cognizant, able to perceive. When we look into this nature of knowing, we see it is not made out of anything whatsoever. It is empty. Being empty and cognizant are not a contradiction; on the contrary, they are an indivisible unity. That itself is what is called 'the middle path'. It is an honest, straightforward path that does not become a sidetrack or an error: it is simply the middle way of unity.

Ordinary people may think, "Oh, the nature of mind is beyond me; I don't have the ability to see it." We may think to truly realize the innate nature of suchness is quite difficult, and indeed, if we hold onto that attitude, it is hard! Fortunately, though, there were many great siddhas of the lineage who personally realized this nature. They very kindly gave pith instructions that we can receive and apply. When we persevere in these instructions and look into this mind, we discover that it's not very difficult to recognize the nature of mind. After all, our mind is just our mind. It's not far away or out of reach. It is simply our own nature of mind, that which perceives. When looking into that which experiences, into this mind, it's not that difficult at all to see it as it is. We can understand first-hand that it is not made out of anything, and yet it is not a complete nothing. There is still experience; there is the ability to perceive and be awake. These two are not two different entities — one empty, another cognizant. Mind is not limited to being one or the other. That is why the Third Karmapa in his fourth line says: "May we realize the unconfined nature of mind."

It's possible in this context to doubt whether we can actually see the nature of mind. This problem arises particularly with people who have studied Buddhist philosophy. For instance, Shantideva, in the chapter on transcendent knowledge in the *Bodhicharya Avatara*, uses examples to show how it is not possible for the mind to know or see itself. One example he gives is that of a sword: it can cut other things, but no matter how sharp the sword is, it cannot cut itself. Likewise, a very strong, agile person can master other creatures. He can tame a horse, or even an elephant — but he cannot ride on his own back, no matter how strong he is. In this same way, the mind cannot see itself. Chandrakirti gave similar examples for how the mind cannot see or apprehend itself. When reading these lines of logic, we may doubt whether it's possible for the mind to see or realize itself. Honestly, though, this is not a problem. What Chandrakirti and Shantideva refute here is the possibility of the mind seeing itself as a concrete thing. They do not speak about the mind looking into itself and not seeing any entity. That is not what they are refuting — no need to be in doubt about that.

Both the Mahayana and Vajrayana traditions of Buddhism speak about the view and how to realize it. Even though the word view is used in both cases, the identity of that view is not exactly the same. The Sutra system's view is called 'the view of utilizing inference'. Here, we arrive at the view by deduction, through a process of investigating or inquiring further and further. In this process, one thinks, "It is probably true that the nature of mind is nothing whatsoever. It seems also to be true that it has a cognizant quality." This is all deduced through intellectual reasoning, and remains in the realm of thought. Yet it is possible through this intellectual understanding to feel convinced, to gain a very clear, precise conviction of how things are. By growing accustomed to this understanding, sooner or later we are able to see in actuality the innate nature of things. Even though this is a quite long path, the innate nature of things is eventually seen directly. The view of Vajrayana, in the context of Mahamudra or Dzogchen, is called 'the view that utilizes direct perception'. That means that our mind is not something we have to think of or find at some other place far away. It is right here – after all, it's our own mind, isn't it? There is no need for a lot of deduction. All that is necessary is to take a look at "How is this mind? Where is it?" We simply look, and by looking, we see directly how it really is. That is why it is called the view of utilizing direct perception.

Although in Mahamudra the view is introduced in direct experience, it is also possible for an individual to mistakenly approach it through inference or intellectual reasoning. One does this by not taking it personally, by not aiming for direct experience of Mahamudra. Instead, one thinks, "This is a profound idea I should grasp. Perceived objects do not really exist and my perceiving mind, my awareness, apparently doesn't really exist. These two are a unity. I must keep this understanding in mind." That is not what is really meant here in the context of Mahamudra. We should apply all these points to our own personal experience in a very clear and straightforward manner, rather than mistakenly intellectualizing our approach.

Next, among the three points, is about the Mahamudra of meditation, first stating the nature of Mahamudra of the basic state:

The first section was about the view. Now we come to the next section about the Mahamudra of meditation, which also has three points. The practitioner is introduced to 'This is how it is', the nature of things, the nature of our minds. Remember, Mahamudra is not apart from ourselves — it is our own nature. Meditation here means the training in growing used to that and making it a continual experience. While the first three points about the view are not hard to comprehend, the next three points about the Mahamudra of meditation are not as easy. This is because it is rather difficult to become genuinely accustomed to our nature. For countless lifetimes in samsaric existence we have been used to the exact opposite of realizing our nature. We have acted out of delusion and ignorance instead of from a state of knowing our minds. Instead of our attention facing towards its own nature, we have been extroverted, looking away from and being occupied with something other than our nature of mind. By repeating this pattern again and again, life after life, this ignorance has created an incredibly strong habitual tendency for not knowing the nature of our minds. Therefore, the training in the Mahamudra of meditation requires equally strong perseverance in the opposite direction.

There is another common doubt people express concerning Mahamudra meditation: "If Mahamudra is merely a matter of relaxing my mind into an unfabricated state of naturalness, then why do Tibetan Buddhists do all those complicated rituals? Why do they beat big drums, blow different types of horns, chant countless texts, perform lengthy ceremonies and jump around in their bizarre dance costumes? What do these elaborate rituals have to do with natural mind?" It is certainly true that Mahamudra is simply a matter of leaving mind in its natural state. Honestly, though, sometimes it just doesn't happen. Sometimes our minds won't remain relaxed and natural, no matter how hard we try. On these occasions we need to apply various methods to relax the mind. The buddhas and great masters have very kindly and skillfully designed different means to focus our attention and guide us to the point where we can simply relax into the state of Mahamudra. These methods take different forms: music, ritual dance, visualizing deities,; reciting great numbers of mantras, prostrating many times, and so forth. All these diverse ways are skillful means leading to the state of natural mind.

When we begin the practice of Mahamudra, although we may have an understanding of its nature, it is often not more than a short glimpse, a flash of insight that disappears and reappears. The continuity of the insight is not sustained at this point; there's no real stability in it, no steadiness, and no deep clarity or brightness. The instruction in shamatha is extremely helpful in dealing with this. There are many different details on how to practice shamatha to attain stability of mind.

Nowadays the most popular method is to focus the attention on the movement of breath. Following the breathing is extremely beneficial. The Buddha himself said: "If discursive thoughts are predominant, place the attention on the inhalation and exhalation of your breath." When we shift our attention over to simply noticing the movement of breath, our thought involvement automatically subsides, and that is definitely very useful.

In the Mahamudra tradition the type of shamatha being cultivated is somewhat more subtle. The attention is not fixed on any specific focus like the breath. We simply pay attention to the empty and awake quality of mind and sustain that. We avoid involvement in thoughts about past, present, or future events. For example, we might spend a lot of time recalling: "Last year I went to such-and-such a place; I met so-and-so and did this and that. It was nice (or, it was not nice)," and so on. As soon as we notice that we are mentally 'following the past', we just take a break from that activity and let it go. Likewise with future thoughts: "Next year I'll go to that country. I'll meet so-and-so and I'll work on this project." That is called 'anticipating the future'. When you notice that you're doing that, just let it go; take a break from that. It's the same with thoughts, feelings or impressions we have about the present moment. Don't sit and make value judgments about them. When you notice you've gotten carried away; take a break from it. It's much easier to see the nature of mind and stay with the empty, awake quality when we are disengaged from our constant preoccupation with thoughts of past, present and future.

Sometimes we get entangled in a thought pattern. There's a method called 'abrupt cutting' that is useful with very strong, forceful thoughts or opinions that we nurture. Abruptly cutting means we simply sever the involvement in that thought. You could say that it is a wrathful approach. A more peaceful way is known as 'letting go into whatever arises without fabrication.' This is easier to do with ordinary and relatively weak thoughts. Simply let the thought slide; let it subside all by itself without accepting or rejecting it. When this type of thought occurs just let it vanish, without trying to do anything in particular. If our mind is overtaken by forceful thoughts, we can cut that involvement abruptly. Using these two methods, we can deal with any type of thought.

II

Earlier I spoke on the view of Mahamudra and on its importance in creating a firm foundation for the meditation practice of Mahamudra. I also discussed the importance of shamatha, of stillness of mind or calm attention. I would like to stress that increasing one's presence of mind and cultivating the stability of shamatha should not be confined to the meditation session. We should try to be more mindful in all situations and at all times in our lives.

There is a famous saying that states, 'the spontaneous arising of the meditation state is due to the power of blessings'. 'Blessings' refers to a power or capacity that we can receive. Due to blessings, someone who has not experienced the meditation state will be able to experience it; someone not stable in the meditation state will become more stable; and someone whose meditation state is not that clear will gain clarity and alertness. In both Mahamudra and Dzogchen, the way to receive blessings from the lineage masters is through the preliminary practices of the four types, especially through the guru yoga practice. Do not apply the guru yoga only once in a while; but in all circumstances, remember to supplicate from the core of your heart your guru and lineage masters. In this way we receive blessings, which are extremely important.

In the Vajrayana tradition, it is often said one should regard the guru as equal to a buddha, or even as superior to a buddha. For non-Vajrayana practitioners, this might seem inappropriate. According to the general teachings of Buddhism only the fully awakened one, the Buddha, can be the object of supplication, veneration and devotion. To put someone else in his place as that supreme object might not feel right. Within Vajrayana, the Buddha is still the supreme object of our supplications and devotion. However, the Buddha appeared in this world quite a long time ago. Even though we have connected with Buddhist practices and become Buddhists, there are centuries and centuries between ourselves and the Buddha. Because we didn't have the fortune to meet the Buddha in person and hear his teachings, we need someone or something to serve as a link between the Buddha and ourselves. This is exactly what our root guru does.

The qualities and activities of our personal teachers are of course not the same as those of the Buddha, in that they don't have the same power and depth. Yet for us as individuals, the blessings of the Buddha's qualities and activities reach us mainly through other people. Blessings are received in the most immediate way through a lineage of teachers. Our lineage gurus are thus extremely important, as they are a conduit. We receive blessings by connecting directly with masters, especially our root guru. For us as individuals, being with our guru is like being with the Buddha in person. Our root guru is therefore considered even more important than the Buddha, in the sense that he connects us directly with the teachings and the blessings. We should supplicate our root and lineage masters as often as possible in order to receive the blessings of the Buddha and the Dharma. For example, we can chant *Calling the Guru from Afar* from the core of our hearts, and make sincere, deep-felt supplications through guru yoga. After supplicating, receive the empowerments by imagining that the rays of light from the guru's fore-head, throat, and heart center dissolve into you, blessing your body, speech and mind.

What we need to realize is the nature of mind, the basic, natural state here called Mahamudra. This nature of mind has always been with us, throughout all our countless former lives in samsara. It is not like we somehow lost the nature of mind and now have to regain it – we simply have to recognize something that has always been with us. But if it's been continuously with us all this time, why haven't we realized it already? What is missing? The answer is that we lack the blessings. To recognize the nature of mind, we need to be infused with the power of blessings of the truth, the Dharma, passed from an enlightened one, a buddha, down through the realized lineage masters. The realization of this truth is what makes the difference. By receiving the blessings, we don't suddenly somehow get a new nature of mind that we didn't have before. Neither is it true that the longer we stay in samsara the more lost our nature becomes. No, it's totally unchanged, right with us all the time. Nevertheless, the ability to realize what is intrinsically present in ourselves depends upon the right circumstances — on whether or not we receive the blessings and are infused with this capacity to realize. The way to receive the blessings depends upon the sincerity of our openness, devotion, and trust. In order to open up our hearts and minds to trust, to devotion, to faith, it is important to make sincere supplications.

When I use the word faith, I don't mean unreasonable blind faith, but an open-mindedness that arises after we receive the blessings and understand they are a definite reality. It is not that we close our eyes and insist that it must be so because of what we have heard (and probably haven't understood). Buddhism advocates 'faith through knowing the reasons' — an appreciation that comes from comprehending the qualities of enlightenment that are deeper than our limited scope of experience. This allows us to open up and receive the blessings. These days, in my opinion, it seems that the scientific frame of mind that dominates Western culture creates somewhat of a barrier to faith and devotion. The rational scientific approach to things is based on the unspoken premise that things must be tangibly perceived and measured before they can be proven to exist. Clinging to such a premise merely traps one within it. Try instead the premise, "Maybe it is possible to have a wider horizon than an ordinary human being." This opens one up to the possibility of receiving the blessings of enlightened beings.

> It is neither something to be corrected nor transformed,
> But when anyone sees and realizes its nature,
> All that appears and exists is Mahamudra,
> The great and all-encompassing dharmakaya.

Among the three points about the Mahamudra of meditation, the first one states the nature of Mahamudra or the basic state. The beginning sentence — "It is neither something to be corrected nor transformed" — is extremely profound. What we are trying to realize is the basic state, the nature of our minds. Whatever the 'it' refers to – be it what is perceived in our experience, the perceiver, our mind; or the Mahamudra of union — we do not need to make up anything artificial about the nature of our minds or fabricate something that wasn't there before. We do not need to correct some flaw in the nature of mind and transform it into something good. We should not think that by training in Mahamudra there is a transformation taking place, that our nature is through the training somehow becoming something other than it already is. Our basic state is and always was the unity of emptiness and cognizance. Mahamudra training is simply a matter of recognizing how it is. By growing accustomed to this through training, it becomes an actuality. That is what is meant by realization. Thus, the Mahamudra of meditation does not involve correcting, contriving, or transforming anything. The next sentence is: "But when anyone sees and realizes its' nature." 'Anyone' does not refer to a special person of an aristocratic family, or someone with a unique talent, but to any person. It doesn't matter whether the practitioner is young or old, important or unimportant, learned or uneducated — none of those things are important in this context. When it's a matter of simply realizing the nature of mind, those specifics don't matter at all. That is why Naropa uses the word 'anyone'. What is necessary is to first recognize, then see, and realize the nature of mind.

The Tibetan word used here for 'nature' literally means 'simply that'. The 'that' refers to the fact that the ultimate true nature is not apart from being the nature of the relative state of mind — it is simply its nature. That's why it's called 'simply that'. Since everyone has this nature, what is important is to be sincerely interested and to trust that it is possible to recognize it by looking. After looking, we need to see it; and after seeing it, we need to fully realize exactly how it is. Do not feel satisfied with intellectually having figured it out, or with inferring that it's probably like such-and-such. That is called 'clouding the nature of mind with inference,' or 'obscuring yourself with intellectual thoughts.' Instead, nakedly and directly see this nature as it is and realize it.

One danger in practicing Mahamudra is that we may confuse inferred knowledge with direct experience and fail to see the difference between what we figure out and what we see directly. These two can be mistaken. Naropa uses the word 'see,' rather than 'know' or 'understand,' to make sure that we don't make that mistake. In this context, the nature of mind is not an object of knowledge. It is not an entity that we inquire about, investigate and finally get an idea about and feel gratified. That would be what is called 'having a deduced or inferred idea of an entity held in mind'. To make sure that we get the point, Naropa uses the word 'to see,' which means like seeing something with the naked eye. When you see something, you don't have to have any idea about what it is in order to see it — you simply see it, directly, and nakedly. What is necessary here is to let our mind simply look into itself and directly see how it is. Our mind is empty of any identity, and is cognizant by nature. These two qualities are indivisible. Knowing this is direct knowledge, attained by seeing in actuality. Milarepa, when giving the pointing-out instruction to Gampopa, said, "The view is what it's about, so look directly into your own mind. It's like the master wrestler looking for his jewel, Gampopa." The analogy Milarepa used comes from an old myth about a master wrestler who had a jewel in his forehead. He often worried about whether he would lose it while wrestling. One day when he was really tired, his forehead wrinkled down over the jewel and covered it. When as was his habit, he touched his forehead to see whether the jewel was still there, he didn't feel it. He got incredibly worried and went everywhere looking for it. He searched and groped around, but he couldn't find it. At some point he finally discovered that actually his jewel had been there all the time. The basic message Milarepa was giving Gampopa was: look into your own mind. Trying to figure out this nature by means of intellectual reasoning is not going to help. What is necessary is simply to relax and see it directly.

When training in this seeing, everything — all that appears and exists — is experienced as Mahamudra. Both that which is perceived and the perceiving mind have the identical nature of being the basic state of Mahamudra. If we grow accustomed to this through training and attain complete realization, everything is the great and all-encompassing dharmakaya. The innate nature is seen as encompassing everything.

I would like to introduce one important key phrase for practice: 'rest freely in uncontrived naturalness'. Uncontrived naturalness doesn't mean deliberately trying to be natural or free. We should not endeavor to rid ourselves of whatever could be considered unpleasant in our meditation state. Conversely, we should not attempt to deliberately bring forth a state that is supposedly good. That's why the word 'uncontrived' is used. Resting freely is the exact opposite of being tight and constricted. Some people, who have a great interest in their meditation practice, sit down in an extremely intent frame of mind. They tighten their body into a stiff posture, while their mind is very resolute that it will be 100% concentrated. This tense state results in the muscles, tendons and spine being held very tightly. Sit like that for a while and it becomes incredibly uncomfortable – so much so that one is unable to continue.

Actually, the best meditation is done in a totally relaxed state, when one is not constricting oneself or tightening up inwardly. Don't sit tensing your muscles and tendons; instead, freely and loosely remain at ease.

If we sit with a very tight posture, we may at times feel a tightness around the heart. Due to our over exertion, we create undue pressure inside ourselves. Sometimes our brain might even feel squeezed from the sides, very tight, and uncomfortable. There's no need to create that kind of situation. Rather, relax by letting be, and have a sense of setting yourself free. Letting be can be misunderstood as meaning to simply allow yourself to get carried away. We may imagine that the mind is permitted to take off and get involved in whatever emotion or thought that arises. That's a little too relaxed! You should be not too tight and not too relaxed, but hold both the body and the mind in a very free and easy way. This is important.

Another piece of advice given by many of the great meditators of the past is: put mindfulness on guard! In other words, place a watchman called 'presence of mind' on sentry duty. Be present and aware of what is taking place in the mind. Such attentiveness helps us to become aware of whether we are distracted or undistracted. Of course, we know the difference between the mind resting naturally in itself or being carried away by memories or plans. But it is momentarily possible, and quite common, not to be fully present and to simply get lost in thought, oblivious to the fact that we are distracted. While mind has a singular nature — it does not have many parts — cognition can have different expressions or mental events. Some may be unvirtuous; some virtuous, and so forth. Among the various expressions of mind, one of the most important is a sense of presence, of being attentive – in other words, mindfulness. Mindfulness is simply mind being aware of what is happening.

STUDENT: You spoke of cutting forceful thoughts wrathfully. How do we deal with forceful thoughts without being an accomplished meditator?

Rinpoche: What I mentioned about 'abrupt cutting' was in the context of shamatha, and referred to dealing with forceful thoughts, not weak ones. Please understand that any forceful thought gains its strength, the power that fuels it, only from oneself. This strength could be a strong fascination, as in, "I like to think about such-and-such!", or "I definitely must do such-and-such." There's a delicious taste we get from being involved in our thoughts. It is that clinging, that savoring of it, that reinforces the thought or the emotion. It's not that the thought by itself has some independent power. It's because we feel "All right, maybe I should be meditating, but this is such an interesting thought that I must spend a little more time on getting into its complete details." Remember that it is our fascination that makes the thought involvement stronger.

'Cutting abruptly' means you return to your senses, remind yourself that what you set out to do is not to sit and daydream about this and that, and then get down to the meditation training. Remind yourself, "I'm wasting my time. I'm not going to continue along that track; I'm going to return back to the main point." That action, that decision, is what cuts the forceful thought. To use an amusing analogy, it's like clubbing a pig on the snout. Imagine a big, hungry pig who sees food. To stop him, you have to whack him over the snout, because that's the only place he can really feel it. To whack the pig anywhere else will not faze him if he's really intent on eating.

Student: Didn't you say that the nature of the mind was beyond the four extremes of existing, not existing, both, and neither? Is understanding that, what 'seeing' means?

Rinpoche: Understanding the nature of mind to be beyond the four extremes of existing, non-existing, both, and neither is different from seeing the nature of mind in actuality. The first statement is a tool used to convince us intellectually about how the mind isn't. Through this we get a certain intellectual conviction about mind, which is different than seeing directly. The aim of inference is to be able to see directly afterwards. However, the focus, what is being inferred, is not the same as what is seen instantaneously through direct perception. There's definitely a difference.

STUDENT: Is clubbing the pig on the snout the same as suppressing thoughts?

RINPOCHE: The word 'suppressing', in Tibetan actually means reducing. The general method of reducing negative thoughts and emotions is to apply an antidote against them. For example, the remedy against anger is loving kindness and compassion. Even though this year we may not have been successful in avoiding being irritated, angry and resentful, we can try during the coming year to be more compassionate and kinder. Then maybe it will be easier to deal with anger. If we look back, we might say that our anger has been 'suppressed.' It's not that it has been entirely squeezed out, but there is less of it – it has been reduced. That kind of reducing is not the same as clubbing the pig on the snout, which is a more immediate method. The force of your involvement in thought is your own clinging to it. When you remind yourself that actually this is a waste of time – when you tell yourself, "I'm supposed to be practicing meditation, I'll give it up" — that's called 'hitting the pig on the snout'. It is not that you just sit and think, "I shouldn't be thinking this." That doesn't help at all.

12

Of the three points on Mahamudra meditation, I have covered the first one, which is "Stating the nature of Mahamudra of the basic state." Now I will discuss the second: "Stating the nature of the Mahamudra of how to realize," The way of realizing means, first, what needs to be realized, and second, the method of how to realize that. Earlier I mentioned the method as being uncontrived naturalness, or resting freely without fabrication, and I will now explain this further.

Second, stating the nature of the Mahamudra of realization:

> Naturally and without contriving, allowed to simply be,
> This unimagined dharmakaya,
> Letting it be without seeking, that is the meditation training.
> But to meditate while seeking is deluded mind.

It is possible to explain this in a very short and somewhat unpolished way. We can also get into all sorts of fine details about how to practice and train in Mahamudra. One of these ways is called 'looking while being still'. 'Still' in this context refers to shamatha, which we have cultivated to some extent. We feel that our mind is quiet, our attention remains calm, and we are concentrated. There is a sense of being fully relaxed and at peace. During this time when our attention remains at peace, look into what exactly it is that remains at peace. Question yourself, "Where does it remain? How does it remain? What is the 'it' that remains? What is its identity?" By simply looking into this, we fail to find any concrete entity that is at peace, that remains calmly. This stillness of mind that has no real concrete identity to be found is how it really is — this is the basic state. Yet, at the same time, it feels as if there is a mind that is calm and resting in stillness. This feeling is only superficial, because the moment we investigate the question: "Does this mind have a dwelling place? Is there something that abides calmly?", we find nothing. At the same time there is a feeling of stillness! The seeming and the real, the relative and the ultimate, are thus indivisible. While remaining calm in shamatha, we can see the mind as it actually is by looking into its nature. Unfortunately, our mind is not always still. Sometimes it moves into a thought or an emotion, and there is also a method to look into its identity at those times.

When we leave our peaceful state of shamatha meditation and begin to think, this thinking seems more tangible than the stillness. Strong thoughts, such as emotions, give us the very distinct impression that: "I am thinking, I am feeling such-and-such about that." Anger, attachment, jealousy, stupidity, and pride are all particularly strong attachments, which create a very clear understanding that "I am feeling." Even during the more subtle formation of concepts or neutral ideas, it still seems like something is arising or being formed in our mind. We must look into this thinking or feeling to discover whether or not there actually is some 'thing', some entity there that thinks or feels. There are two ways that we could do this. One is to label thoughts when they arise or move: "Well, now there's a thought; there's another thought." With this method, we are one step behind in pursuit of the thought, always attaching a label to it. This is not a technique of Mahamudra. In Mahamudra, the practitioner looks directly into that which thinks. He or she doesn't label it as being such-and-such. Through this type of practice, we discover that thoughts and emotions have no concrete identity, in exactly the same way as we discovered that stillness had no identity.

The great siddhas of the past used a very nice analogy for thought movement, comparing it to the movement of wind through empty space. Like the wind, it seems like there is something, but there is nothing to see when we look. The wind has no visible color or form, does it? It is the same with thoughts and feelings. If we are unaware of our fixated attention and do not look into the thinker, we will not recognize that there is no entity there. We continue along with our fixation unaware and unknowing. On the other hand, the moment we look towards the thinker, into the identity of what thinks, we are at a complete loss to see anything. This is not because we somehow missed the point: it is simply because there is no 'thing' to see.

Whether we look into the essence of the knower while being still or while thinking, in both cases there is no concrete 'thing' that is still or that thinks. This is simply our basic state; how it is all by itself. This is the unimaginable dharmakaya, which is only a matter of simply looking and seeing it as it is. There is no need to form a description of how it is or to conceptualize it. This is what was mentioned before as 'being beyond thought, word and description'. The word 'unimaginable' means 'impossible to think of as an object of thought'. The nature of mind is empty in essence and cognizant by nature; these two are indivisible. This dharmakaya is the real condition, the basic state. "Letting it be without seeking," without thinking. This is not something that we will discover at a later point in time; nor is it something that we need to seek in a far-away place. "Letting it be without seeking, that itself is the meditation training."

Remember the line in one of the chants we do, the Dorje Chang Chenma, which says: "The essence of thought is dharmakaya, it is taught."? If we try to understand that statement in terms of intellectual reasoning, it seems impossible. It doesn't make sense. After all, isn't it thinking itself which obscures dharmakaya? From our personal point of view, it seems like when there is thinking there is no dharmakaya, and when there's dharmakaya there is no thinking. As a matter of fact, the basic nature within the thinking — meaning the very identity of what thinks — is itself dharmakaya. From this perspective, there is no conflict whatsoever. It's true that being involved in a thought is not dharmakaya, but remember: the very essence of that which thinks is dharmakaya. Don't keep the attitude that thought is impure and has to be cast away, while dharmakaya is pure and should be held on to. Such intellectualization only makes it more difficult to realize this nature, how it really is.

As I mentioned several times before, while training in knowing this, we can fall prey to intellectualizing. Instead of seeing what basically is, we set up our own version by making concepts about it, thinking, "This is emptiness! This is the clarity, the cognizant quality." Rather than acknowledging that our basic state is simultaneously empty and cognizant, we create our own conceptual model of an empty and a cognizant quality, and try to fuse them together. That effort is nothing more than a creation of more thoughts — 'thought building,' we could say. Such involvement, however subtle or intelligent it might be, blocks the direct seeing of the natural state. Hence the last line, "But to meditate while seeking is deluded mind."

Third, stating the nature of the Mahamudra of indivisibility:

Just as with space and a magical display,
While neither cultivating nor not cultivating,
How can you be separate or not separate!
This is a yogi's understanding.

Now for the third among the three points of the Mahamudra of meditation, "Third, stating the nature of the Mahamudra of indivisibility." The indivisibility of the perceiver and the perceived means that their essence is not two different things. It simply manifests different aspects of the same identity, which form an integral unity. Mipham Rinpoche, in his commentary on the chapter of transcendent knowledge in the *Bodhicharya Avatara*, mentions that some people misunderstand the nature of the perceived, meaning of phenomena, and of mind. They think that what we experience is real and concrete, while emptiness is totally non-existent, like the horns of a rabbit. When one has such concepts in mind, the unity of appearance and emptiness is like tying together a white and a black string and calling that 'the unity of appearance and emptiness'. If one insists on misunderstanding the nature of things this way, one will also misconstrue the unity of what is perceived and its emptiness. We should instead understand the perceived to be more like a magical illusion, while emptiness is like the space within which this magical illusion occurs.

It is also necessary to realize that appearance and emptiness do not cancel each other out. It is not that emptiness is lost once there is appearance. At the very instant of appearing, the identity of this appearance is empty — intangible like a dream. It is not necessary to negate the presence of what was dreamt for a dream to be empty. For example, when you dream of a mountain with all its distinct features, it is vividly present, crisp and clear. At the same time there is no real mountain whatsoever — it's empty. This emptiness of the mountain does not get lost in any way because of its apparent presence in the dream. The lucid experience of a dreamed mountain occurs even though it has no true existence. Similarly, we perceive at the same time that the object of our perception has no concrete identity. In other words, its emptiness coexists with its being present.

That is why Naropa says: "Just as with space and a magical display." 'Space' here represents the empty quality, while the magical display is what we perceive while experiencing. The magical display is not other than space itself. When a magical display is visible, it is not that it had to move out of space to another location in order to manifest. It occurs in space – in a way we could say it is space that is somehow made visible. The magic is indivisible from the space itself.

In the next sentence, "While neither cultivating nor not cultivating," the word 'cultivating' and meditating is the same in the Tibetan. We don't have to make an artificial creation through an act of meditation. We should not construct a fake state and call it Mahamudra. On the other hand, looking into the essence is not without cultivating, in some sense. It is not that we totally let go and carry on forming ordinary deluded concepts as usual.

The result of that kind of training is described in the line "How can you be separate or not separate!" It is not the case that we are divorcing or separating ourselves from the thinking that is some entity that we have to throw away. At the same time, being not separate means acknowledging that the very basic state, the identity of that which thinks, is no 'thing' whatsoever that needs to be gotten rid of. In this way, we are neither separate nor not separate. We can say that cultivating and not cultivating is like the path, while being neither separate nor not separate is the fruition.

"This is the yogi's understanding" means that this is what can be accomplished. When we become truly trained in this way, we will realize the basic state. While trying to train, of course, we inevitably encounter some difficulties. One possibility is that we become dull and absent-minded. Maybe we feel a little bit shut down, tired and drowsy. Another difficulty is to be carried away by thought and become agitated. On these occasions, thoughts seem to be a little too vigorous, too active. It becomes impossible to abandon thinking about this and that. While these obstacles do not exist in the nature of mind, unfortunately they can arise on the path. The different manuals on how to train in Mahamudra offer techniques on ways to handle these two situations.

Let's examine the two problems of dullness and agitation a little further. There are different reasons why we become agitated when trying to practice. First is attachment, or desire. Thinking of some situation we were in where we enjoyed ourselves, we want to get back and re-experience the happiness we felt. We feel attached to that experience and we start making plans about how we can recreate it and feel that same joy we had. Another way we can make ourselves agitated is through anger or aversion. We focus on our enemy or someone we hold a grudge against, thinking, "He did such a terrible thing to me! It was wrong; and now I should do something to hurt him back." This kind of feeling belongs to anger and ill-will. Making plans about what to do about someone we don't like definitely disturbs our meditation state. Then there's regret, where we feel guilty about an action we did in the past. While practicing, we think: "I really shouldn't have done that. It was inappropriate. I'm a bad person." We make ourselves feel guilty and cultivate that feeling. A fourth way to produce agitation is indecisiveness, doubt, feeling unsure about what to do: "Should I do such-and-such, maybe it's a good idea — wait a minute, no, maybe I shouldn't do it." We waver back and forth, creating thought after thought. These are four basic ways of being agitated.

There are many different remedies for agitation, including changing our attitude, shifting our physical position, or adjusting our visual focus. When trying to change your attitude, remind yourself that nothing lasts. This situation, like everything else, changes. It's guaranteed to be fleeting. Happy moments never last, and neither do unhappy feelings of hurt or sadness. There's no point in all this involvement. It's futile. Since everything is impermanent, why bother? That kind of reminder is very helpful in this situation.

We can remedy agitation by shifting our physical situation. The ways to do that may sound a little strange, but they may prove beneficial. One method is to draw the window curtains to make the room a little dimmer, which might help calm your mind. Another solution is to put on more clothing and make yourself warmer. Or, if you are sitting too straight, relax slightly so that your body loosens up a little. These three methods can help reduce agitation.

The other major disturbance to the meditation state is dullness or drowsiness, both of which cause us to feel unclear. First, we feel a little drowsy, then dull, and eventually we fall asleep. Since that definitely obscures the meditation state, we need to apply a remedy. One is to inspire our attitude by thinking of the qualities of the awakened state of the Buddha, of the Dharma, of the practice of samadhi. Think of the great benefit and the immense fortune to have the opportunity right now to progress on the path to enlightenment. If we inspire ourselves and deeply appreciate this great fortune, we'll wake up and won't feel as drowsy. Second, we can change our physical situation by removing some layers of clothing so that we're less warm. We might also open up the curtains and the windows, making the room brighter and airier. Straighten your physical posture, consciously concentrating and tightening up your body. All those things help us to wake up and not feel obscured or dull.

The third way of remedying both agitation and dullness is to adjust our visual focus and to imagine something. In the case of agitation, imagine a tiny black four-petaled flower facing downwards at your heart center. Visualize it as being, the size of a pea, with a little sphere, also black, in the center. It sinks down and remains beneath our body, on the seat. Keeping the attention on that helps to reduce the feeling of agitation. To remedy dullness, imagine a white flower facing upwards. It also has a little sphere the size of a pea in the center, which ascends and hovers at the top of our head, bright and clear. This helps to remedy the feeling of being drowsy or dull.

13

Up until now I have covered the Mahamudra of the view and the Mahamudra of meditation. Now we have arrived at the third point, which is the Mahamudra of conduct. The first part of this is combined with the view, in other words, conduct combined with the view.

Once more, for the three points about the Mahamudra of conduct, first, stating the nature of the Mahamudra of self-liberation:

> All the good deeds and harmful actions
> Dissolve by simply knowing this nature.
> The emotions are the great wisdom;
> Like a jungle fire, they are the yogi's helpers.

These words are particularly suited to those who have understood the basic view and have realized it in actuality – those who have reached a high level of experience. Since we are beginners, it is not quite appropriate for us to follow these instructions to the letter. In the case of ordinary sentient beings, there is always something that we need to avoid or to abandon.

We may have tremendous interest in spiritual practice, in the Dharma. We may have pursued that interest and succeeded in meeting a qualified master, to the point where we have received profound instructions. We may even have put them into practice, and to some extent, have had personal experience of the state of samadhi. All that is of course very well, it's excellent. But maybe we are not really progressing in meditation training. We may feel, "I've practiced meditation all these years but I haven't gotten any genuine results; I haven't reached fruition yet. Why is this?" It is because of not having 'made use of the conduct' in the sense of using every moment in our lives as part of the training. The conduct hasn't taken effect. Remember the quote from Gampopa that says, "Although your view is as high as the sky, be scrupulously careful in your actions and behavior." Regardless of whether or not we have realized a very high view and experienced the natural state; be very careful in what to accept and reject.

As sentient beings we create karma through our physical actions. It's crucial that we do our best to avoid creating any negative karma and that we act to create positive karma instead. Since we create karma through the words we say, we should make up our minds to avoid saying words that harm others and to use our voice to create positive karma. It's the same with our thoughts, which likewise create both positive and negative karma. It is extremely important to form the attitude to avoid indulging in harmful thoughts as much as possible. Try to cultivate the perspective of wanting to improve both self and others. Please be conscientious and careful in all actions. This is incredibly important.

As ordinary people, we of course make mistakes, but that's not what matters here. What matters is that we make up our minds to sincerely attempt not to indulge in negative actions any longer. Sometimes we succeed in this, while other times we'll fail. Still, we should engender the attitude that "I will try my best to avoid the ten unvirtuous actions as much as I'm able, and to do what is helpful and beneficial for myself and others." Most of you probably know the ten unvirtuous actions — the three of body, the four of speech, and the three of mind. We should form the resolve that "In the past I wasn't that careful in avoiding what is negative to others; but from now on I will be." Forming a determination to refrain from harm in the future and a sense of remorse for the harm we've done in the past is important. We shouldn't think, "Well, there's nothing I can do about it. It's my nature." Then it will be very hard to progress, to create what is positive and avoid what is negative. Instead, develop the frame of mind that "I will strive to avoid evil and do what is good." This is essential.

You might notice that becoming intoxicated or drugged is not mentioned among the ten unvirtuous actions. Since it is not openly referred to, it may not seem to be particularly harmful. Still, it does cause the practitioner to be less careful, attentive, and discriminating. For those reasons it is not a particularly good idea. We should put emphasis on being conscientious and developing presence of mind. Always be mindful in any situation and cultivate the state of meditation as much as possible.

Concerning good deeds, the Buddha taught extensively on the six transcendent actions, the six paramitas. The first one is transcendent giving, or generosity, which is explained as three kinds: the giving of material things, the giving of protection against fear, and the giving of the truth, which means Dharma teachings. Giving material things means to give other beings what they need, be it food, medicine, clothing, or shelter. By this type of generosity, we are able to relieve their suffering and distress. The second, protection against fear, is to give the means to relieve suffering. Whether beings endure physical or mental pain, we should provide care so that they will feel more at ease and not be unhappy. The third, the giving of the truth, is giving Dharma teachings. This entails offering the methods on how to reduce disturbing emotions, advice in what to avoid and adopt, and giving special teachings on how to practice the true spiritual path.

The second of the six paramitas is that of transcendent discipline, which is also of three types. The first is the discipline of refraining from evil — in other words, avoiding any action, speech or attitude that is harmful towards others or to oneself. The second is the discipline of creating goodness, which means to act, speak, and harbor an attitude that is benevolent and helpful. The third one is called 'the discipline of acting for the welfare of other beings.' The first two refer to our own behavior, what we avoid or adopt, while the third is to do something that helps and benefits other beings.

The third of the six paramitas is that of transcendent patience. The first type is called 'the patience of taking no offense when hurt'. When ordinary people are harmed by others, the natural response is to retaliate. If we investigate the outcome of taking revenge, however, we find the end result is only more pain, as it is motivated by anger or resentment. Retaliation doesn't delete the previous hurt; nor does it bring happiness. Thus, to seek revenge is a mistaken idea. Instead, try to continue the practice you know, especially that of sustaining the natural state. In that way, be carefree about being hurt.

The second type is called 'the patience of having definite confidence in what is to be realized,' which means not to fall prey to discouragement. Do not be disheartened and think, "I do all this practice and nothing comes out of it. Maybe there is nothing to be realized; maybe all this effort is worthless." This is not true. Meditation training definitely leads us to a positive result. Having confidence and trust in that realization is the second kind of patience. The third is called 'the patience of gladly undertaking hardship,' — not minding if there are difficulties. We shouldn't give up, even when working for the benefit of self and others is not easy or smooth. To gladly undertake any hardship encountered and carry on is the patience of happily undertaking difficulties.

The fourth of the six paramitas is that of exertion, perseverance, or diligence. It refers to diligence in doing what is good or beneficial and in avoiding what is harmful. Basically, it is laziness that prevents us from being diligent. There are three types of laziness. The first is the basic laziness of being indolent, feeling "I can't do anything," and not wanting to either. The second one is the laziness of clinging to habitual activities, for example, having a strong tendency towards killing animals. Because it's a habit, we aggressively feel, "I don't want to give it up; I don't even want to question it."

The third form of laziness is called 'the laziness reinforced by oneself'. This the laziness of self-deprecation, or discouraging oneself. We may have all the circumstances that are necessary for persevering in special practice: we have a precious human body, complete with the eight freedoms and ten riches; we have met a spiritual teacher and received the teachings, and so forth. There is nothing that should prevent us from practice, yet, still we harbor thoughts like: "I cannot, I'm unable, I'm no good, I'm a bad person, I'm weak." Those types of indulgent thoughts are a form of laziness. These three types of laziness should definitely be abandoned.

The fifth paramita is that of meditative concentration. There are two types: the mundane or worldly and the supramundane, beyond worldly states. Mundane concentration refers to meditation states we get into without having entered the practice of the true Dharma, the sublime truth. In other cases, we may have entered Dharma practice, but we have not fully formed a true resolve towards enlightenment, towards benefiting others. Our concentration thus lacks a sound basis. It's true that the meditation state we cultivate without this true foundation can give temporary relief from suffering, and may provide states of subtle pleasure and peace. However, since there is no substance within it for liberation and enlightenment, these experiences are temporary and always wear off. Because we always return to ordinary samsaric situations, these are called mundane levels of concentration.

Supramundane meditation comes about from fully forming the resolve of bodhichitta. Engender the wish to abandon all obscurations, disturbing emotions and thoughts, and to truly accomplish the basis for benefiting others. Any practice we do on that foundation, even ordinary shamatha, becomes the support for bodhichitta. Furthermore, it unfolds as the support for the profound insight of vipashyana that can be discovered and cultivated. This is why it is said that the true shamatha, which is the source or root of all virtues, is called transcendent concentration.

The sixth paramita is that of transcendent knowledge. Knowledge is the most important of all because the root cause of samsaric existence is ignorance, the opposite of knowing. How do we develop knowledge? The Buddha has taught that we begin by learning. A certain type of knowledge results from studying what the Buddha taught. But it is not only the words of the Buddha from which we can learn. From the Tibetan Vajrayana perspective, the shastras — treatises that are commentaries on the Buddha's words — are considered even more important. The reason is that in the sutras the Buddha would sometimes teach the definitive meaning, and other times would teach in a way that was more expedient. It was not always clear to people as to what was what. The commentaries by great panditas clearly distinguish what is the definitive and what is the expedient meaning. Studying these clarifies the words of the Buddha. Even more important than the treatises are the pith instructions. Instructions by the mahasiddhas of the past sometimes came in the form of *dohas,* spiritual poetry such as the vajra songs of Mahamudra. Even more beneficial are oral instructions from our own root teacher, which condense the essential points into a very applicable, concise way. We need to study, listen, and learn. That is the first step, the knowledge of learning.

The second type of knowledge is the knowledge of reflection. The Buddha said: "Analyze my teachings as carefully as you would test gold before buying it." You don't unequivocally believe the seller who claims that the gold is pure. You need to test it yourself before buying it. There are various ways that people check gold: they can cut it, rub it on a stone, or melt it. Melted gold should have uniform properties all the way through. To feel confident a piece of gold is pure, we need to examine it thoroughly and gain certainty about it. The Buddha continued: "Don't accept my words without questioning. You must discriminate and examine them for yourself." It is always possible that a statement could have been misquoted or some extra words added. Perhaps we cannot easily differentiate whether the Buddha was referring to the definitive or expedient meaning. Therefore, we must investigate and analyze before reaching assurance. This certitude we arrive at is called 'the knowledge from reflection'.

The third type of knowledge is called 'the knowledge from meditation training'. We do not relinquish disturbing emotions by simply knowing how to do so: that comes about from growing used to abandoning them. It results from training, and from personal application of the knowledge that arises from that. By training in a sustained way, we come to the point where we can actually abandon disturbing emotions.

I have now briefly mentioned the ten virtuous actions, the ten unvirtuous actions and the six paramitas. Occasionally differences arise as to what is correct or not correct. Ultimately it depends on the circumstances and the individual's attitude and motivation. We have to judge very carefully the distinction between what is right and wrong. For example, to take a life is usually a very negative evil action that creates suffering and conflict. Nevertheless, there are rare occasions when taking a life can be very beneficial. For instance, there's a famous story about one of the past lives of the Buddha, when he was captain of a ship with 500 merchants traveling aboard. On the same ship was a criminal who wanted to kill the 500 merchants by sinking the vessel. The captain discovered this and decided to kill the criminal before he killed the others. It may have looked like a negative action, but actually it was very expedient; as the lives of 500 people were saved. Back to the text, and the line that states, "All good deeds and harmful actions dissolve by simply knowing this nature." In general, without knowing this nature, it is definitely important to avoid all involvement in evil actions; and to do as many positive actions as possible. During the actual situation of knowing the natural state, however, there's little reason to be either attached to virtuous actions or be afraid of unvirtuous ones, because all frames of mind dissolve into the basic state.

14

I will now continue with the Mahamudra of conduct. The root verse says: "All good deeds and harmful actions, dissolve by simply knowing this nature." It is not only good and bad thoughts that are liberated by knowing the nature of mind. Disturbing emotions, are transformed as well into the great wisdom, original wakefulness.

The Buddha mentioned different types of disturbing emotions in various contexts. For instance, in the collection of scriptures that belong to Abhidharma, he spoke of the ten primary disturbing emotions and the twenty subsidiary disturbing emotions. However, the most familiar classification for the disturbing emotions in both Sutra and Tantra is the three or five poisons, which are attachment, anger, delusion, pride, and envy.

These five disturbing emotions have the nature of the five great wisdoms. When speaking of transforming disturbing emotions into wisdom or original wakefulness, we should first of all understand what the root of a disturbing emotion is. They all have a common basis — ignorance or unknowing, the source from which all disturbing emotions unfold. Ignorance means to be unaware of the real condition, the basic state. It is because of ignorance that confusion can take place and unfold as disturbing emotions.

Disturbing emotions lack the quality of being clear and lucid. Wisdom is seeing things exactly as they are. There are two aspects of wisdom, the first being the wisdom of knowing the unconditioned nature as it is, and the second being the wisdom of seeing all conditioned things that can possibly exist. The first one is to realize that no phenomenon has any true identity, that all things are empty of any essence. Does that mean that an enlightened person in a state of wisdom does not perceive anything? Is enlightenment a vacant, dull state? No, absolutely not. While knowing the innate nature, there is a clear and distinct seeing of the relative aspect. That is the second type, 'the wisdom that sees all possibly existent conditioned things.'

To go into more detail, the five wisdoms represent five aspects of original wakefulness. The first, the quality of seeing the empty essence, is called dharmadhatu wisdom, while seeing that all phenomena are equal in nature, or are of the same taste, is the wisdom of equality. These t wisdoms primarily belong to the wisdom that knows the nature as it is. The remaining three aspects of wisdom – the mirror-like wisdom, the discriminating wisdom, and the all-accomplishing wisdom — primarily belong to the wisdom that sees all possibly existing things.

To reiterate, ignorance is to be unaware of our basic nature. Some teachings, when speaking of transformation or of purifying the five disturbing emotions, say that by abandoning the five poisons one realizes the five wisdoms. Other scriptures that have a slightly higher perspective say that the five disturbing emotions are basically transformed into the five wisdoms. Whichever way it is phrased, the five disturbing emotions dissolve and the five wisdoms unfold as part of the transformative process. Let's look at this process more closely, examining the disturbing emotions and their accompanying wisdoms one by one.

The first of the disturbing emotions is delusion. The opposite of delusion is to be aware of the innate nature. By growing accustomed to that, the quality of not knowing gradually fades away. We call that the transformation of ignorance or delusion into the wisdom of dharmadhatu. The nature of all phenomena is seen as 'nonarising'; and is indivisible with the basic sphere or dharmadhatu.

The mirror-like wisdom is the basic purity of or the transformation of anger. Due to not knowing our innate nature, there is an instinctive attachment to the belief in a 'me'. At the same time, there is an instinctive aversion towards that felt to be 'not me' — the 'other'. This clinging is very deep-rooted and gives rise to intense fixation and manifold complexities. At the same time, there is always the possibility for mirror-like wisdom. The analogy here is that of a mirror: an image reflected in a mirror appears very distinctly, even though there is no 'thing' in the mirror. It is empty of any substantial entity and yet visible. Once someone realizes the basic state and sees the empty nature of all things, experience still takes place. Experience unfolds like the images reflected in a mirror. Everything is seen, but there is no attachment to these images as having any concrete substance. In this way, there is no opportunity for anger to arise.

The wisdom of equality is the transformation of pride. Seven kinds of pride are mentioned in the scriptures. Basically, pride or conceit, however, is the attitude of regarding others as inferior and oneself as superior. It is based on cultivating a fondness for ourselves as special and then focusing on that in a sustained way, out of ego-clinging. There are different degrees of being conceited, for instance, the fixation on oneself as extraordinary and other people as inferior. To regard oneself as superior among equals is a medium type of pride, while feeling superior to people who are even better than oneself is extreme conceit. Then there is the pride of believing oneself to have qualities that one doesn't, and the conceit of thinking oneself to be free of faults that one does have. These types of pride all dissolve when one grows more accustomed to realizing the real condition. It fades away and leaves place for what is called the wisdom of equality or sameness. This wisdom comes from seeing that everyone in their basic nature is equal. There is not even a mustard-seed of difference in the qualities of the basic nature of anyone. That is called the wisdom of equality.

Discriminating wisdom is the transformation of attachment. Not knowing the basic state, we lack clarity as to what is beneficial and harmful, what is good and evil. Real discrimination is missing. This attachment and involvement create a tremendous amount of complications because we are unable to see clearly what is valuable and what is unwholesome. Conversely, as we grow more accustomed to knowing the nature of Mahamudra, the real condition, this attachment dissolves and is changed into discriminating wisdom. Discriminating wisdom means realizing emptiness, through which everything is seen exactly as it is, distinctly and unblurred.

All-accomplishing wisdom is the transformation of envy. We often become envious when seeing other people's qualities, happiness, good fortune, wealth, and enjoyments, thinking: "Why shouldn't I have that?" We are unhappy when others have something we don't, and based on this feeling, we may wish to harm them. This envy prevents us from carrying out the tasks we need to accomplish. When we try to undermine other people, we cause unhappiness not only for ourselves but for them as well. Any involvement motivated out of envy creates misery. The more we train in the nature of Mahamudra, the more envy subsides and dissolves. It transforms into the ability to carry out what needs to be carried out, which is called the all-accomplishing wisdom.

Exactly how do the five poisons transform into the five wisdoms? In the Sutra teachings, the Buddha taught how to deal with disturbing emotions through five different methods of changing oneself. The first method is to keep one's distance from emotions. Try to be clear about the negative characteristics of involvement in disturbing emotions. Understand that being hateful and undertaking actions that cause disquiet brings nothing but suffering. Out of attachment we become involved in various miseries. Remember that the disturbing emotions of anger, delusion, pride, and jealousy are not beneficial in the slightest, but are extremely harmful. Again and again, they create problems for ourselves and others. Engender the attitude that, "It's a bad idea to continue like that. I should change." This frame of mind doesn't totally eliminate our tendencies to be involved in disturbing emotions. Still, it makes it easier to not leap directly into them the next time the opportunity arises. Hence the first step is called 'keeping distance'.

The second remedy is called 'reducing disturbing emotions.' This doesn't mean suppressing them, in the sense that we take a disturbing emotion and force it down. It is a progressive occurrence that takes place naturally as a result of shifting our attention away from normal involvement in an emotion. We do this by cultivating a concentrated, calm state of mind repeatedly. Through practicing shamatha, through deeply relaxing, we keep out of complex entanglements, and our mind gradually becomes more peaceful. By developing a sense of presence of mind that helps us to be attentive and alert in any situation; we are more likely to notice whether or not we are getting carried away by disturbing emotions. Before training in the concentrated, calm state of mind of shamatha, we didn't even notice ourselves becoming lost in anger attachment, jealousy, pride. Now, because of being more mindful, we become aware of when these emotions take place. Due to the cultivation of mindfulness, calmness and openness, it's easier to refrain from getting further entangled in a disturbing emotion. This natural subsiding or diminishing is therefore called the remedy of 'reducing disturbing emotions.'

The third remedy the Buddha taught is called the remedy of 'uprooting disturbing emotions', which means to totally obliterate the emotion from its very core. This elimination is thorough and complete, not merely a temporary release. In terms of the Sutra teachings, it becomes possible when one has become accustomed to directly seeing the basic state of the emptiness of disturbing emotions. According to Vajrayana, involvement in disturbing emotions falls away through cultivating insight into the natural state of Mahamudra, or the Great Perfection of Ati Yoga. This is not the case for someone who hasn't fully stabilized insight into the basic nature. This insight is called 'clear seeing' or vipashyana in the Sutra system. If our level of proficiency in recognizing our nature is sporadic, with no true sustained stability, then we will not always be able to allow a disturbing emotion to dissolve. It is necessary is to apply the practice of Mahamudra directly in these instances. It does not help much to merely claim that the basic nature of this emotion is emptiness. Rather, at the moment the disturbing emotion arises, look nakedly into that which feels angry or attached. You will immediately see the reality of the nature of this disturbing emotion as being totally devoid of any concrete identity. We see it as it is because it is empty. In the moment of seeing that there is no substance to that which gets involved in the disturbing emotion, the disturbing emotion dissolves and is liberated. When we grow stable in recognizing and make this practice an actuality, we no longer become involved in the disturbing emotion. That is 'uprooting' in the true sense of the word, isn't it?

Naropa says: "The emotions are the great wisdom, like a jungle fire, they are the yogi's helpers." When a jungle catches fire, the bigger the jungle the bigger the fire. Since we are beginners, the more we can apply the remedy, the more opportunity there is for realizing wisdom, basic wakefulness. In this way the emotions are helpers or assistants for the practitioner.

Second, stating the nature of the Mahamudra of equal taste:

> How can there be staying or going?
> What meditation is there by fleeing to a hermitage?
> Without understanding this, all possible means
> Never bring more than temporary liberation.

To continue: "How can there be any staying or going?" This means that even while walking or moving about, of course we can still realize this nature. Our nature does not go anywhere or stay anywhere; it is always with us. It cannot possibly be some 'thing' that either stays or goes. Similarly, it does not become more present by going to the mountains and living in a hermitage. Our nature does not change according to circumstances. Therefore, moving about, staying somewhere, going or not going to the mountains — all these are superficial attributes that are not found in the basic nature itself.

If you have any questions, you can ask now.

STUDENT: Could you please clarify what it means when Naropa says: "While neither cultivating nor not cultivating, how can you be separate or not separate!" I didn't fully understand.

RINPOCHE: Let's look at the beginning part, "While neither cultivating nor not cultivating." The basic nature of Mahamudra is not made out of anything whatsoever — it's just naturally so. It's definitely not some 'thing' that is gradually cultivated. Does this mean we should be totally frivolous and let things run wild? No, it doesn't; it's incorrect to simply let go and get carried away into disturbing emotions and distraction. The basic nature is not something to be cultivated, but it shouldn't be forgotten either. We still need presence of mind. The next line, "How can you be separate or not separate!" means that our nature itself is already free from disturbing emotions, free from conceptual thought and obscuration. It does not need to be separated from or divested of anything. Yet, at the same time we cannot possibly be separate from this nature. Even while involved in conceptual thoughts or disturbing emotions, the very identity of this involvement, the essence, is still dharmakaya, so it is never apart or separate.

STUDENT: What is the connection between the "jungle fire" and the yogi?

RINPOCHE: The jungle fire is an analogy for the strength and power of the yogi's realization. The denser the jungle is, the stronger the fire will be. If the yogi in actuality experiences the basic nature of Mahamudra, then the more thoughts and emotions he has, the stronger the clarity, the bliss and the experience of the basic wakefulness will be.

STUDENT: Rinpoche, do you, personally, think? That is my first question. The second is that every day we finish with your long-life supplication. Why do you sing along?

RINPOCHE: In answer to the first question, I must say that I have no special or superior qualities, nor any extraordinary realization. I do have thoughts; I have disturbing emotions — I have them all. Just because I give teachings doesn't mean that I have totally realized Mahamudra. What it means is that I have been fortunate to meet some very great masters and to have received pith instructions that I consider extremely profound and beneficial. Out of this appreciation I try to practice them myself, and I feel if other people could understand these instructions, take them to heart and realize what these teaching are, they will receive strong benefit. This is the reason that I give teachings like these on Mahamudra.

About the long-life supplication: my students chant it, and they mean it. They want me to have a long life and good health, which is very nice. Whether it actually helps or not, it's still expressed out of a good heart and a sincere attitude, so from that angle it is very nice. When they're chanting, I feel that there's no point in me sitting quietly. There's no specific value from keeping silent. And as there's no real harm in me joining the chant, I feel like I can just as well sing along. Why not?

STUDENT: What is the cessation of thought like for someone who has realized Mahamudra? Does he become numb and insensitive, like a vegetable or a stone?

RINPOCHE: You must realize the difference between 'thought' and 'supreme knowledge'. The Tibetan word for an ordinary thought is *namtog,* which automatically means that there is fixation in terms of feeling something is pleasant or unpleasant; in terms of liking or disliking it. A feeling of attachment or aversion characterizes involvement in namtog. Practitioners who have realized Mahamudra do not at all become insensitive like a vegetable or a stone. They experience supreme knowledge, and are fully endowed with the five aspects of wisdom. Everything is known clearly and distinctly, but not in the same way as ordinary thought activity, which conceptualizes, labels, likes and dislikes.

I am happy that you wonder "Will the practice of Mahamudra eliminate conceptual thoughts?" Please use that interest to continue the practice of Mahamudra, and later you can look back and see: "Are there any thoughts left now, or not?" Then you will clearly know.

STUDENT: Rinpoche, when you talk about uprooting disturbing emotions, does that entail a physical act of abruptly turning about, or is it a mental act to meet the emotion head-on?

RINPOCHE: The phrase used is 'mind looking into mind', and the word 'looking' is in the sense of using the eye. This is of course an example, an analogy. What it means is to see directly. We experience the emptiness instantaneously, not in a roundabout way through constructing an idea about it to facilitate understanding. We simply let mind experience directly how its nature is. That is what is meant. Dealing with disturbing emotions can be a direct looking into the identity — or the lack of identity — of that which feels the emotion. It can also be the realization that comes about naturally by growing more accustomed to recognition. So, whether the disturbing emotion is cut through and dissolved at that very moment or whether it already has dissolved and does not arise any more — these two are actually basically the same.

There's a particular and profound reason to use the word 'looking' or 'seeing' rather than 'figuring out' or 'understanding', because this is not merely a personal problem — it's a general problem. When it comes to looking into the nature of mind, most people have a tendency to get caught up in understanding the nature of mind in conceptual terms. This conceptual understanding obscures the direct knowing of the nature. It is remarkable, in a way, that someone who is simple-minded and uneducated often has an easier time understanding instructions in Mahamudra. When he hears the instruction, "Look into your own nature," that person will simply and directly look into his or her own nature, without making too many ideas about it. On the other hand, someone who is educated and clever, will, when told to look, not look immediately. Instead, he will conceptualize something to be understood out of that — "This is what I understand and it's such-and-such," and he will create all kinds of labels. Instead of perceiving directly, he tries to deduce from the experience what the nature of mind is. This problem needs to be overcome. Do not confuse the inferred understanding with the direct experience!

So: is it all right if I sing along with my long-life supplication? [Laughter.]

15

Earlier I explained how the five disturbing emotions are transformed into the five wisdoms. In connection with that, I will now define the different aspects of mind. The Vaibhashika and the Sautrantika schools of Buddhist philosophy describe mind as being the six collections of consciousness, the six aspects of cognition, while in the Mind-Only School, eight aspects are defined. It is these eight aspects of cognition that, through practice, are transformed into the five wisdoms.

These six or eight aspects of consciousness are, of course, defined by means of intellectual analysis. These divisions are not about external things outside of ourselves, but are various aspects of our inner minds. Knowing about them will help us notice progress in meditation practice when we check to see how our meditation is improving.

The first of these aspects are the five sense consciousnesses, or sense cognitions. Consciousness becomes involved in the five sense objects through the five senses, as I briefly mentioned earlier. Through the eyes there is seeing, through the ears hearing, through the tongue tasting, through the nose smelling, and through the skin tactile sensation takes place. These five sense cognitions happen without any further involvement as to whether what is perceived is good or bad, pleasant or unpleasant. No particular concepts are formed within those cognitions themselves. Therefore, it is said that the five sense cognitions are non-conceptual. The sixth aspect is the mind consciousness that performs the function of associating the sense input in terms of past, present and future, good and bad, etc.

The seventh aspect of consciousness is called 'disturbed mind consciousness', and is something that is ongoing. It is definitely a quality of ego-clinging but is not as pronounced in the way of the thought "I am" as is the sixth consciousness. Rather, the disturbed mind consciousness is like a subtle background noise; an ongoing feeling of holding onto itself. This is present in every situation, whether we are awake or asleep.

The eighth is called the 'all-ground consciousness', or the alaya-vijnana in Sanskrit. It is also a type of background consciousness in the sense that it is the ongoing clarity or the conscious quality of mind. The alaya is what allows for any experience to take place, whether there is or isn't any thought involvement, whether or not we are interpreting the input that is presented through the senses. The quality of being able to cognize, to be awake, aware, and so forth, is something that is steady and continuous. Through all our beginningless lifetimes, this all-ground consciousness has been the basis for the habitual tendencies that recreate the different ways we perceive things. This is why it is called the all-ground consciousness.

The seventh and the eighth are called ongoing aspects of consciousness because they are continually present. Of course, all composite things are impermanent, being of a momentary nature, but this moment-to-moment presence of the seventh and eighth consciousnesses is continuous in the sense of being incessantly repeated. When we practice meditation, what is it that practices? It couldn't be the five sense cognitions because they are not always present. When there is seeing, the cognition of sight is present, but when the mind switches away from paying attention to a visual object, there's no seeing; there is no cognition of sight present. Sound cognition is present when we hear a sound, but when we don't hear anything, it's no longer present. There's no steady occurrence of the five sense cognitions at all. They are sporadic, occurring only from time to time. So, when we are asked, "Is it the five sense cognitions who practice meditation?", we have to say, "No, it isn't." They simply occur from time to time in a thought-free or nonconceptual way.

What about the seventh and the eighth aspects, the disturbed mind consciousness and the all-ground consciousness — are they the ones cultivating the meditation state? No, they aren't; because they are, respectively, a vague lack of clarity and a steady ongoing conscious presence. They don't cultivate anything in terms of stillness or insight, shamatha and vipashyana. As we progress through the bhumis, the bodhisattva levels, they are transformed and gradually fade away until they vanish. That's why you can't say that the seventh and eighth consciousnesses are the ones practicing meditation.

So, who or what exactly is it that practices meditation? We have to say it is the mind consciousness, the sixth aspect, which refers to that which thinks. We see sights, and notice various sounds, smells, tastes and textures. Accompanying those experiences is an act of conceptualizing which attaches labels and values to what is perceived — "This is nice, this is not nice." It's the mind consciousness that associates judgments with these sense impressions. Is it conceptual or non-conceptual? It is certainly conceptual, as it creates an untold number of different thoughts, ideas and notions about this and that.

This mind consciousness does not perceive objects directly. The learned masters of the past had a name for what the sixth consciousness apprehends — *dönchi,* which means 'mental image'. This mental image is presented in our mind and is then fused together with all sorts of different associations – for instance the name of the particular object. Let's take the example of a pillar. The sixth consciousness will create the idea of 'pillar' by fusing together a conglomeration of various impressions based on all of one's past memories about different pillars — thin, thick, ornamented and unadorned. These are put together in one generic image that we connect with the word pillar. The sixth consciousness associates and identifies a certain sense imprint — what is simply presented through the senses — as being a pillar.

This is different from the visual cognition, which is simply a direct sense impression of what is present. Sense cognition does not attach any labels or values — it is non-conceptual. It is the mind consciousness that starts to classify and define the current image. Through this process it creates an idea and some structure as to what it is we perceive. It culls memories from the past and premonitions of the future, melts these together with many other things and labels that mix with the name pillar.

So, among the eight consciousnesses, only the mind consciousness meditates. In other words, it is the thinker who cultivates the meditation state. Instead of giving in to the normal tendencies of thinking and being involved in emotions; catch hold of the activity of this mind consciousness with attentive presence. Being careful and relaxing this mind consciousness can generate a new habit of being more quiet and less lost in thoughts and concepts. When mind consciousness relaxes and becomes less involved in conceptualizing, that is exactly what is called shamatha, the calm state of concentrated attention.

How is vipashyana or insight cultivated through the sixth consciousness? Up until this point I have said that the sixth consciousness is conceptual, but that only refers to when it is extroverted. Thoughts and concepts are created when it faces away from itself, towards externally perceived objects. When the sixth consciousness is turned on itself, however, it has a non-conceptual, thought-free quality. This is entirely possible because the eight consciousnesses all have a self-knowing capacity; described as *rang-rig* in Tibetan. This quality of 'knowing-by-itself' does not need any other agent in order to know. When we see, we don't need somebody else to tell us that we see. We know that a visible object is being seen. It is the same with the other senses: we naturally hear, smell, taste, and feel. When thoughts and emotions occupy our attention, we know that we are thinking or feeling. This self-knowing is a sense of being naturally aware. What exactly is it that experiences? What is it that sees when the sixth consciousness is turned on itself to see? There is a direct self-knowing that the experiencer is not made out of anything whatsoever. It's like a breeze moving through empty space. To phrase it another way; there is a seeming yet insubstantial movement that is possible to perceive directly without any inference at all.

Buddhist philosophical logic makes use of an amusing example. It is said that the five sense cognitions are like a mute person who can see objects but can't talk about them. There is a bare seeing, hearing, smelling, tasting, and touching, with no concepts connected to them. They are direct impressions through the senses. Mind consciousness, on the other hand, is like a very talkative person who is blind. He can describe things quite eloquently but can't actually see them. Obviously, there's a problem here. How do we get these two aspects together? This is where the self-knowing quality comes in. It links together the mute sense cognitions with the blind act of conceptualizing. It creates a connection between the sense impressions and the conceptual mind consciousness.

Practicing meditation is unlike the ordinary state of mind that is always occupied by this and that. When not meditating, there is no real noticing of this naturally cognizant, self-knowing quality. Meditation training means to cultivate, grow used to, and be aware of this self-knowing quality. During the meditation state all the thought activity and general busyness of the sixth consciousness is allowed to calm down, to subside. All eight aspects of consciousness have a peaceful, tranquil quality. During this state it is possible to have clear seeing, in other words, to know this naturally cognizant quality.

How are these consciousnesses transformed into the five wisdoms as we progress in meditation training? The five sense cognitions accomplish the tasks at hand, but in their present ignorant, mistaken state, they function in an imperfect way. When we see, we don't see completeness, we don't see things exactly as they are. Something may be too far away or concealed, or most often our way of perceiving is not really correct. It is the same with the other sense impressions. However, as we progress in the meditation state, whatever needs to be carried out is fully and truly done; the tasks are all accomplished. That is why the transformation of the five sense cognitions is called the all-accomplishing wisdom.

The sixth consciousness, the mind consciousness, usually performs the function of discriminating between what is good and evil, pleasant and unpleasant, clinging to and fixating upon the notions we form. This mistakenness falls away and subsides as we gradually transcend it through practice. Eventually the sixth consciousness is transformed into discriminating wisdom.

The seventh, the disturbed mind consciousness, is usually described as subtle ego-clinging that is continually present. The inherent feeling that this 'I' here is more important than that 'other' over there is the basis for disturbing emotions. It is the act of clinging to the duality of perceiver and perceived, to self and other, regarding self as more important than other. The great master Chandrakirti in his Madhyamaka Avatara says that the disturbed mind consciousness is transcended at the eighth stage of the bodhisattva path. From that point onwards there is a sense of equality of self and other. Even though duality hasn't totally fallen away, the tendency to regard self as more important than other has subsided. It is said that the transformation of the disturbed mind consciousness is the wisdom of equality.

Now we have only the eighth left — the all-ground consciousness, often explained as the basis for habitual tendencies. The habitual tendencies that we created throughout past lifetimes ripen in this life, in the sense that they structure how we hear and see, perceive and think. It is exactly like a fruit ripening, in that something created in the past gradually and naturally unfolds. At the same time, we are currently creating new habitual tendencies. Our moment-to-moment frame of mind forms new habitual tendencies that will ripen at some time in the future. The habitual tendency is the cause, the seed. It's just like putting money in a bank. Think of the all-ground consciousness as the storehouse or the bank where all these tendencies are kept. We speak of two aspects, causal and resultant. When the transformation of the resultant aspect is completed, it is called dharmadhatu wisdom, which is the empty quality. When the cause, the seed quality of this all-ground is transformed, it is called mirror-like wisdom.

Let's go over this once more, briefly. Among these eight aspects of consciousness, that which practices meditation, that which cultivates and performs the training, is the sixth. This mind consciousness also makes most of the mistakes in what we do and how we experience. When we apply the trainings of shamatha and vipashyana to this mind consciousness, the confusion and busyness of thought gradually subsides. We train in knowing the very nature of this consciousness and getting more and more accustomed to realizing exactly how it is. By becoming used to the natural state, this consciousness is liberated. This is why Naropa says: "Without understanding this," — without realizing one's nature — "All possible means can never bring more than temporary liberation." This is the way to be liberated. Trying to accumulate merit and experiencing the results of that merit in samsara does bring temporary freedom, but it is only through realizing the natural state that any permanent liberation is possible.

Third, stating the nature of Mahamudra of indivisibility:

> When understanding this nature, what is there to bind you?
> While being undistracted from its continuity,
> There is neither a composed nor an uncomposed state
> To be cultivated or corrected with a remedy.

The numberless troubles that we undergo, all the hardship and anguish that accompany samsaric states come about from one cause — the lack of knowing our basic nature. All this bewilderment and confusion is due to ignorance. As long as this ignorance persists, we will continue in pain. When we clear up ignorance, all its resultant problems, obstacles and hindrances no longer occur. Or, as Naropa says, "When understanding this nature, what is there to bind you?"

When training in Mahamudra, we are supposed to practice in a way in which shamatha and vipashyana, stillness and insight, are united. We speak of the samadhi of the meditative practice and the samadhi of post-meditation, when one is walking, sitting, talking, or doing various kinds of physical work. At that time do not let your mind wander but be as attentive as you are in your meditation practice. It is especially important to sustain the experience of the nature of mind during the activities of your daily life. This way of training in the samadhi of post-meditation will assist the samadhi of the main practice, the meditation state itself. Likewise, training in the meditation state itself will help improve the samadhi of the post-meditation.

Sustaining the practice of post-meditation is not necessarily that easy for a beginner. It is difficult to mingle the experience of this practice with daily activities, or when involved in disturbing emotions. We find that we get distracted again and again. We forget to practice or feel it's inconvenient to practice while doing something. Don't give up just because it's hard. The more we persevere in the training, the easier it will be. In the beginning, apply short moments of recognition. Later on, you'll find your ability to remember to practice in daily life situations will naturally increase. There is a definite benefit from training during daily life situations. Practice does not prevent or impede carrying out daily tasks, and at the same time is extremely helpful for progressing in the meditation state itself.

Now we are at the third point about the Mahamudra of conduct, at the line where Naropa says: "While being undistracted from its continuity." While we are training in the experience of the empty and cognizant nature; we are not distracted. Remaining like that, "there is neither a composed nor an uncomposed state." 'Composed' means trying to place the mind in a way that it stays in equanimity. This is not necessary when recognizing the nature of mind. There is no need to make an extra composed state in addition to being undistracted. While experiencing the nature of mind, there is no opportunity to be involved in thoughts or emotions, so therefore it is also not an uncomposed state.

Let's look at the next line: "To be cultivated or corrected with a remedy." A beginner inexperienced in the nature of mind may think: "I don't have any great qualities, so I must try to somehow create them through this practice. If I try hard enough, eventually they'll appear." In this way we attempt to bring forth and cultivate something that is not present. Or we might think that, "I have thoughts, but through this practice they can be eliminated," and try to get rid of our thoughts in meditation practice. This is not the way to practice Mahamudra. Please understand this point: It is essential to discern that the nature of mind does not possesses any flaws in the slightest. There is no need to remove any imagined faults. The nature of mind is naturally tranquil, with the quality of luminous wakefulness inherently present. There is no need to put effort into cultivating these qualities either. What we must do is to acknowledge and recognize what is already present and allow it to be fully realized.

There is still another way in which we could misunderstand this line, by mistakenly thinking that there is nothing to do, no meditation to carry out. To believe it's not necessary to remedy anything by practicing is incorrect. Once again, I will repeat: we need to recognize our mind and experience the nature of Mahamudra. However, that which is recognized or experienced is inherently present within our basic nature. From that perspective, it is not necessary to recreate or fabricate what we already possess. This is an essential point. When we engage in meditation training, it may look like we are trying to sit and do something new. It may appear that we are creating a new entity or a sublime state that is not present in our minds. That is not the case. Instead, we are simply relaxing the habit of mistakenness that constantly stirs up confusion and concepts. We are releasing that tendency and letting it dissolve. What we experience is not something new that never was. Rather, it is our intrinsic nature itself.

16

In this teaching on the view, meditation, conduct, and fruition of Mahamudra, we have now come to the fourth, the Mahamudra of fruition. There are different results of practice, temporary and ultimate. When training in meditation, we need to distinguish between primary results and experiences and ordinary ones.

Ordinary experiences can take the form of visions that appear in various types and ways. They may feel sublime or be horrible. We could hear voices and have manifold sensations. Ordinary experiences are not to be regarded as amazing, a great virtue, nor as some kind of huge mistake on our part. It is most beneficial if we attribute very little significance to such experiences.

Read *The Rain of Wisdom,* also called *The Ocean of Songs of the Kagyü Masters.* In the chapter on Gampopa's songs, there is the story of how he received oral instructions from Milarepa. Gampopa had incredible experiences. Sometimes he would see the entire mandala of the yidam deity as white or red. Other times he had extraordinary experiences that were immensely pleasant. Occasionally he had downright awful experiences, like having a vision of the hell of black lines. Each time he would relate what he experienced to Milarepa and ask for advice about its meaning. Every time, Milarepa's response was: "This is not something good, nor is it something bad. Just continue your practice." So Gampopa simply continued his practice.

Milarepa gave an analogy for how to regard these different experiences. If you press your eyeball slightly while looking at the moon, immediately there's a vision of two moons. You might think this is extraordinary. "Hey, normally people only see one moon, but now I see two. This is incredible, a great experience!" Honestly, there is nothing special about that. Somebody else might think: "Oh no, normally people only see one moon and now I see two. I'm in great danger! What do I do about it? Maybe I'm making a big mistake." Milarepa's reply was that these experiences are neither special nor a great danger. They only come about because one is pressing one's eye. It's neither good or bad. In the same way, he instructed Gampopa, "These experiences come about because of focusing wholeheartedly on practice. Since all experiences are mental, all sorts of different visions take place, but they're neither extraordinarily good nor horribly bad. They're just experiences."

If we attach great importance to what or how we feel and experience, we can make it quite unpleasant for ourselves. When good experiences occur, we start to think: "This is extraordinary. I must be someone special" and become conceited because we had such-and-such an experience. Such pride decreases our diligence in practice, causing an obstacle for progress. Or perhaps the experience we considered as being so important ceases, and we yearn to relive it. We try to recreate it through our practice, thinking: "I want to feel like that again." When we don't, the longing makes us unhappy and creates problems for our practice.

On the other hand, we may become very fearful about our experiences, worrying that what we feel is dangerous. Perhaps we are making a mistake, we feel. While the fear is not that strong in itself, it can become intense once we start to invest all of our attention into that little worry. We can blow it totally out of proportion and become obsessed by it, at which point it does become a big problem. Actually, though, a little fear about how we feel is nothing special. All we have to think at that time is think, "There is nothing important to worry about. This is simply another experience."

It's also possible to have a sudden experience of emptiness and become either terrified or enthusiastic, feeling, "This is extraordinary — I am remarkable." Or we may have experiences of immense bliss or clarity. These are the three traditional experiences that are mentioned: bliss, clarity, and nonthought. In none of these cases is it necessary to attach great value to how we feel. If we do, the attachment itself creates the obstacle. It's best to continue in a way where we feel at peace and tranquil.

The great masters of the past mention that we need to bring everything we encounter onto the path, that we should utilize whatever we meet as the path. The traditional way of describing this practice is the 'four-fold taking as path.' The first of these four is called 'bringing joy and sadness onto the path'. The first one, joy, is when everything is going fine — we are successful, have enjoyments, wealth, good health, and friends. We naturally take joy in that, and feel happy about what is happening in our life. That is of course not such a bad thing, because all sentient beings want to be happy and enjoy. However, once we start to cling to the particular situation that brings us happiness, this fondness for the joy will turn to pain once the situation changes, since everything is impermanent and eventually perishes. Instead of being caught up in the frame of mind that takes joy in these circumstances, we should rather look into the very identity of that which feels happy. We will discover that it is not made out of anything whatsoever. It is empty of any identity. That is called 'bringing joy into the path'.

Conversely, we feel pain when we feel sad or hurt, when we have misfortune or bad health. Often the thoughts come: "This is agonizing. I cannot bear it. It is just too much!" Just as you did with pleasure, look into what it is that feels this sadness. Once again you will not find a concrete entity anywhere. It is empty of any real substance. This is how to utilize joy and sadness as the path.

The second is called 'taking sickness onto the path'. Occasionally we experience physical pain. When our body is sick, it is not a mental state; we actually ache physically. We can neither ignore nor deny that something is wrong with our body. An ordinary person turns their hostility towards the sensation, thinking, "I don't like it. I don't want to feel this." The pain then appears to be even more unbearable. As practitioners training in the profound meditation, we should try to bring physical pain into the path, to use it as the path. Severe sickness is not easy to deal with when one is a beginner, but a little pain is not too difficult. For example, if you take your fingers and squeeze them slightly it hurts a tiny bit, it's unpleasant, but not unbearable. At that moment, instead of getting involved in the aversion, look into what is it that feels this dislike, the hurt. As before, we find out that the feeling of pain is not made out of anything. It's empty in essence. While being empty, sensation is still present, but it's not unendurable because it is insubstantial. By experiencing bodily pain in this way, we are not overcome by it, and therefore it is called 'utilizing physical pain as the path'.

The third is called 'utilizing disturbing emotions as path'. Disturbing emotions are unlike mental or physical pain. Our attention directs itself in a coarse, almost concrete way. The strongest disturbing emotions that we have of course are desire, anger, pride, and jealousy. There is also guilt and doubt. When these emotions take over our minds, we feel overpowered, we lose control and get caught up in the negative feelings. Take desire, for example: we become attracted towards some concrete thing in our life or a living being. We may become completely preoccupied with being near that person or possessing that particular object. Desire creates disquiet and restlessness, and we are uncomfortable. It is similar with anger: we feel hostile towards a thing or person. It takes over our focus continuously and makes us deeply disturbed. It's the same with jealousy, pride, guilt, and so forth. These emotions make us uneasy, they unsettle us.

A practitioner needs to bring disturbing emotions onto the path. Instead of getting totally caught up in what we feel so strongly about, look into that which experiences the emotion: "Where is it felt? Where does this feeling arise out of? Where is it right now? How does it look? What is it made out of?" When we fail to find any concrete thing whatsoever, we are utilizing disturbing emotions as path.

The fourth method is called 'bringing the bardo onto the path'. The bardo is the intermediate state between this life and the next. After this life has dissolved and the next rebirth has not yet unfolded, there is an in-between period where the consciousness undergoes various experiences — sounds, colors, lights, and other manifestations. Because of the attachment to the normal events in our lives, we are deeply unsettled and intensely worried when we arrive in the bardo state. We think: "I don't know where to go. Oh no! Where will I take rebirth?" We are terrified and overcome by all sorts of immense anxieties. This situation, the bardo experience, needs to be brought onto the path. Here's how to do this.

As Buddhist practitioners, we should strive to not be like an ordinary person, who wants only to enjoy and be comfortable in this life. An ordinary person, by definition, doesn't give any thought to the fact that sooner or later we all die and whether we like it or not, we arrive in the bardo state. During the bardo ordinary people have nothing to hold onto, and they experience immense fear. Overcome by panic, distress, and despair, they may feel incredible regret for how they spent their life. Their intense uncertainty about what is going to happen to them is terrifying. In order to avoid this, we need to make sure right now that we do not end up totally unprepared for the bardo phenomena. Whether we do or not is entirely in our hands right now. We should repeatedly picture ourselves in the bardo state and imagine how it would be. This will help us to become more settled and self-assured so that we will not be totally bewildered or at a loss as to how to deal with that circumstance. It is extremely beneficial to bring the bardo state onto the path in this way.

Whether we are alive in a physical body or have passed on and are in the bardo state, the most important thing is to be stable-minded and level headed. Be steady in yourselves, and do not become totally overwhelmed by experiences; do not immediately get carried away by whatever takes place. This is an important quality to cultivate. Otherwise, whenever we feel pain or anxiety, we will be totally caught up in it. Train now to be more balanced in your response to your emotions. Cultivating this quality through Dharma practice makes an incredible amount of difference as to whether we take an unfortunate rebirth or a good one. During the bardo state, it is said that we encounter the natural sound of dharmata, the intrinsic and empty lights, colors, and sounds. We can grow accustomed to these right now.

Train first by sitting with closed eyes. In the beginning, everything is dark and we don't see a thing, but eventually shapes start to appear. There are bits of light that takes different forms, perhaps moving; maybe green, yellow, blue or red. After a while it is possible that these formations of light will start to become bigger. They could even become quite overwhelming, but you should remain completely relaxed. These appearances are not made out of anything. They are insubstantial, and there is no real place that these formations come out of, or dwell. There is nothing to be astonished about; they are merely an expression of the empty nature. Once we grow slightly accustomed to these light formations that are the naturally empty lights of the innate nature, we have developed a kind of steadiness that will help us not to be overcome by the natural lights of dharmata in the bardo.

Similarly, we can grow accustomed to the intrinsic sound of dharmata that occurs in the bardo state by sitting down in a quiet place with no noise and paying attention. We should direct our concentration towards our hearing, not in an extroverted way, but tuning into a subtle sound that is present all by itself. Sometimes it helps to clench your teeth slightly and listen. There is a subtle roaring which you can hear more and more if you focus. It is not the sound of physical things clashing together, like a drum or any outer material objects. It is the sound of our own nature. When we pay attention, we find that the sound is not coming from anywhere, it remains nowhere, and it is not made out of anything at all. While looking into the identity of this intrinsic sound, there is no identity to find. It's totally insubstantial. Simultaneously, there is the hearing of this sound vividly and distinctly. This is identical in nature with the natural sound of dharmata during the bardo state. If we can relax into the hearing without being apprehensive or caught up in it, we can avoid being overwhelmed by the natural sound of dharmata in the bardo state.

We do encounter all these situations that I have described. We have pleasure, pain, joy, and sorrow, we fall sick, we have disturbing emotions; and sooner or later we will have to go through the bardo. We need to accept the inevitability of these things. Not wanting to think about them doesn't help; they will still happen. We need to prepare ourselves for those situations without falling prey to anxiety, fear and unhappiness. It is much better if we become fully capable of encountering all circumstances right now, without being at a loss about what to do and where to go. The key point in all these four situations mentioned is settling into the equanimity of knowing the natural state of mind. The more we train in recognizing our nature, the more accustomed we become. We need to persevere diligently in order to reach proficiency. This is an essential point.

In the Buddhist teachings, everything depends on the karma we created. However, two dominant factors are at play: the ripening of former karma and temporary circumstances. We may have a certain karmic course, but if we fall prey to temporary circumstances, panic, and start to be bewildered in the bardo state, we may make a terribly wrong choice. It's very important to be level-headed so that we can be calm about what we encounter in the bardo state. In this way we don't force ourselves into an unfortunate rebirth. We will have the opportunity to choose and will be free to exert ourselves in taking the correct rebirth. From this perspective as well, this teaching is extremely important.

Once more, for the three points about the Mahamudra of fruition, first, stating the nature of the Mahamudra of what appears and exists:

It is not made out of anything.
Experience self-liberated is dharmadhatu.
Thinking self-liberated is great wisdom.
Nondual equality is dharmakaya.

Let's go back to the text: "It is not made out of anything." The 'it' here refers to any experience you encounter, no matter what it is. There is no concrete substance; everything is empty in essence. Nevertheless, experience occurs unimpededly. The content of experience is a transitory circumstance. Every moment of experience naturally vanishes — "Experience self-liberated is dharmadhatu." The thinker, that which perceives and labels, likewise dissolves by itself — "Thinking self-liberated is great wisdom." Thinking is like a bubble on the surface of water or like a gust of wind: neither is solid. Yet there is a seeming presence of awareness that is not made out of anything whatsoever. Ordinary people do not pay attention to the reality of this. Practitioners should look into that which thinks and see its insubstantiality; watch the seeming thinker vanishing by itself. This is original wakefulness. In short, the perceived is dharmadhatu, while the perceiver is the luminous wakefulness. Hence, "Nondual equality is dharmakaya."

These two aspects of experience — the perceiver and the perceived — are not only utterly insubstantial and empty of any concrete identity, they are an indivisible unity. This indivisible unity, here described as nondual equality, is the basic state, the reality of experience. Whether we realize it or not, it is our natural state. When through practice it is fully actualized, there's a state of great serenity. That is what is called the dharmakaya, the final fruition.

If you have any questions, feel free to ask.

STUDENT: What's the connection between the bardo state and the eighth consciousness, the all-ground consciousness?

RINPOCHE: Where does experience take place? Whether an experience belongs to this life, the next life or the bardo, it unfolds within the all-ground consciousness. The all-ground consciousness is like the environment or atmosphere within which the ripening of past habitual tendencies manifests. It is also the place where the new tendencies we form are kept. For example, a small child, when shown a tiny circle, does not at first have any real ideas connected to that. He is then taught or imprinted with the association of the sound 'O' to the circle. Later on, when he's reading a text, he sees the circle amid other letters and the sound 'O' immediately comes to his mind. It does so spontaneously, without him having to think, question, or ask someone else. It has become a habit to associate a circle with the sound 'O'. It is the same way with all habitual tendencies. The experiences that occur in the bardo state are also structured. Whether they are clear or unclear, or whether we feel at ease about them or uneasy, all depends upon the habitual tendencies that are stored in our all-ground consciousness.

STUDENT: In the context of becoming accustomed to the practice of the natural state in the bardo experiences, is that training stored in the sixth or in the eighth consciousness?

RINPOCHE: The predominant aspect of the consciousness that practices is the sixth mind consciousness. This is true whether we are in this life, the next life or in the bardo. The sixth consciousness is what accepts or rejects joy and sorrow, pleasure and pain. It creates thoughts about all the different experiences. However, the habitual tendencies formed by doing so are stored within the all-ground consciousness. In the context of bringing the bardo onto the path, we train in relaxing into the natural state while experiencing the intrinsic colors and sounds. The looking into the nature of that which experiences these is the nonconceptual aspect of the sixth consciousness. The habitual tendency for that training, however, is stored in the eighth consciousness.

STUDENT: What are the signs that you are proceeding correctly when you are practicing the path?

RINPOCHE: It is generally said that the sign of learning the Dharma is to be peaceful and gentle. The sign of being adept in Dharma practice is to be free of disturbing emotions. What that means is the more we learn about Dharma practice, the more easy-going we should become — gentle, disciplined and self-contained. The more we practice, the more in charge of our minds we should become, not immediately getting caught up in anger if we don't like something. We should be in control and not be immediately overrun by emotions. That is a sure sign of progress on the path.

17

Among the three points about the Mahamudra of fruition, the first point was about the natural liberation of the perceiver and the perceived. The second point is about the indivisible nature of samsara and nirvana.

Second, stating the nature of the Mahamudra of samsara and nirvana:

> Like the continuous flow of a great river,
> Whatever you do is meaningful.
> This is the eternal awakened state,
> The great bliss, leaving no place for samsara.

The first line — "Like the continuous flow of a great river," refers to diligence, exerting ourselves. We may be able to recognize the nature of mind; but to sustain it; exertion is necessary. Naropa uses the flow of a great river as an example. A great river flows continuously and effortlessly, at its own natural pace. That is a wonderful image for the type of diligence that is indispensable.

The general teachings mention two kinds of diligence: one is called 'devoted application', and the other 'constant application'. In devoted application, we try our best, our utmost, to apply effort and carry on in that way. Constant application means one is not just diligent for a few days, weeks, months or years, but continuously, in a sustained way. Devoted application is very important, but a sense of constancy in our exertion, especially in this context of training in the natural state of Mahamudra, is what is needed. The ordinary attitude of being diligent and pushing doesn't allow our exertion to increase and develop.

I will now explain the six types of diligence that the great bodhisattva Shantideva mentions in his *Bodhicharya Avatara*. The first step towards being truly diligent is sincere interest. Sincere interest comes about once we appreciate the value of something, that it's meaningful and worthwhile to pursue. Our attention is directed towards that and we exert ourselves. If we don't really understand the value, it's very hard to be really interested and diligent in accomplishing any task.

The second factor is pride. The word 'pride' figures among the six primary disturbing emotions, but here the meaning is not the same, but rather has the connotation of confidence. It is the self-assurance that "I can do this; it is not impossible; not beyond me. I can practice and train in samadhi. It is meaningful and worthwhile." If we don't have self-confidence and we think, "I'm weak, I cannot eradicate my faults or promote good qualities, I cannot practice meditation," it's hard to ever be diligent. On the other hand, if we have a sense of pride that, "This is possible, I can do it," we can be diligent.

There's another reason for why we can feel confident in our ability to practice. Think of the life examples of the eighty-four great mahasiddhas of ancient India, who trained in samadhi in all sorts of different ways and attained accomplishment. As I mentioned before, many of these realized masters had occupations and lived and worked in the world. King Indrabhuti, for example, was very powerful. He had immense wealth and luxuries and many enjoyments. As ruler of a country, he had innumerable tasks to attend to. Still, within this situation he focused his mind on the practice of realizing Mahamudra, and in that very lifetime attained supreme accomplishment. So, no matter what situation we find ourselves in; whether overindulgence in luxuries or overburdened by work, we can still continue and persevere in the practice.

Another example is that of Nagarjuna, an extremely learned great master who wrote many treatises and established various modes of reasoning. We might think that he had to engender immeasurable concepts to figure out and define all these different things. Yet, by looking into the nature of what thinks within all this activity, Nagarjuna was able to continue the training in samadhi and attain supreme accomplishment. Even if one is a scholar and does a lot of intense conceptual thinking, there is the possibility of pursuing and reaching enlightenment.

Tilopa had very low-class jobs like pressing sesame seeds into oil. He even worked as the doorman at a brothel! While doing so, he cast away all pride and continued training in realizing Mahamudra. Later he was known as the mahasiddha Tilopa. Another mahasiddha actually worked as a coolie, digging and carrying dirt. While working he remained mindful, focusing on the practice of realizing the nature of Mahamudra. Eventually he too attained supreme accomplishment.

It makes no difference whether one is male or female. There were female mahasiddhas as well, like the great masters Niguma and Sukhasiddhi, who attained supreme enlightenment and were able to display miraculous powers like flying through the sky. Thinking of all of these great practitioners, we can feel confident that we too can practice.

The basis for being able to persevere, the basis for fortitude, is that all sentient beings do have a buddha nature, an enlightened essence. No matter who one is — whether an inferior or superior person — we all, without any exception, have an enlightened essence. Based on that, good qualities can unfold and negative traits can be eradicated.

That type of perseverance was rooted in mind, our essential buddha nature. The next type is based on our physical situation as human beings. If we were born as another life form where we didn't have these capabilities, we wouldn't be able to persevere in Dharma practice to the same extent. Right now, we possess what is called 'the precious human body' endowed with the eight freedoms and ten riches. We are capable of carrying out what needs to be carried out. We can be diligent in what is meaningful. Therefore, in regard to the body we have at the present time, we can feel confident that we are able to practice, and in this way be diligent.

The second factor was pride or self-confidence; the third factor is enthusiasm. If we take pleasure in what we do, it doesn't seem difficult at all and it is easy to be diligent. Watch how children play. When they are engrossed in their games it doesn't matter if it's cold outside or whether they are a little hungry — they are happy to continue playing. Even if the game is difficult, they don't mind the difficulty at all; they continue joyfully. In the same way, if we take joy in practice, then no matter what difficulty we encounter it won't seem hard at all. Enthusiasm is thus another factor in diligence.

The next one is the courage that comes from abandonment. Abandoning means not holding onto a particular practice we have become quite good at, thinking that "This is sufficient simply because I have trained in it." For example, we may feel very competent in shamatha practice because we have attained some proficiency in it. We might think "Maybe it's not necessary to expand into vipashyana. Why enter a new area that I am not familiar with? Maybe I'd better hold onto what I know and do well in." That is clinging, the opposite of abandonment. When we have a brave escort on the path, we have the courage to proceed further. Courageous abandonment thus helps us to be more diligent.

The next factor for diligence is determination, making up our minds that, "What I'm involved in is the main thing, it is significant, I will focus on it." A determined frame of mind helps us to persevere and be diligent.

The last factor, the sixth, is the strength of taking charge. We do not have to feel weakened or victimized by samsaric tendencies – this is our own choice. We shouldn't feel lazy and excuse ourselves by thinking, "I'm sorry, I can't help it; it is not within my power to do much." We should instead take charge of our lives, deciding what to focus our attention on. Whether we will allow ourselves to be lazy or not is basically in our own hands. The strength of taking charge allows us to carry on with practice, to persevere and be diligent.

When Naropa describes being diligent in the sense of "the continuous flow of a great river," it means not to lose presence of mind in any given moment. Always try to be alert and attentive, and frequently remind yourself to practice. It doesn't matter what position we have in life. Simply continuing the practice, being mindful and diligent, we can carry on like a river.

"Whatever you do is meaningful," means that by acting in this way, our lives will have some consequence, some meaning. Keeping the continuous awareness of the nature of mind is itself what is called the eternal awakened state — eternal in the sense of being uninterrupted. 'Awakened state' here means the real buddha. In the continuity of that awakened state there is no room for ignorance. There is no opportunity for any samsaric state to occur with all its accompanying suffering and misery. This is why it is called "the great bliss, leaving no room for samsara."

Maybe some doubts are surfacing at this point. For example, you might think that understanding all outer things to be empty and devoid of concrete nature, as well as understanding the perceiver to be free of any substantial identity, could exclude the possibility of compassion. One might worry that through realizing emptiness one might become uncompassionate, heartless and cruel. That's not the case at all. For the individual, all suffering vanishes when the nature of mind is realized. The absence of personal suffering is in itself great bliss. Unfortunately, it is not the same for others, who still experience suffering, even though they have the same essential enlightened nature. The Third Karmapa said that the essence of all beings is continuously the awakened state, just as what the practitioner realizes. Even though their nature is the awakened state, it doesn't help much if they are unaware or ignorant of it. In most situations sentient beings are unable to realize how the nature of their mind is. Seeing that, one cannot help but feel compassion.

Another reason we do not become uncompassionate from practicing Mahamudra is that we are practicing within the framework of the bodhisattva vow. Even at the beginning stage when compassion does not spontaneously arise out of realization, we can still generate compassion through developing bodhichitta. All sentient beings possess the enlightened essence, and are therefore able to be enlightened. They are able to train in the state of samadhi and fully realize it. However, certain circumstances must be complete for them to understand how to train. Maybe they don't have even the interest or the merit to learn how to practice. If that is the case, realization will be very difficult. Thinking of this again, even in a conceptual way, we can feel compassion. Thus, from both the relative and the ultimate points of view, we can be compassionate while practicing Mahamudra.

On the other hand, we might fear that compassion prevents realization, feeling that being compassionate could prove to be a stumbling block for understanding emptiness. It is not like that either. Whether we practice Mahamudra or Dzogchen, in the moment of being compassionate, we can look into what it is that feels compassion. Whether it is a natural compassion or a generated one, the moment we look, we see that there is no entity to find. As the Third Karmapa Rangjung Dorje said: "In the moment of love, the empty essence dawns nakedly." When feeling love and compassion for others, that which feels compassion is not some kind of hard, solid lump or blob. It is totally insubstantial, as in the case of any other emotional or conceptual state. By looking towards that which feels compassion, we can realize this emptiness in actuality. In this way, emptiness and compassion are indivisible. By progressing in our practice of the natural state and developing further compassion, we accomplish the benefit of ourselves by cultivating insight into emptiness. Through cultivating great compassion, we will be able to undertake the immense task of accomplishing the benefit of others.

If you have any questions, please ask.

STUDENT: When there is perception, is it the self-knowing quality of mind that apprehends? Is it the same principle for both conceptual and non-conceptual experiences?

RINPOCHE: The word self-knowing, rang-rig in Tibetan, is defined as 'one's mind not being hidden from oneself'. In other words, you can say your personal cognition is not hidden from yourself; but is 'self-known'. When you see something, you don't have to be told that you see it — you know that you see. You don't have to wonder, "Am I really seeing the pillar or not?' or wait for someone else to tell you, "Now you are seeing a pillar." That is the self-knowing quality. Whether the experience is conceptual or non-conceptual doesn't make any difference; it's still self-knowing, or as you might say in English, 'auto-knowing.'

STUDENT: Concerning doubt, isn't it healthy to doubt when making up our minds in problematic situations? Isn't it possible that sometimes in meditation one can resolve problems?

RINPOCHE: It depends on the circumstances you're in. If people are waiting for you to apply your attention to a certain problem, you should make up your mind, and solve it in an intelligent way. You should be able to discriminate between what is and is not beneficial, to weigh the possibilities and decide on what is best. Eliminate all doubt, then announce your decision. That's the course to take. In a different situation, nobody is waiting for you to make up your mind. You're simply sitting on your meditation cushion and your mind keeps churning: "Maybe I should do this. Maybe I should do that. I wonder. I'm not really sure." Such a situation, when no imminent decision needs to be taken, yet doubt keeps developing, creates an obstacle for meditation practice. At that point, it's much better to look into who is it that doubts. Dissolve the doubt by recognizing its empty essence and relax into the calm, quiet state.

STUDENT: If I am unable to experience emptiness and compassion in an indivisible and united way, should I alternate between the two?

RINPOCHE: It is important to know from the beginning that emptiness and compassion neither alternate nor obstruct one another. It's not like we can experience one without the other. If we maintain that it's only necessary to focus on emptiness, that compassion doesn't matter; we will go in a wrong direction. If we think that the most important thing is to be loving and kind, and that understanding emptiness is not important; we will likewise go in a wrong direction. Even if at present you are not able to experience emptiness and compassion in an indivisible way, it doesn't matter that much. Just continue the practice. Sometimes recognize emptiness, and sometimes cultivate compassion. As we train repeatedly, we discover that within emptiness there is the possibility of having full compassion for all sentient beings. Likewise, being compassionate doesn't prevent insight into the empty nature of all phenomena. Gradually you will realize the state of original wakefulness in which emptiness and compassion are indivisible.

STUDENT: It seems that enlightenment is far away. How can we explain it in an understandable fashion to our children?

RINPOCHE: On one hand, we may believe that enlightenment is far away, that it takes a long time. It's true that if we don't practice, it is extremely far away. However, if we practice continuously and steadily, the state of enlightenment, the awakened state, will draw closer. The point is simply to practice as much as you can. I don't feel there is any particular special way to make understanding emptiness easier for children. It is more a matter of allowing them to decide to practice by themselves when they grow up. That is quite good.

STUDENT: I have a question from the text. I understand that it's a mistake to believe in eternalism or nihilism, but here in the text it says:

"This is the eternal awakened state." How is that different from the misconception of eternalism?

RINPOCHE: The view of eternalism is the idea that things last forever, and this belief obstructs the understanding that all composite things are impermanent. Falling into the extreme of permanence thus becomes a hindrance. The view of nihilism maintains that there is no consequence to one's actions; and that there is nothing after death. Using these definitions, the understanding of the awakened state doesn't fall into the extreme of eternalism. Simply because it's the original, primordial, basic state doesn't mean that it's eternalistic.

18

We have now come to the third point about the Mahamudra of fruition, called "stating the nature of the Mahamudra of ultimate perfection," which means the ultimate result.

> All things are empty of their own identities.
> The concept fixed on emptiness has dissolved in itself.
> Free of concept, holding nothing in mind,
> Is, itself, the path of all buddhas.

In the first line, 'all things' includes both entities made out of physical substance that we perceive as well as the consciousness that cognizes and perceives. Both physical things and consciousness are devoid of individual identity. When we closely inspect any particular entity, we find every single one of them are composed of many parts. It's only in our minds that we apprehend things as being singular. Actually, they are a composite of many smaller sections. When we look at the smaller parts, we find they are also a composite, and so on and so on, down to the tiniest atom. When we examine the atom we discover that even an atom, literally an indivisible particle, does not withstand our scrutiny — it doesn't hold up as being a single entity either. It is as insubstantial as a bubble. Therefore, as Naropa says, all things are empty of their own identities.

Secondly, consciousness is similarly empty of its own identity. There is no concrete substance to it. There are two ways that we can establish this. One is through direct experience, turning consciousness directly onto itself to look directly into what it is that experiences. In that moment, we do not find any concrete entity that experiences. We see it in actuality as being empty of any definite substance.

The other way is through reasoning, which also allows us to find certainty about the emptiness of consciousness. Normally we think of 'my mind' as a continuity that is sustained from the past into the present, and through the present into the future. We decide conceptually that 'my consciousness' is one singular entity. In fact, this is mistaken. Those instances of consciousness that occurred in the past are gone and have ceased. Future moments of consciousness have not yet occurred, so they cannot be said to be right now. The present moment of experience, no matter how short or subtle it might be, must have a beginning, a middle and an end. If the moment has any duration at all, it can be divided into parts that belong to the past, are present right now, and are connected to the future. However intelligently or minutely we search, we are at a loss to find a real continuous 'thing' that is the perceiving consciousness. In this way, through reasoning, we can conclude that consciousness is empty of its own identity.

As a side remark, the word 'all things' in Tibetan is *chö*, in Sanskrit dharma with a small 'd'. The word dharma has many connotations. Sometimes dharma refers to that which needs to be applied in practice, while other times it means the teachings of the awakened ones. Dharma can also mean knowable entities, anything that can be known or experienced. That is the connotation here; the word 'dharma' refers to knowable entities like physical things and consciousness.

The statement in the second line is that "conceptual mind fixed on emptiness has dissolved in itself." We can understand that all things are empty of their own identities. However, to rigidly hold onto the concept 'everything is empty' is definitely no good. As the great Mahasiddha Saraha said, "To believe that things are concrete is to be as stupid as an ox." Attaching concrete existence to that which doesn't have it is as foolish and ignorant as the perception of an ox. However, Saraha adds, "If one fixates on the idea of emptiness, that is even more deluded."

The idea 'all things are empty or insubstantial' is dependent upon and negates the idea that things are concrete and substantial. Without the original premise, 'all things are substantial,' — which is untrue — there couldn't be the opposite idea that they aren't. These two concepts, substantial and insubstantial, are thus mutually dependent. The great bodhisattva Shantideva gave an example for this type of mutual dependency. A woman falls asleep and dreams that she had a child. First there is the idea that something is. Later in the same dream, the child dies. Based on the idea that there was a child, there idea arises that there isn't a child anymore. But remember, both are false — because no child was ever born! After all, it's a dream. In the same way, no child died either. There is no real birth, and no real death. This example shows us how, since all things do not really exist to begin with, it is equally deluded to hold onto the concept that "things are unreal" The concept of emptiness must be dissolved as well, but naturally.

Through using reason and logic, we can settle with certainty that everything is empty of its own identity, both things as well as consciousness. In Mahamudra practice, we do not reason intellectually. Rather the training is simply to let consciousness look directly into itself and see that there is no concrete entity that perceives or experiences. Mind is empty of any identity, any concrete essence. Not only is it empty — there is a natural quality of being conscious, awake. This lucidity is a cognizance that is always present throughout all states. Likewise, this conscious or cognizant quality is not made out of any concrete identity either. Through seeing this directly, any concept of emptiness vanishes.

In Mahamudra training it is possible to go astray in three particular ways. The first of these three is called 'the basic straying from the nature of emptiness'. One thinks that the emptiness of the nature of all things is an absence of what already is. This is a mistaken idea. Emptiness is not like the normal concept 'empty', which means 'nothing'. An empty room means there are no things in the room. but emptiness does not imply that something has to be totally absent to be empty. Rather, it is that all things are already empty by nature. The true state of all things is inherently emptiness, and this emptiness is indivisible from dependent origination. One does not prevent the other. The emptiness of mind does not block off its cognizant quality. While perceiving, this cognizant quality is at the same time empty of any concrete substance. It's unconfined. By understanding in this way, we avoid slipping into 'the straying of emptiness as to the nature of things'.

The next way of going astray is called 'basic straying into generalizing emptiness'. When this occurs, your attention moves into a thought or a disturbing emotion, and you remind yourself, "This thought is emptiness!" This method superimposes emptiness on top of the thought or the emotion, rather than directly seeing the emptiness that is naturally present. Of course, it's not totally bad to remind ourselves of emptiness, but this way of impressing emptiness on top of thoughts and emotions prevents us from seeing emptiness in actuality.

The third type is 'emptiness straying into the remedy.' In this case, when we get attached or angry, we think, "I shouldn't be feeling angry or attached. The object of my desire or anger is emptiness, so I should give up this anger or attachment." Objects are certainly empty of any true existence but using the idea of emptiness as a remedy is not a totally effective way to realize the natural state of emptiness.

Rather than training in the three ways of going astray, we should, as Naropa says, allow ourselves to be "free of concept, holding nothing in mind." We should understand that there is no such 'thing' as an emptiness that can be held in mind as an object. Acknowledge this to be as it is, and do not hold anything in mind. Then there is nothing that needs to be pinpointed as being emptiness. As the text says, that "is, itself, the path of all buddhas." All buddhas of the past, any awakened ones in the present, and any buddha appearing in the future will all traverse exactly this same path of being free of concepts and holding nothing whatsoever in mind.

As you know, Milarepa sang many songs, which were very pithy and extremely beneficial to those who listened and understood. Among these songs is one he sang for a woman called Paltabum. In the song she is referred to as *Nyama* Paltabum. The word nyama, maiden, has a special connotation of being a female lay practitioner. In those days, there were women who would practice a lot but still led the life of lay people. They took vows to do intensive practice on the eighth, fifteenth, or the thirtieth day of the Tibetan month, and in between they would carry on their normal work. Milarepa had many such disciples. Paltabum was very bright and devoted and she asked Milarepa many questions. One of the responses he gave her is in the form of a song that I would like to share with you now.

Paltabum had asked Milarepa: "Who is your teacher? What teachings did you receive? Having received teachings, where did you practice? How did you practice? Having practiced, what kind of realization have you achieved? What disciples do you have?" Milarepa's reply combined an outer, inner, and innermost level of meaning. He sang about what he himself practiced, how he practiced, where he practiced, how his state of realization was, and so on.

Paltabum also asked questions about how she herself, being an ordinary woman, could combine Dharma practice with her daily life. As she related, "In the daytime I have to work, at nighttime I sleep, in the morning and evening I need to cook. I am a servant to all these tasks that fill up my life. In spite of this, I still want to practice. How can I do this? Please give me some advice."

In reply, Milarepa sang a song of four analogies and one meaning, five points. First, he said: "Look at the mountain. The mountain is unshakable. Like that, train in being like a mountain, always steady and stable." Then he said: "Look at the sun and the moon. Though sometimes covered by clouds and haze, the sun and the moon in themselves never change; their brilliance doesn't increase or decrease, they're forever the same. Train yourself in being constant, without waxing and waning." The third analogy he gave was: "Look at the sky. Space is not made out of anything. Its nature is empty, and has neither center nor edge. Train yourself in being free from center and edge." Then he said: "Look at the great lake: Though its surface ripples, the body of water remains unwavering. Train yourself in being unwavering." Finally, he gave the fifth point, the meaning, singing, "Your mind is the most important. Simply settle into yourself and look into your mind. Without being carried away by thoughts about this and that, be totally steady and meditate. That is the heart essence of meditation."

Paltabum connected her next questions with the analogies Milarepa had just given. She said: "I can at times train in being as stable as a mountain. However, on the mountain various plants, shrubs and trees grow. What should I do? I can at times practice in a way that is unchanging like the brilliance of the sun and moon. But occasionally the sun and moon are eclipsed. When that happens, what should I do? I can at times train in being as steady and unchanging as the sky, but sometimes many clouds gather. At that time, what should I do? I can train in being as stable as the ocean, but sometimes great waves appear. At that time what should I do? In the same way, when I'm simply looking into mind, sometimes many thoughts come. At that time what should I do?"

Milarepa's reply continued with these themes. He said: "When you practice in a way that is like a mountain, remember this; shrubs, trees, and plants grow naturally on the mountain, sprouting, growing and perishing there. This arising, dwelling and ceasing of growth does not change the mountain in any way whatsoever. It is merely different expressions that don't affect the stability of the mountain at all.

"Sometimes you are able to practice in a way that is unchanging, like the brilliance of the sun and moon. However, remember that the eclipsing of the sun and moon is not real and constant; it's a momentary event that does not any have concrete substance in itself. It vanishes. It's only the different expressions of the sun and moon, and does not affect their inherent nature, as they continue to shine naturally.

"Sometimes you are able to practice in a way that is unchanging, like the sky. Remember this: when clouds gather, they do not change the sky itself, no matter how dense or dark they are. The many different types of weather are a varied display, but the sky remains beyond change.

"Although you can practice like the ocean, remember this; when the surface is in turmoil with waves, there is no wave that exists apart from the ocean. It's the ocean itself that manifests different expressions. No wave has a separate identity from the ocean.

"When different thoughts crowd your mind, remember that no thought has any existence separate from the empty cognizance of the mind nature. It is the empty cognizance itself that takes the form of a thought, and is like varying facial expressions or moods, without any separate identity." This is Milarepa's instruction in sustaining the nature of mind.

The practice of the development stage involves visualizing many different details. First imagine the buddhafield, the environment, within which there is an immense celestial palace housing the deity. There could be either a single deity or a chief figure surrounded by a retinue of other deities. These deities wear all sorts of ornaments and rich attire and hold various attributes in their hands. In the center of the heart of the chief figure, visualize the awakened state of mind in the form of a seed syllable. This syllable can be *hrih or *tam or *hung or any other. At the end of the development stage comes the completion stage, where everything held in mind gradually dissolves. First the buddhfield dissolves into the celestial palace, which dissolves into the deities. All the deities gradually and slowly dissolve into the seed syllable in the heart center. This seed syllable gradually dissolves into light. At the end there is no 'thing' held in mind as a focus. We allow ourselves to remain like that, not developing anything. This is called 'the method of realizing emptiness through the completion stage'.

This training in the completion stage after dissolving the visualization into emptiness is a little different from the training in the emptiness of Mahamudra, but the end result of realizing that all things are empty of any substantial identity is the same. Thus, as we train more and more, we will find that they are mutually supportive and there is no conflict between them at all.

19

Some teachers keep these Mahamudra instructions secret, and choose not to teach them openly or widely to just anyone. When they do teach Mahamudra it is only to people who have done a considerable amount of practice, so-called 'worthy recipients.' There are several reasons for doing so. When those who are truly ready to receive these teachings are told how to place their attention, how to settle their mind and train in Mahamudra, there is no problem. The problem comes when, instead of getting down to the heart of the matter, the practitioner spins a web of concepts to create an understanding of how to practice. By continuing that way, the person eventually finds that he or she is making little progress. He or she may lose faith or even turn against the teachings, saying, "Mahamudra practice is useless! Nothing comes out of it!" That is a serious problem. If we don't genuinely understand the practice, we should not pretend that we do, or give up, saying: "This is too difficult to assimilate." Rather, we should put effort into achieving both correct understanding and practice. We shouldn't lose courage but persevere.

Here's another problem some people encounter. We may discover we are talented and easily comprehend the practice of Mahamudra. It seems to immediately fit "our way," and we discover we can settle our minds into the state of Mahamudra almost effortlessly. When that happens, we may start to think we are incredibly special. We may tell ourselves, "I don't need to do anything other than Mahamudra practice. To get involved in accepting good or rejecting evil is an inferior way of practice; it's unimportant. Creating merit is not anything I need to spend my time on." Such a proud attitude can cause a serious predicament. Just because we occasionally glimpse the awakened state, or even have a sustained experience of it, doesn't mean it will continue. There is no guarantee that the experience will deepen or that we will progress. What is essential is to not only have an experience, but to continuously practice in order to deepen and expand that experience. If we think that the point we have reached is sufficient, it's very difficult to progress further. Among the two factors — cause and conditions — the cause is the experience of Mahamudra, but one of the conditions that helps it to develop is to pay close attention to the consequences of our actions. We need to accept good and reject evil deeds, to create merit, purify the obscurations, and gather the accumulations. When we do this, we can definitely progress in Mahamudra practice.

To conclude, instructing and stating the dedication:

> I have given these concise words of heartfelt advice
> For the most fortunate ones.
> Through this may every single sentient being
> Be established in Mahamudra.

The great pandita Naropa condensed the teachings on Mahamudra into concise words and gave them as heartfelt advice. These teachings are meant for the most fortunate ones, those who have the karmic destiny to enter the Buddhist teachings, and to have the interest, the opportunity, and the capability to apply the teachings. Many people in this world seem to have no inclination towards spiritual practice, and thus lack this fortune. Even among those people interested in Buddhist spiritual practice, it's not everyone who has the ability and opportunity to receive Vajrayana teachings. Among those who enter the gateway of Vajrayana, it's not everyone who can assimilate and trust in the practice of Mahamudra. Even though they may have the opportunity to receive the teachings, not everyone can actually apply themselves diligently — in other words, have the precious fortune. The teachings here are meant for those people who are the most fortunate ones. Not only have they pursued a spiritual path; they have entered Buddhism. They have met the Vajrayana and most especially are fortunate enough to receive Mahamudra teachings, trust them, and apply themselves diligently. It is for these people that Naropa has given this summary of profound guidance.

The great pandita Naropa states "I have given these concise words of heartfelt advice." Naropa bestowed these teachings with great affection and love. Mahamudra instructions can be taught in a very detailed and precise way. In this song, all the aspects of the view, the practice and the stages are explained very succinctly. Teachings like these are very precious and beneficial when one is studying to attain certainty about the view. When it comes to training our mind in Mahamudra, too many details can encumber direct application. To touch base with the practice itself, sometimes it is more helpful to have everything condensed into short, concise words. That way we can remember, understand, and remind ourselves to utilize them from time to time. Naropa has given us a summary of Mahamudra structured as twelve verses — three each for view, meditation, conduct, and fruition — plus an extra verse for the conclusion, making thirteen verses altogether.

The teachings of the Buddha and the commentaries of the great panditas are very extensive, vast in their scope and perspective. It requires a person of broad intelligence to be able to embrace all the meaning contained in the sutras. For this reason, a few of the great masters composed treatises that compressed the immense meaning into a few brief verses. Their efforts were specifically directed to benefit people of later eras, who lack the capacity or simply the time to assimilate the meaning of all the Buddha's words. In the sutras we occasionally find that certain vital points are not fully clarified, and are even concealed. In order to emphasize what has real importance and to fully bring to light that which was held back by the Buddha, panditas wrote treatises — shastras — that fully disclose the hidden meaning. In this song by Naropa, we have both. The term "heartfelt advice," means he openly revealed his innermost heart to the listener. You can say that he fully uncovered the hidden meaning, the vital points. The word concise implies that the vast meaning is brought together into a few key points.

The first two lines express Naropa's knowledge, his capacity to create a text like this. The next two lines are about compassion. He wrote this out of great love and kindness for all sentient beings. The words he uses are: "Through this may every single sentient being be established in Mahamudra." The benefit of this teaching is not restricted to a certain caste of people, for those from a particular area of a country, or from only a few countries, or even for only human beings. It is meant for every single sentient being, without any exception. His aspiration is that the effect of this teaching may be of benefit to everyone. People are truly benefited by realizing Mahamudra, and all the manifold teachings that the awakened ones give out of skillful means do bring benefit to whoever practices them — there's no doubt about that. Among all the teachings given, the pithiest ones that have the deepest impact and are the simplest to apply are those of Mahamudra.

"May every single sentient being be established in Mahamudra." When Naropa expresses this wish, it is out of compassion. By showing this, he shows us, his followers, how to behave as well. We should follow this example of kindness towards everyone without exception. In our lives, when we look at other beings, we see that they suffer in various ways. Some are hungry, some are sick, some have mental problems, others physical ones. Very often people with an altruistic frame of mind feel saddened and frustrated by seeing the suffering in the world. Often, they feel the need to do something to help others. Through our compassion we can alleviate suffering to some extent. In the Buddhist teachings there is the famous wish: "May all beings be free of suffering and the causes of suffering." Not only is it important to alleviate the actual suffering that sentient beings feel; it is essential to work on removing the causes that bring about the experience of pain and misery. The teaching of Mahamudra is exactly what can remove the causes of suffering.

Out of compassion, we should try our best to ensure that the teachings of the Awakened One, the Buddha, do not disappear and vanish. Please work to make the teachings accessible for others, which will ensure that the teachings do not disappear. This is particularly true for the teachings of Mahamudra. Spreading them all over the world makes the actual remedy against suffering and the causes of suffering available. This is a way to express compassion in a true manner. When doing this, it is important not to focus on selfish or materialistic aims, but to act out of a true, kind heart.

In general, compassion is a feeling that is overwhelming. You could call it a deep-felt sadness. It is often described by the great masters as the feeling a crippled mother has when she sees her only child being carried away by a river. She desperately wants to help save her child, but she cannot – she is powerless. That is how the tenderness of compassion in our heart is. It's not totally the same as ordinary frustration or feeling incapacitated or depressed, however, because within this compassion is the understanding that by practicing, one will be able to help others. One thinks, "Since I am a practitioner, the opportunity exists for the virtues I cultivate to be used for the benefit of others." It's not a completely hopeless situation either, as 'boundless joy' is combined within the compassion. It's a happy/sad feeling at the same time; kind of bittersweet.

This was given orally by the great pandita Naropa, to Marpa Chökyi Lodrö at Pullahari.

As I mentioned at the beginning of this book, Naropa was a great scholar in the first part of his life. He was entrusted with the position of guarding the northern gate of Nalanda Monastery during the time when the Buddhist teachings truly flourished. The gates to Nalanda functioned as an entry point, and the pandita in charge of each particular gate would sometimes meet with the people who entered. If people came out of sincere interest, the pandita would teach them how to begin Buddhist practice. If they were devoted and wanted further instruction, he would give them further instruction. If someone had doubts or uncertainty, he would clarify them. If someone came to object against Buddhism, to raise controversial points and dispute, the pandita's responsibility would be to defend the Buddhist point of view, to refute any wrong notions.

Remember the story of Naropa's meeting with Vajra Yogini at the northern gate? His encounter with her taught Naropa that he needed to be learned in meaning rather than words. Vajra Yogini told him about the great mahasiddha Tilopa. Simply upon hearing the name Tilopa, Naropa experienced incredible devotion and trust, and the intense wish to meet Tilopa welled up inside him. So, he set out to find Tilopa, whom he finally met with and followed. Naropa received the pithy instructions of Mahamudra that he practiced and realized. At some point, Tilopa gave him the prediction that, "In the future your chief disciple will be a Tibetan by the name Marpa Chökyi Lodrö. It is to him you should entrust your lineage." That is how we have this text, which was given orally by the great pandita Naropa to the Tibetan Marpa Chökyi Lodrö at Naropa's hermitage at Pullahari.

I would like to add that I am not someone who is accomplished in any significant way. I have neither attained the common nor the supreme siddhis. However, I have met extraordinary masters and received these wonderful teachings, which I consider very precious. I feel that that you students must also value them, as many of you have come from far-away places and have taken quite a bit of trouble to reach Nepal. I am extremely happy for this opportunity to teach Mahamudra to all of you who attended this seminar. It seemed to me that you listened well throughout the teachings, and I am also pleased at how you practiced during this time. The most important aspect about Mahamudra teachings is not simply to have heard or received them. The real importance lies in applying them — in practicing and training in them. When applied, these teachings will be of immense benefit, not only for oneself, but also for others. When we have trained further and become stable in the practice of Mahamudra, we can undertake the task of helping others to similarly understand. In this sense, the benefit is not limited to ourselves. Since the basis for this lies in practicing, please practice these teachings.

Song of Lodrö Thaye

Within Nonconcept, Wisdom Dawned

The Song of Lodrö Thaye was composed by Lodrö Thaye, Jamgön Kongtrül the Great, and expresses his realization of Mahamudra. It is contained in the collection of songs called the *Ocean of Songs of the Kagyüs*, known in English as *Rain of Wisdom*.

Jamgön Kongtrül Lodrö Thaye was foretold by Buddha Shakyamuni in the *King of Samadhi Sutra*. When I taught this sutra, I mentioned that Gampopa was predicted but I did not say much about Jamgön Kongtrül. In the sutra the Buddha is recorded as saying, "In the future, when the time of degeneration has begun, there will be a great bodhisattva named Lodrö who will vastly benefit beings by means of the five types of knowledge." In fact, Jamgön Kongtrül Lodrö Thaye established the body of the Buddha's teachings, which he collected and composed, within five treasuries. In this way, he delayed the disappearance of the Buddhadharma. When he realized the view of Mahamudra, he spontaneously wrote down this song.

Traditionally, when writing a composition, one first explains the reason and purpose for doing so. Jamgön Kongtrül elaborately describes this in this song. Then he divides the topic of Mahamudra into three parts: ground Mahamudra, path Mahamudra and fruition Mahamudra.

The first section is a detailed exposition of the reason for composing the song. Jamgön Kongtrül mentions the special fortune of having met his root-guru, Nyinchey Wangpo, a very extraordinary person and one of the incarnations in the line of Situ Rinpoches. Because of having connected with his own root guru and with the sublime masters of the lineage, experience and realization could take place within his stream of being. Furthermore, he mentions receiving the instructions which served as the catalyst for the birth of extraordinary experience and realization.

The unique qualities of his root guru are mentioned under five points. First, Jamgön Kongtrül relates his connection with his incredible master. By virtue of that connection, he was able to receive the extraordinary pith instructions. By practicing and taking them to heart, he was able to give rise to experience and realization. Everyone who follows in his footsteps should understand that it is of primary importance to first connect with a qualified master. He likens his master to Vajradhara:

> The illustrious one, Vajradhara,
> Who is said to possess the eight good qualities,

Vajradhara, regarded as sublime among the Three Jewels or Three Roots, embodies both the dharmakaya and the very heart or essence of the sambhogakaya buddhas. This 'illustrious one,' the precious, world-renowned, most extraordinary buddha, is endowed with eight qualities. These eight great qualities expressed in many sutras, treatises and tantras are the utter purity of the earth element, the utter purity of the water element, the utter purity of the fire element, the utter purity of the wind element, the utter purity of the space element, the utter purity of the element of the sun, the utter purity of the element of the moon, and the utter purity of the element of consciousness. In short, these are the eight qualities of purity.

Jamgön Kongtrül continues describing Vajradhara, saying:

> Is seen in human form by ordinary men like us.
> You are the refuge called Padma, endowed with the blessings.

Vajradhara appears as a human being to ordinary people with ordinary impure perception. Yet, in his own personal experience, Jamgön Kongtrül perceives Vajradhara to be 'Padma, Endowed with Blessings.' This refers to Padma Nyinchey Wangpo, from whom he received the pith instructions on Mahamudra that formed the basis for his experience and realization.

The Indian siddha Tilopa received teachings directly from the dharmakaya buddha Vajradhara, and, having practiced these oral instructions, gave rise to experience and realization. In the same way, Jamgön Kongtrül connected with a great master, received the pith instructions, practiced them and attained realization. With great trust, strong devotion and pure perception, he regarded his own root guru, Padma Nyinchey Wangpo, as Vajradhara in person. Likewise, we should regard our own root guru as Vajradhara in person and entrust ourselves to him with complete confidence. If we do so when practicing the oral instructions, we too will be able to give rise to experience and realization.

Having met our root guru and received the pith instructions we need to supplicate from the core of our hearts in order for the blessings that engender realization to arise. Jamgön Kongtrül's song continues:

> From the eight-petaled lotus dome of my heart,
> I supplicated you not to be separate even for an instant.

The heart-center is sometimes called the 'jewel-octagon.' Here, it is described as an 'eight-petaled lotus dome.' Within this poetical rendition of the heart-center, likened to a tent of light, we continuously imagine our root guru without separating from him or her for even a single instant. This acts as a constant support for our prayers and supplications. The teaching for us, Jamgon Kongtrül's followers, is to proceed in exactly the same way as he did. When practicing Mahamudra, if we have connected with a qualified root guru it is extremely important to supplicate him from the core of our heart while imagining him in our own heart-center. What is the purpose of supplicating the root-guru with utmost faith and devotion? It is to receive the blessings. By receiving the blessings, we can give rise to realization.

Depending upon our own capacity realization can occur in either of two ways, gradually or instantaneously. The 'instantaneous type' is someone in whom realization and liberation occur simultaneously. Such was the case of the great king Indrabhuti who received the empowerment of *Guhyasamaja* from Lord Buddha Shakyamuni himself. Simultaneous with realizing the nature of things and the nature of his own mind, he was completely liberated from obscurations and disturbing emotions. This is an example of the instantaneous type of person who is liberated in the very same sitting as realizing the nature of mind. Liberation in this example is not through a gradual process. Jamgön Kongtrül says:

> Although I did not have the good fortune of realization and
>   liberation at once,
> I was blessed with just recognizing my own nature.

Here 'own nature' means the nature of our mind that is forever present within us. However, ordinary beings do not have the ability to realize this nature directly. Merely thinking about it, deducting and inferring by means of normal conceptual knowledge, will not enable us to realize the nature of our mind. So, how is it recognized? It is recognized by receiving the blessings of our guru through deep-felt supplication. In that moment, it is possible to 'see' or recognize the nature of our mind.

Jamgön Kongtrül then explains what happens when we receive the blessings and recognize the nature of our mind:

> Therefore, concern for the eight worldly dharmas diminished,

What are the 'eight worldly dharmas?' Worldly dharmas here means the attributes of a worldly person. When we experience pleasure, praise, material gain or fame, we feel very happy and even delighted. But when the opposite occurs, we are sad and downcast. To be involved in this is called 'being subject to the eight worldly dharmas' and it is an obstacle for spiritual practice as well as normal mundane pursuits. It is difficult to be free of these eight worldly concerns or dharmas unless we stabilize the recognition of mind nature. In the very moment of recognizing mind nature, it becomes possible to accomplish the welfare of self and others.

What is the outcome of receiving the blessings of the guru and recognizing the nature of mind? The guru's realization is transmitted so that we ourselves can experience and give birth to realization. Jamgön Kongtrül declares:

> And I clearly saw the famous luminous dharmakaya
> By mixing my mind with the guru's.

This luminous dharmakaya is renowned throughout all Buddhist scriptures, regardless of whether they belong to the vehicle for shravakas, the Mahayana, or Vajrayana. The ultimate and final achievement is always the realization of dharmakaya, the body of enlightened qualities. There is nothing higher than this. What differs, though, is the amount of time and energy it takes to actualize this achievement. In some instances, it takes many aeons — sometimes three, seven, or thirty-seven incalculable aeons. Over these vast stretches of time the practitioner must gather a tremendous accumulation of merit, otherwise, it is said it will be impossible to realize dharmakaya. Especially in the case of a bodhisattva, it is necessary to perfect the paramita of generosity.

Within the paramita of generosity, there are three acts of giving: giving, great giving and extremely difficult giving. 'Extremely difficult giving' means giving what is very hard to part with, what is treasured most dearly — our own body and life. When in his past incarnations the Buddha was requested, he gave away his head, his eyes, the flesh of his body, and so forth without any feeling of stinginess. In this way, by giving what is extremely difficult to give away, he gathered an immense accumulation of merit.

But if we have the great fortune to meet a qualified master and receive from him the Mahamudra pith instructions, we will not have to wait innumerable aeons to realize the famous luminous dharmakaya. It can occur in this very body and lifetime, through resting in the state in which the guru's mind and our own mingle into one.

The realization that takes place when mingling our mind with the guru's and receiving the blessings is as follows:

> I discovered nonthought in the midst of discursive thought,
> And within nonconcept, wisdom dawned.

'Discursive thought' refers to a moment of distraction, after which we form concepts about what is occurring. Yet at the same time, the very essence or identity of this discursive thinking is nonthought, meaning nonconceptual original wakefulness. This is the state of realization of all the buddhas, the wisdom of Mahamudra. It is possible to realize this within discursive thinking. Within 'nonconcept,' meaning the absence of conceptual mind, the realization of Mahamudra, which is wisdom, dawns. This is what Jamgön Kongtrül declared. Similarly, if we supplicate our root-guru and receive the blessings, realization can occur.

As the fifth point, due to having received the pith instructions from his extraordinary master, some degree of realization took birth in

Jamgön Kongtrül's being, so that he was overjoyed and delighted. He equates this joy and delight with arriving at the first bhumi, which is called the 'exceedingly joyous' level. This is reached after an immense accumulation of merit. Arriving at the first bhumi is the path of seeing the nature of things directly. At that point, immense joy and appreciation takes place. This is what he describes upon realizing Mahamudra.

> Now, with the joyous appreciation of a lineage son of the
> Dakpo buddha,
> I am inspired to speak out.

He felt moved to express his realization out of nonconceptual great compassion for all other beings, his disciples and followers. He thought "I must share my experience so that they, too, can realize this." He was overwhelmed, overpowered by strong compassion, he could not help but sing this song.

After describing the qualities of connecting with a root guru, Jamgön Kongtrül also describes the qualities of the lineage masters under six points. The first point is about Tilopa.

> In the west, in Uddiyana, the secret treasure ground of the
> dakinis,

This is the place where Tilopa had direct vision of Vajradhara and received the pith instructions in person.

> The great siddha, Tilo
> Opened the treasure of these three gems.

These 'three gems' refer to the wishfulfilling gem of the path of ripening, the wishfulfilling gem of the path of liberation, and the wishfulfilling gem of transmission. Having received these extraordinary three gems, Tilopa transmitted them to the subsequent lineage masters.

The person to whom Tilopa transmitted the teachings was Naropa:

In the north, in the hermitage of *Ravishing Beautiful Flowers*
The learned Mahapandita, Naro
Showed the mark of a siddha, indivisible prana and mind.

The name *Ravishing Beautiful Flowers* is translated here from Tibetan, but in Sanskrit the name is *Phulahari.* Jamgön Kongtrül considered this a very important location. His third incarnation went, together with Gyaltsab Rinpoche, to try to locate the exact place where Naropa lived and practiced. They did find the spot, but discovered it had been taken over by Muslims and that there is nothing to do about it. Out of their great aspirations and prayers, Jamgön Kongtrül the Third established a place in Nepal to invoke the blessing and spiritual qualities of *Phulahari.*

I feel it is very important for present-day practitioners to embark upon a pilgrimage to the newly established *Phulahari* temple, practice in retreat, and offers prayers and supplications there. This will partially fulfill the aspirations of the first, second and third incarnations of Jamgön Kongtrül.

Having met with Tilopa and received the pith instructions, Naropa practiced at the location called *Phulahari, Ravishing Beautiful Flowers*, and there he gained mastery of his own *nadis, pranas,* and *bindus* by utilizing their extraordinary key points. Reaching mastery over the nadis, pranas, and bindus, or the channels, energies, and essences, he realized the nature of mind. Through this realization, he showed the mark of a siddha, meaning the sign of accomplishment, which is the indivisible nature of prana and mind.

In the south, in the land of herbs, the valley of *Trowo*,
The translator, emanated from Hevajra,
Established the source of the river of all siddhas.

In Tibet, in the district of the Valley of *Trowo,* the great master who received the lineage from Naropa was a Tibetan named Marpa, the Great Translator, who himself was an emanation of Hevajra. Through his great level of realization, he became one of the chief mahasiddhas in the land of Tibet.

Knowing One Liberates All

In Jamgön Kongtrül's song, the verses first extol his root guru, then the lineage masters. In each case, geographical locations are mentioned: Tilopa in western *Uddiyana,* Naropa in the northern *Ravishing Beautiful Flowers* Hermitage, Marpa in the southern Valley of *Trowo,* and Shepa Dorje or Milarepa in the western *Labchi* snow range. We may wonder why ordinary geographical locations are included when talking about enlightened masters. Why bother stating their dwelling places in the context of describing the qualities of samadhi, the wisdom present in their state of being? There is a reason for this.

These masters were born as human beings in our world, the southern Jambu Continent. Having taken birth here, they received Dharma teachings and practiced them. Through this practice, they attained realization of the supreme and common accomplishments. Afterwards, they were capable of guiding other people and there are stories of how they did so. If this were not the case, if these masters were superhuman celestial beings from beyond this world, we would feel alienated from them and consider their accomplishments completely beyond our reach. For instance, had they been dharmakaya buddhas from beyond our normal world that would be very disheartening because it would seem impossible for us to emulate them. But because they were human beings, we as human beings can follow in their footsteps, practice the Dharma and attain realization. In this way, we experience a strong feeling of reassurance and confidence.

> In the west, in the *Labchi* snow range,
> Attained the state of unity in one lifetime.

Among the lineage masters, the fourth mentioned is Shepa Dorje, Milarepa. The Six Fortresses were among his many retreat places. The most well known of these is found in the *Labchi* snow range.

Shepa Dorje was one of Milarepa's names, but he had other aliases. He was called Dorje Gyaltsen, which means 'Vajra Banner of Victory,' *Thu Chen*, 'Great Sorcerer,' and Milarepa, 'Cotton-clad Mila.' But Shepa Dorje, 'Laughing Vajra,' was his secret name. It was given to him by the dakas and dakinis who appeared above the mandala during the Chakrasamvara empowerment, conferred upon him by the great master Marpa. The dakas and dakinis declared that his name should be Shepa Dorje, which in Sanskrit is *Hasa Vajra.*

Milarepa was a disciple of the true meaning. Possessing diligence and intelligence, he was able to purify all his obscurations and negative karma and in that very body and lifetime realize what is called the unified state of a vajra-holder or Vajradhara. As I mentioned earlier, Milarepa himself stated that he was not the emanation of any buddha or bodhisattva. He professed to be a 'great sinner.' But he was able to meet a uniquely qualified master and receive the extraordinary teachings on Mahamudra and the Six Doctrines of Naropa.

> In the east, in heavenly *Dakla Gampo,*
> The honorable physician, the second Victorious One,
> Realized the samadhi of the tenth bhumi.

The fifth master mentioned in the lineage is Gampopa, who was predicted by Buddha Shakyamuni as the future incarnation of the bodhisattva Youthful Moonlight. The prediction stated that he would be seated amid the mountains upon a king's throne. Such a place actually exists.

Gampopa met Milarepa and received the pith instructions. Later, he went to practice in solitude in an extremely remote place called *Dakla Gampo*, which is likened to a buddhafield or celestial realm. When he arrived in this totally unpopulated area, Gampopa vowed, 'Now, for thirteen years, I will concentrate one-pointedly on samadhi training, and not depart for any other place.' He formed the resolve to remain in a small retreat hut and focus strictly on practice. But that same night, he dreamed that a dakini appeared before him and said, 'Compared to spending thirteen years in meditation, it is better to spend thirten years benefiting others.' When he woke up, he thought, 'How can I benefit beings by staying in this remote place?' Yet, that same day, a meditator, who became his first disciple, appeared. Afterwards, disciples kept arriving until eventually there was a gathering around him of 800 meditators whom he taught. This is what is mentioned here.

In the chakras of Body, Speech, and Mind,
The hosts of siddhas of the four great and eight lesser lineages
Obtained the life-force of Mahamudra
And could not help but attain enlightenment.

After Gampopa, there appeared innumerable other masters among his disciples. They are mentioned as the 'four great and eight lesser lineages.' In this context, Gampopa's chief disciple was the first Karmapa, *Düsum Khyenpa*. Gampopa himself gave him the prediction, 'My son, go to *Khampo Gang-ra* in the east and make that your seat of accomplishment. By doing so, your activity will spread throughout central Tibet, Tsang, and Kham. The first Karmapa did as he was told. First, he established his seat in *Khampo Gang-ra* in Kham. This is his Body seat. Afterwards, his Speech seat was established at *Karma Gön.* Later, his Mind seat was established at *Ogmin Tsurphu* in central Tibet. From that time forth, the lineage continued.

Another of Gampopa's chief disciples, named Dorje Gyaltsen or *Phagmo Drubpa,* initiated many of the other Kagyü schools. Practitioners in these lineages who attained supreme accomplishment, the enlightened state, have been as innumerable as drops of rain.

The next lines describe the qualities of abandonment and realization of all the lineage masters from Tilopa down until Jamgön Kongtrül's own root guru, *Situ Padma Nyinchey Wangpo.* Due to their great qualities, they 'could not help but attain enlightenment.' In other words, enlightenment was unavoidable. Why did all these masters in the four great and eight lesser lineages, from Tilopa down to Jamgön Kongtrül's own root-guru unavoidably attain enlightenment? Because they established the life-force of Mahamudra in their stream of being. This is the special quality, the strength and power of Mahamudra training, that makes the attainment of enlightenment unavoidable.

Skilled in magnetizing through bodhichitta,
They could not help but benefit beings.

These masters of the four great and eight lesser lineages were extremely successful in benefiting beings. Vast gatherings of followers and many disciples flocked around them. This was not the result of some political trick or deceitful manipulation on their part. They did not try to acquire greatness by gathering many disciples. It happened in a spontaneous way. Why? Because they were 'skilled in magnetizing through bodhichitta.' Due to their motivation by the attitude of awakened mind called 'bodhichitta,' the strong wish to benefit all beings, they did not have to deliberately try to attract followers. When people come in contact with someone who is very kind, generous, and protecting others, they naturally feel, "This is my friend. This is the kind of person I can trust." Conversely, when someone spreads slander and harms others by wrong conduct, other people will feel, "This hostile person is unpleasant to be with. This is not a friend and is not someone I can trust." The reason why all the great masters had tremendous success in benefiting beings, had numerous disciples, and vast activity was due to their precious motivation of enlightened mind. Bodhichitta fully unfolded within their stream of being and they worked solely for the sake of other sentient beings.

> Having obtained the profound wealth, the perfection of the two accumulations,
> They could not help but become prosperous.

The great splendor and wealth belonging to the mahasiddhas of the Kagyü lineage was not amassed by means of a deliberate pursuit on their own part. This also occurred spontaneously due to their vast gathering of the two accumulations: the accumulation of merit with reference point and the accumulation of wisdom beyond focus. Because of this enormous accumulation of merit and wisdom, 'they could not help but become prosperous.' Extraordinary wealth and splendor was naturally gathered.

The fourth quality mentioned in the song is:

> Fully understanding that knowing one liberates all,
> They could not help but fulfill the great prophecy.

This means that they possessed immense learning that was not the result of spending years studying or attending university. Rather, it arose from 'knowing one that liberates all.' The one thing to be known is the natural state of Mahamudra. Because of seeing directly, as it is, the essence of original wakefulness, the wisdom state of Mahamudra or the supreme discriminating knowledge itself, the darkness of ignorance and unknowing is utterly eliminated. Therefore, there is no longer any ignorance or lack of knowledge. In fact, when there is no doubt whatsoever, immense learnedness results.

Having described the superb qualities of the root and lineage masters and the excellent fortune of following such a lineage, Jamgön Kongtrül gives two examples to support this. The first example is:

> Lineage sons of these wealthy fathers
> Possess the great self-existing riches of this previous karma.

The son of a rich father is naturally rich, due to his merit. Such a person does not need to do anything other than possess the merit to have been born into a rich family. He does not need to be intelligent or diligent or lucky; he only needs to have a rich father. In the same way, if we have the tremendous fortune to connect with the lineage of these sublime masters, without having to be especially intelligent, we still inherit the immense wealth of the lineage.

The second example:

> They are the children of snow lionesses and great garudas.
> By the power of their family bloodline, they are completely matured at once.

The offspring of a snow lion or garuda do not need to engage in a lot of training, eat vitamins or special foods in order to develop their prowess. The tremendous strength and capacities appear naturally, due to the power of their family bloodline or species. These attributes do not come from some other source.

This means that:

> As followers of the lineage of Kagyü siddhas,
> Their meditation is naturally born through the power of these blessings.

The greatest quality stems from receiving the extraordinary oral instructions from our root guru as well as the blessings of the lineage, not from being smart or especially lucky. Nor does it come from merely pretending to practice, as Jamgön Kongtrül says:

> Bragging of their pain in many years of practice,

Simply having spent many years trying very hard to engage in practice is, in itself, not sufficient. This is not where the blessings of accomplishment come from. Someone can say, "I've practiced in difficult conditions for all these years," and then consider himself quite special due to this. But hardship in itself is of no benefit whatsoever. Someone may even be:

> Proud of dwelling in indolence.

Although we may have spent many years in retreat in a remote, unpopulated place, if we have been unable to intelligently penetrate to the core of practice, unable to resolve our doubts, or unable to be diligent in the true meaning, just relaxing for some time in a quiet area will not be very helpful.

> Boasting of having endured such pain,

Some people may be tremendously diligent and undertake great hardships in their practice, but if it is done blindly, without really knowing the key points, that is not something to brag about.

> Undermining others and haughty,

This means one considers oneself incredibly special because of engaging in profound practices, and demeans others who have not done such practices. Criticizing others while exalting oneself is not how to attain blessings and realization.

> Keeping score with discursive thought of self and others
> In counting up the realizations of the bhumis and the paths,

Some people compare themselves with ordinary people, 'keeping score with discursive thought of self and others.' Every time they gain a little experience, such as an unusual dream, they consider this event very special and superior. They count these experiences and try to figure out which bhumi or level of realization they have arrived at. Such activity is totally futile. About this list of faults, Jamgön Kongtrül says:

> These are the qualities of the ignorant meditators in this dark age.

These characteristics come from not really understanding how to practice or to receive the pith instructions. Just spending time engaging in an ignorant, stupid way of meditation will not lead us to become a siddha or an accomplished being.

> We do not possess these, and though I do not have the title of a siddha,
> Nevertheless, through the excellent oral instructions of the example lineage,
> I have seen the wisdom of the ultimate Mahamudra.

Jamgön Kongtrül himself says he had the immense fortune to receive the precious, excellent oral instructions of the pure lineage. This is why he has seen the wisdom of ultimate Mahamudra. 'Seeing the wisdom of ultimate Mahamudra' by means of the extraordinary instructions and blessings of the lineage usually occurs in the form of the ripening empowerment. There are two types of empowerments: 'unique' and 'common.' The unique or special empowerment is the pointing-out instruction or an introduction to the state of original wakefulness, the wisdom which is the nature of the empowerment. This is what is pointed out during the empowerment ceremony.

Through the vase empowerment, we are empowered to practice the form of the deity. Through the secret empowerment, we are empowered to practice the total purity of the channels, energies, and essences. Through the wisdom-knowledge empowerment, we are empowered to realize or recognize what is called the example wisdom. These three of the four empowerments, the vase empowerment, secret empowerment, and wisdom-knowledge empowerment, are conferred in order to realize the ultimate, which is the fourth empowerment, also called the precious word empowerment. The fourth empowerment is the direct introduction to the wisdom of ultimate Mahamudra. This empowerment is often given by means of a symbolic gesture such as showing a crystal. The vajra master introduces the original wakefulness, the nature of mind, the nature of all things, the natural state of Mahamudra. This is the meaning of the 'unique or special empowerment.'

There is also a common or ordinary way of empowerment, in which we simply participate in the ceremony and receive some degree of blessings. Simply receiving the blessings ensures that at some point in the future we will have the fortune to realize the true empowerment.

In the tradition of Mahamudra, the natural state of Mahamudra is not only pointed out during an empowerment ceremony, it can also be pointed out based on the pith instructions. By the means of the oral instructions, the disciple can be introduced to the wisdom of ultimate Mahamudra.

> Ground Mahamudra is the view, understanding things as they are.
> Path Mahamudra is the experience of meditation.
> Fruition Mahamudra is the realization of one's mind as buddha.

Jamgön Kongtrül mentions that, having been introduced to Mahamudra, there are three aspects: ground Mahamudra, path Mahamudra, and fruition Mahamudra. As described here, ground Mahamudra is, in the sense of intellectual understanding, arriving at the correct view of understanding things as they are by means of inference or deduction. Path Mahamudra is to be directly introduced to the nature of Mahamudra in our own experience. By training in the correct experience of the nature of Mahamudra, we actualize fruition Mahamudra. Fruition Mahamudra is what all the masters of the Kagyü lineage describe as 'realizing the perfectly enlightened buddha within the nature of our own mind.'

Based on ground Mahamudra, we can experience path Mahamudra, and realize fruition Mahamudra. For Jamgön Kongtrül this took place within his stream of being, not because he was great or special, but as he says:

> I am unworthy, but my guru is good.
> Though born in a dark age, I am very fortunate.
> Though I have little perseverance, the oral instructions are profound.

Jamgön Kongtrül declares that he lacks any extraordinary qualities or virtues whatsoever. He acknowledges he was born into a dark age and has 'little perseverance.' Even though he has realized the ground, path and fruition, it does not make him feel special. He regards himself as just an ordinary, 'unworthy' practitioner. He is saying this to humble conceit.

So, how did he reach such attainment? Jamgon Kongtrul attributes it to the excellence of his guru. He had the excellent good fortune to be accepted by a sublime root master with manifold qualities and blessings. Furthermore, although he was born in a dark age in which the 'five degenerations' are rampant, and not during the Age of Perfection, a Golden Age, still he had the tremendous fortune to connect with a pure lineage and receive the pith instructions and blessings necessary for practice. In that sense, he did possess very immense fortune.

In terms of faults, Jamgon Kongtrul describes himself as being lazy and unpersevering, indicating that he was not a very vigorous or diligent practitioner. He humbly states that the reason realization was able to arise was solely due to the profundity of the oral instructions.

In this song up till this point, Jamgön Kongtrül has presented the qualities of his root guru, the qualities of the lineage masters, and the faults of the practitioners of the Dark Age. He has done so in order for us to understand, and later to experience and realize, the true state of Mahamudra. In the next section of his song, he will begin to explain the view of Mahamudra in terms of ground, path, and fruition.

We have covered the section describing the reasons for singing this song. Now, begins the main part of the song, which is on Mahamudra.

Mahamudra here is divided into three points: ground Mahamudra, path Mahamudra and fruition Mahamudra. The meaning of ground Mahamudra has two sections: one is stated in terms of inference, the other through direct perception.

> As for ground Mahamudra:
> There are both things as they are and the way of confusion.

The first, ground Mahamudra in terms of what we can intellectually understand by means of inference, is divided into two points: 'things as they are,' and the 'way of confusion.' 'Things as they are' refers to how the natural state really is, the basic condition of things. There are reasons why we fail to realize or clearly perceive the nature of things. The second point, the 'way of confusion,' describes the causes and circumstances through which we become mistaken about the nature of things.

This basic state of ground Mahamudra encompasses both the way reality truly is, and how it seems to be. In essence, how it really is, there is no difference between what is called samsara, not having realized the basic condition, and what is called nirvana, having realized the nature as it is. The very identity or essence of both the confused and the realized states — of both samsara and nirvana — is not different. Within the essence itself, no distinctions exist. Their very nature is indivisible. The very heart or core of samsara is nirvana. Nirvana is not separate from or apart from samsara either. Therefore, it is said:

> It does not incline toward either samsara or nirvana.
> And is free from the extremes of exaggeration and denigration.

'It' refers to ground Mahamudra. 'Exaggeration' means adding something that is not already present. The state of ground Mahamudra is not superimposed upon anything in any way whatsoever. At the same time, it is also free from the extreme of denigration, meaning subtracting anything that is already present. In other words, it lies totally beyond any kind of extraneous formulations that we try to make about it. By being unchanging in nature, it is:

> Not produced by causes, not changed by conditions.
> It is not spoiled by confusion
> Nor exalted by realization.

It is primordially and spontaneously present. Since the essence is unchanging, it cannot be altered by conditions or circumstances.

When deluded about the natural state and roaming about in samsaric existence, is our nature in any way worsened? No, it is not. The basic state of Mahamudra, the natural state itself, is not spoiled by confusion. It is not changed in any way whatsoever. Is the natural state of Mahamudra improved through being realized? No, it is not. It is not an entity or identity that can be either worsened by confusion or exalted by realization.

The great treatise called the *Uttara Tantra* says:

> The nature remains unchanged
> Like a jewel, like water, like space.

When a jewel is encrusted by rock or dirt, its inherent identity is not changed in any way whatsoever by means of polishing. Whatever it was before polishing, is exactly what it is after. In the same way, although water may be muddied by dirt, the water itself has not changed. And while space can be covered by clouds, the space itself remains unchanged by them. In the same way, the basic state of Mahamudra is not spoiled by confusion and not exalted by liberation.

> It does not know either confusion or liberation.

The natural state, the basic condition of Mahamudra is empty in essence. Although it seems as though we are deluded and roaming about through samsaric existence, our basic identity or nature is not changed or confused in any way whatsoever. When there is no 'thing' that is deluded or confused, there is also no entity to be liberated either. What is the reason for this? Shantideva gives an explanation using the rough example of dreaming that one has given birth to a child that died. But if the child was never born, how could it have died? Since our nature has never been confused in samsara, it cannot be liberated either. Our innate nature is subject to neither confusion nor liberation. The unmade essence, the ground, the natural state of Mahamudra, is naturally, from the very beginning, emptiness. Emptiness is uncreated. That it is unmade does not imply that it is nothing whatsoever, like the child of a barren woman or the horns on a rabbit. All types of appearance, all experience, is unobstructed; anything can arise, all the various pure and impure phenomena.

> Since no essence exists anywhere,

This means the natural state of Mahamudra, our basic nature, is not comprised of or made out of anything whatsoever.

> Its expression is completely unobstructed and manifests
> everywhere.

In other words, any content of experience — in any form whatsoever — can arise and be experienced unobstructedly.

This basic state of Mahamudra encompasses, or is present, throughout all samsaric and nirvanic states. Therefore, it is said to be all-pervasive.

> Pervading all of samsara and nirvana like space.

This was about the basic state of Mahamudra, the ground itself.

Next, Jamgön Kongtrül explains how the ground is experienced, first in accordance with the view of the Mind Only School, by establishing that all appearances — all experience — is mind. Then he explains this in accordance with the view of the Middle Way, in which even this experience is empty of any independent nature, as it is emptiness. Here, the song says:

It is the ground of all confusion and liberation.
With its self-luminous consciousness
And its *alaya-vijnana.*

The basic state of Mahamudra forms the ground, or basis, for all confusion, meaning the deluded state of samsara. When realization and liberation are attained, this same basic state of Mahamudra forms the ground or basis for such attainment. Without falling into any category whatsoever, it is not confined to either samsara or nirvana. That is why it is said to be the basis or ground of all, the alaya.

Regarding the alaya, in terms of the Mind Only School, the six or seven aspects of consciousness are always limited or confined to one particular function. For example, the eye consciousness is the experience of visual objects; it is seeing. The ear consciousness is confined to hearing. The nose consciousness is restricted to smelling, and so forth. The mind consciousness formulates thoughts and concepts about everything. The seventh consciousness, called the defiled mental consciousness, is thas at which adheres to the concept of self, of ego. All these aspects are limited to their particular function, while the alaya vijnana, the all-ground consciousness, is not limited or confined in any way whatsoever. It simply remains 'self-luminous,' meaning consciousness that is cognizant by itself.

As for the view of the Mind Only School, all experience is nothing but mind. When we perceive a visual object by means of the eye consciousness, the object seen by the eyes seems to somehow exist in our own experience, separate from and outside our own mind. The same applies when a sound is heard: it appears to us that the sound exists somewhere other than in our own mind. The other consciousnesses or aspects of cognition evoke the same assumption. But in fact, what we experience does not exist in any other place at all, it exists only as the contents of our experience. In other words, all appearances, whatever is perceived, are nothing but mind. They are mind only.

'Realization,' according to the Mind Only School, occurs when realizing that all appearances are illusory and lack any independent existence apart from being mere perceptions. The basis for this, which is the self-luminous consciousness — the alaya vijnana — is neutral by nature, neither virtuous nor unvirtuous. It allows all phenomena to arise. It does not belong to either of the categories called 'samsara' or 'nirvana.'

According to Buddhist philosophy, the Mind Only School is an excellent and correct view. So, what can be wrong with it? There is still some holding on to the notion that mind itself does truly and ultimately exist. This view is taught because it may be too frightening to immediately have a view in which no entity whatsoever possesses any true existence, that everything is emptiness. Therefore, a view is presented in which a basis, called mind or consciousness, does exist. Yet, sooner or later, one must face the facts and establish the real condition of what is — that even mind, experience itself, lacks any true or concrete existence; that its nature is emptiness as well. This is done by means of the view of the Middle Way School, *Madhyamika.*

Regarding Madhyamika, there are two different approaches towards the ultimate truth. One approach places more emphasis on space, dharmadhatu. This approach emphasizes the nonexistent nature of mind and all phenomena — in other words, the space-like nature of all dharmas. The view is called the *Rangtong Madhyamika* school.

While all things, meaning mind and phenomena, are empty of nature, it is not a complete nonexistence. There is simultaneously a wisdom quality, the cognizant, conscious aspect. To place more emphasis on that is called the *Shentong* school of the Middle Way.

In terms of the progressive stages of meditation in the Mahamudra system, we begin by training in the fact that all appearances are mind. Then we train in the fact that this perceiving mind is empty. Still later, we train in the meditation that this mind is not a blank, void state of emptiness; at the same time, there is some spontaneously present quality. Although these three progressive stages are not exactly the same as the philosophical viewpoints expressed in either the Mind Only and Middle Way schools, including the Rangtong and Shentong views, still there is a connection. Realizing that all appearances are mind is linked to the view of the Mind Only School. Realizing this mind to be empty of any entity whatsoever is linked to the view of the Rangtong School. Although this mind is empty of any entity whatsoever, it still has a spontaneously present quality of cognizance; this realization is linked to the view of the Shentong school.

As for the cognizant aspect of this neutral state,
Its essence is empty and its nature is luminous.
These two are inseparable and are the quintessence of insight.
It is space, ungraspable as a thing.

'Essence is empty' means the nature of mind is not comprised of or made out of any entity or essence whatsoever. It is utterly empty. But, at the same time, 'its nature is luminous,' meaning cognizant. These two aspects of emptiness and luminosity are not two separate entities. They are an indivisible unity — empty awareness suffused with knowing. This indivisible nature, being both empty and cognizant, is ungraspable as a thing. It is unidentifiable, like space. Jamgön Kongtrül gives some analogies:

It is a spotless precious clear crystal.

Imagine a crystal that is totally unblemished and flawless, transparent, and utterly clear. When looking inside the crystal, no thing or entity is found whatsoever. It is entirely translucent. This example is often used as a symbol in the empowerment ritual to point out the true nature of mind. Whether we call this the view of Madhyamika or whether we call it 'pointing out the empty essence of mind,' it is a fact that this essence is completely devoid of any concrete entity whatsoever, just like a spotless clear crystal

It is the glow of the lamp of self-luminous mind.

While being empty, it is also by nature cognizant. This empty mind is spoken of in the Shentong view of Madhyamika as having a spontaneously present quality. Here the cognizant aspect is likened to the 'glow of the lamp of self-luminous mind.' This means that even though mind is empty of any entity, transparent like a clear crystal, it still has a radiant presence of natural, independent cognizance. The word 'self'-here means that it is by nature independent and does not require any other agent in order to cognize. This empty essence and cognizant nature are an indivisible unity. Mind is not an entity that can in any way be pinpointed, described or expressed by means of any analogy.

> It is inexpressible, the experience of a mute.
> It is unobscured, transparent wisdom.

At the same time, it is also unobscured. There is a knowing or conscious quality we call 'wisdom.' Mind is not a complete nothingness. In order to avoid any nihilistic tendency, the word 'wisdom,' which means 'original knowing,' is used. At the same time, mind is described as transparent, which also has the connotation of being all-encompassing or unimpeded.

> The luminous dharmakaya, sugatagarbha.
> Primordially pure and spontaneous.

This nature of mind is not something that can be achieved by attaining enlightenment. It is present in the unawakened state in exactly the same way as in the enlightened state. In the awakened state it is called the 'luminous dharmakaya' while in the unawakened state of an ordinary sentient being it is called 'sugata-garbha' — the essence of the sugatas. From primordial time, it is by nature utterly pure and empty. But at the same time as being empty, it is also spontaneously present. In other words, it is both empty, meaning primordially pure, as well as cognizant, meaning spontaneously present.

> It cannot be shown through analogy by anyone.
> And it cannot be expressed in words.

In the context of the progressive stages of meditation in the Mahamudra system, the next stage is called 'training in the naturally free, spontaneously present quality.' Whether we establish the nature of mind as empty, as in the case of the Rangtong school that focuses on the quality of space or dharmadhatu, or whether we establish the nature of mind as luminous, as in the case of the Shentong school which emphasizes the wisdom quality, these two facets are not separate entities.

The nature of mind is in itself the indivisible unity of space and wisdom, dharmadhatu and original wakefulness.

This indivisible nature cannot be shown through any analogy whatsoever. No example can truly demonstrate how this indivisible nature actually is. At the same time, we cannot find any words that adequately express how the nature of mind, the indivisible unity of space and wisdom, really is. Any words we try to use will always confine the nature to being one way or another. We can try to find words to affirm a certain aspect, saying, 'This is how it is,' or we can try to find words that deny some quality, saying, 'This is how it is not,' but the basic nature itself lies totally beyond any affirmation or denial. This is what is meant by the famous statement: "Prajnaparamita, transcendent knowledge, is inexpressible, inconceivable ,and indescribable."

'Transcendent knowledge,' meaning the nature of mind, cannot be conceptualized, expressed by means of words, or described by means of analogies. It can only be known through personal experience within the domain of our individual wakefulness. Otherwise, the intellect or conceptual mind can in no way fathom or inspect how the nature of mind is. Conceptual mind or intellect is by nature ignorant of its own essence. Therefore, any kind of deduction or reasoning that we try to apply in order to figure out and conceptually establish how the nature of mind is will always fall short. The nature of mind is beyond thinking: it is inconceivable. This is what is meant by:

> It is the dharmadhatu, which overwhelms mind's inspection.

The song continues:

> Established in this to begin with,
> One should cut all doubts.

'Established in this to begin with' means at the very outset we should, by means of intelligent reasoning, establish the nature of mind as totally devoid of any concrete entity. The naturally empty mind, unmade and beyond beginning, middle, and end, is primordially so. 'One should cut all doubts' about how the nature of mind is by arriving at an understanding that completely cuts through any attachment to nihilism, any attachment to eternalism, and any attachment to the mind as being real or concrete in any way whatsoever.

> When one practices meditation with the view,
> It is like a garuda fathoming space.
> There is no fear and no doubt.

After having described how to establish the view, Jamgön Kongtrül then explains how important it is to unify or combine view and meditation. Whether we have approached the meditation practice by first intellectually establishing the view of the Mind Only School, in which all appearances are said to be empty, or whether we have done so through the view of Madhyamika's Rangtong school, which adds that the perceiving mind is also empty, or whether we have done so through the view of Madhyamika's Shentong school, which focuses on the luminous quality or buddha nature — in any case the view should be implemented in meditation practice. It should be assimilated and brought into our own experience. When doing so, it is said that we become like a garuda bird: the right 'wing' is the view while the left 'wing' is actual meditation practice. By flying with two wings, the garuda bird is able to soar throughout the sky. There is no limit to where we can fly, no limit to what can be realized when combining view and meditation practice. This is exactly what the great master, *Chandrakirti,* mentioned when he said: "Stretch out the two wings of the two truths. Extend the wing of realizing relative truth, extend the wing of realizing ultimate truth, and soar through the sky like a swan."

When a garuda bird flies through the sky, it is totally free from fear and doubt. It has no fear of falling and no dread of being captured by an enemy. In the same way, when we practice meditation after having arrived at a true and correct view, we need not fear going astray and taking an errant path in any way whatsoever.

> The one who meditates without the view
> Is like a blind man wandering the plains.
> There is no reference point for where the true path is.

The 'one who meditates without the view,' meaning one who stubbornly and stupidly tries to practice what one has not understood or has no knowledge of, has no guarantee about where he or she will end up. Without the correct orientation regarding the view, we will be unable to progress in the right direction. It's like a blind person finding himself alone on a vast plain. He does not know for sure whether he is going in the right direction to reach his destination. He does not know whether he is moving south, west, east or north. In this way, it is extremely important to combine the view and meditation practice.

> The one who does not meditate, but merely holds the view
> Is like a rich man tethered by stinginess.
> He is unable to bring appropriate fruition to himself and others.

On the other hand, we may have comprehended the correct view, but if we are incapable of applying it in our personal experience through meditation practice, it is like a rich man who is hampered by his stinginess. If we tight-fistedly hold onto our wealth, we are unable to enjoy it ourselves and are also unable to be generous and share it with others. In this way, being wealthy does not benefit anyone in any way whatsoever. Similarly, even though we may be able to understand that the mind is empty and the nature is luminous, unless we apply this in practice it does not benefit us at all. Obviously, there is no real benefit in expounding this view to others.

> Joining the view and meditation is the holy tradition.

This last line is the real advice, the precious instruction. Combining the practice of meditation with the view that realizes the mind is empty yet has the nature of luminous wisdom, the cognizant quality of wakefulness, is the 'holy tradition' — meaning the tradition of all noble beings.

This section covers the first of the two points that describe ground Mahamudra — the way things are, meaning the basic state, and the way of confusion, which refers to the ground that forms the basis of delusion.

The nature of things is 'as it is,' but fault arises when this natural state is not recognized. This is called the deluded or 'ignorant aspect.' This is also called all-ground consciousness, which is neutral in nature, meaning it is neither virtuous nor unvirtuous but is indeterminate. Because of not recognizing itself, it has the deluded aspect and forms the basis for samsaric existence. It is said that the alaya, which means the ground of all, is the basis for everything, but it is not the basis for complete perfection, meaning the state of nirvana.

Because of the ignorant aspect we fail to know our nature, which is empty in essence and, at the same time, luminous or cognizant. Failing to recognize our nature occurs due to five causes. Our nature is the natural state of dharmadhatu, not made from any entity whatsoever, empty in essence yet, at the same time, possessing the quality of cognizance. This essence is also described as unborn or nonarising. Nevertheless, at the same time, the expression or manifestation is unobstructed. This is the first cause. Because of this unobstructed expression or manifestation, which is usually called the 'luminous nature,' all possible types of experience can occur. This is the second cause. Incorrect thinking, or a wrong way of conceptualizing, takes place; this is the third cause. Due to this, we become involved in the arising of the five disturbing emotions, which acts as the fourth cause. And because of this we create karmic deeds which result in the arising of all different kinds of deluded phenomena. This is the fifth cause.

To reiterate, the lack of recognizing our nature occurs due to the five following causes: the unobstructed nature, the manifold manifestations, incorrect thinking, disturbing emotions, and the creation of karmic deeds.

This is what is referred to as the ignorant aspect of the alaya-vijnana, or all-ground consciousness, failing to recognize its own nature. This is known as coemergent ignorance. Here in our text, it is compared to an ocean:

> In the ocean of coemergent ignorance,
> The waves of ego-fixation's confusion roll.

In terms of the eight consciousnesses, the eighth being the all-ground consciousness, the waves of the seventh roll. This seventh consciousness is ego-fixation. Here 'ego-fixation' does not merely refer to the formulated thought 'I am' — which belongs to the sixth consciousness, the conceptualizing 'mind consciousness.' Whether or not the formulated thought 'I am' is present, it is a deep-rooted or continuous holding onto the feeling of self that persists. This is like waves continuously rolling on the surface of the ocean.

The seventh consciousness is also called the 'defiled mind consciousness.' Here, 'defiled' is in the sense of the disturbing emotions. Based on this, the concepts of 'I' and 'other' are formed. The text says:

> Cognition becomes a self, and projections become objects.

'Cognition' refers to the cognizant quality, which is the luminous, cognizant aspect of mind — that which perceives. It is conceptualized into being 'me' — the 'self' — while all the different contents of experience are conceptualized into being external objects — external to the perceiver. This is what is called 'grasping' and 'fixation.' The outer objects are grasped by the inner fixating or perceiving mind. The habitual tendencies or patterns for this gradually solidify, becoming more and more rigid.

> And the habitual patterns of grasping and fixation solidify.
> Thus, karma accumulates and fully ripens.

When this mistaken duality of experience solidifies, we create karmic deeds. These ripen, creating the experience of the six realms with its six classes of sentient beings, wherein we spin from one realm to the next. This is like being on the rim of a water wheel.

> The rim of the water wheel of samsara turns,
> But even while it turns, its essence is unstained.
> Even while it appears, it is empty of reality.
> Mere appearances are the vividness of the trikaya.

Now we begin a new section of the text, which describes the taking of direct perception as path. Prior to this, the meaning has been described as it is understood through inference or deduction. Not realizing the natural state is what creates samsara. At present, we are spinning around in samsaric existence. But even though we are circling in samsara, the essence remains flawless and completely untainted. At the same time, we experience seemingly external appearances that are devoid of reality and empty of any real existence. These appearances are nothing other than our own personal experiences perceived as 'other' or outer phenomena.

Whether we are discussing the inner mind that perceives or the outer appearances that are perceived, it is all the vividness of the three kayas. The empty essence is dharmakaya, the cognizant or luminous nature is sambhogakaya, and the unobstructed arising of manifestations is the vivid display of nirmanakaya.

> Unborn is the nature of birth.
> That unborn is unceasing.

Next, Jamgön Kongtrul explains that the nature of mind is beyond arising, dwelling, and ceasing. Whether discussing the essence of that which perceives or that which is experienced, in both cases it does seem as though thoughts, feelings, and appearances arise and come into being. But when we look closely into what it is that seems to arise, it becomes obvious within our direct experience that we do not find a place from where anything arises, nor an entity that arises.

The nature of birth is unborn. When something does not arise or come into being, there is no 'thing' to speak of as ceasing. Since there is neither an entity that arises nor ceases, there is no way to speak of an entity that abides. A thought or appearance cannot therefore be said to abide anywhere in between either. Therefore, the text says:

> On the threshold of nonduality, there is nowhere to dwell.

This nonarising, nondwelling, and unceasing nature of both mind and appearances is very difficult to express.

From this mind, difficult to express,
Various magical displays of samsara and nirvana arise.

We cannot really formulate the nature of mind as truly existing in this way. Nor can we formulate or express it as not existing in any way whatsoever. It is very difficult to describe exactly how it is, yet from this difficult-to-describe nature of mind, all the innumerable magical displays of samsara and nirvana still do occur — but as magical displays.

All these innumerable magical displays of samsara and nirvana do not consist of any real or concrete entity in themselves. This is what is meant by the magical displays being 'naturally free' or 'self-liberated,' which is the next topic here.

Recognizing these as self-liberated is the supreme view.
When this is realized, everything is suchness.
When there are no obstructions or attainments, this is the
innate nature.
When conceptual mind is transcended, this is the ultimate.

That which does not exist and is not formed from any substance whatsoever can therefore never bring about any harm or create any negative effect. When we realize that all the magical displays of samsara and nirvana are self-liberated or naturally free, then 'everything is suchness.' This 'suchness' is not an entity which we need to deny, remove or obstruct; nor is it an entity that we need to establish, affirm or attain. This natural state, the innate nature, lies beyond concepts. It is not something we can keep as an object in mind with the idea, 'This is how it is' or the idea, 'This is how it isn't.' It totally transcends any of conceptual mind's ways of formulating how the natural state is. That itself is the ultimate view.

This completes the section describing 'ground Mahamudra,' which is what should be established within our own understanding, either through deduction or through direct perception. In any case, we need to establish clearly and with certainty how the natural state is, how ground Mahamudra is.

Path Mahamudra is what must be experienced in our personal meditation training. We need to experience path Mahamudra in order to assimilate its meaning, which is the view. Now, for an explanation of the Sanskrit word Mahamudra. I mentioned before that mudra means 'seal' in the sense of a seal or stamp representing a nation's king. The seal automatically carries the power of the king's command. Even a small seal at the bottom of a decree or edict issued by the royal palace signifies that it should be obeyed throughout the kingdom. In this way, maha means all-encompassing, very vast.

Similarly, even though the nature of mind may be very small, this same nature encompasses or embraces all that appears and exists, all of mind and the phenomenal world. In this sense, the word Mahamudra is used.

> As for path Mahamudra:
> Mind and the phenomenal world are Mahamudra.

Why is the phenomenal world and its beings, all that appears and exists, said to be Mahamudra? Because everything is established or ascertained within the nature of our own mind — even what is perceived as 'outer' phenomena. In this sense, both mind and the phenomenal world are Mahamudra.

Next, Jamgön Kongtrül discusses 'coemergence,' which means 'arising together,' and refers to what has arisen together or what has coexisted with one's nature since beginningless time. In this context, 'coemergent' means 'primordially or originally present,' in the sense that the nature of mind and the mind itself, the thinking, emotions and so forth, have always been together, primordially coexisting.

> Coemergent mind is dharmakaya.
> Coemergent appearance is the light of dharmakaya.

The nature of this mind, which is indivisible from the nonarising empty nature of dharmadhatu, is what we can experience directly by means of the 'pointing-out instruction.' When we look towards the perceiver, that which we call our mind, we discover that it does not consist of any concrete entity whatsoever — its essence is empty. This is the empty nature of dharmakaya. In this sense, coemergent mind is dharmakaya. Nevertheless, at the same time, all kinds of appearances do occur as the expression or manifestation of this empty mind. In terms of external appearances there are what is seen, heard, smelled, tasted or touched. In terms of internal appearances, thoughts and emotions do occur. All of this is the 'light of dharmakaya,' which is empty in essence and not comprised of any entity whatsoever.

At the same time, due to the cognizant quality of the nature of mind, these appearances do take place, like sunlight issuing forth from the sun itself. In this case, dharmakaya is like the sun and coemergent appearances are like the sunlight.

Now, we reach the next section that is about meditation proper. Meditation practice consists of shamatha, vipashyana, and the unity of both shamatha and vipashyana. In order to approach the practice of meditation, we must receive the blessings. This happens by means of a qualified master combined with our excellent karma, and by undertaking the preliminary practices, the ngöndro, which consists of four common practices and four special practices. The very root or heart of all the preliminary practices, which facilitates the state of samadhi taking birth in our stream of being, is guru yoga. By practicing guru yoga, we receive the blessings for recognizing the natural state of mind, the state of samadhi. That is why Jamgön Kongtrul says in this song:

> When the blessings of the glorious guru
> And one's karma come together,
> One realizes one's nature, like meeting an old friend.

Through the combination of receiving the blessings and the fortunate residual of the continuation of past karma, recognizing the genuine state of samadhi is like reconnecting with an old close friend. This is not something that needs to be talked about a great deal; rather, it is something that should be assimilated within our personal experience.

Now, we come to the actual instructions on shamatha practice. Shamatha practice in the context of Mahamudra is unlike the usual training in stillness. Therefore, it is called the 'extraordinary nonconceptual shamatha.' The instructions for it differ from the normal instructions on training in stillness.

There are three instructions. The first is called 'directly cutting the sudden-born.' Here, 'sudden-born' refers to the sudden arising of thoughts, which must be directly cut through. This, perhaps, is not so easy, because our suddenly arising thoughts about this and that are accompanied by some degree of obsessiveness or fascination. We prefer to be involved in thoughts because we think they may be very important or very special. We believe that the way in which we sit and think about things is endowed with incredible significance, so it is not so easy to just let go or disconnect.

Nevertheless, when training in Mahamudra, the first step is to cut through and be able to relinquish our attachment to the thought that we are involved in by thinking, 'This is a direct obstacle to the practice of Mahamudra. I will not be totally engrossed in this thought pattern. Let's just cut it right here.' This is what is meant by 'directly cutting the sudden-born.'

Here, Jamgön Kongtrül says:

> There is no point in much talk,
> But the beginner needs various things.

This means there are some techniques needed at the outset.

> One should abandon both welcoming and sending off thoughts of past and future.

This means that when we are practicing meditation, we may have thoughts of what occurred in the past, such as certain activities we were caught up in which we turn over in our mind. This is like giving past thoughts an escort to usher in the past. We should disconnect from this process. Sometimes we send out a welcoming party for future thoughts, meaning we sit and anticipate what is supposed to happen, what we will do and so forth in the future. Inviting thoughts of the future should also be avoided.

The instantaneous mind of nowness
Is the unfabricated innate nature.

What is left? The instantaneous mind of nowness, meaning the present state of mind, the present instant, which should not be altered or changed in any way whatsoever. We do not need to improve it, we do not need to worsen it. If it is empty, we do not need to fill it. If it is not empty, we do not need to try to make it empty. Just allow it to remain exactly as it is, which is the unfabricated innate nature. Simply relax and let be within that.

In meditation, there should be no trace of deliberateness.
One should not stray for an instant in confusion.

Cutting the sudden-born, meaning suddenly arising thoughts, is compared to being concentrated, or focused. On the other hand, it does not help to be too concentrated: we also need to be relaxed. So, the first instruction is to tighten while the second instruction is to loosen. In Tibetan, this instruction is called *gangshar somey,* which means 'not fabricating or modifying whatever arises.' The key point of meditation is the absence of any trace of deliberateness. This means we should not sit with the thought, 'I am engaged in this meditation. This is what I am trying to do.' Not even a trace of a deliberate act of meditation should be present.

On the other hand, there should not be any distraction either. We should not stray from the attentiveness of meditation, from mindfulness and conscientiousness, for even an instant. In other words:

Nonwandering, nonmeditation, nonfabrication are the point.
With freshness, looseness and clarity,

'Nondistraction' means 'not straying away,' 'nonmeditation' means 'not deliberately trying to do something,' and 'nonfabrication' means 'not fabricating.' These three key points are also expressed as freshness, looseness, and clarity. 'Freshness' means being concentrated in the sense of being undistracted. 'Looseness' is 'nonmeditation,' not dwelling on something deliberately. 'Clarity' is like a clear crystal that allows whatever is to just be, without trying to tamper or modify in any way whatsoever. Simply remain in that state.

In this way, the second of the three instructions in shamatha is to leave whatever arises without fabrication. This emphasizes the looseness aspect. The first instruction, 'direct cutting of the unborn,' emphasizes the tightness aspect. In other words, first concentrating, and then relaxing.

The third instruction is called 'skillful in the method of resting.' This is knowing the correct balance between tightness and looseness. Here the teaching says:

> In the space of the three gates of liberation,
> One is mindful, establishing proper watchfulness.
> Always keeping the mind balanced between tight and relaxed,
> One pacifies the accumulation of subtle, tangible and gross thoughts.
> Rest in the state of natural, unfabricated mind.

The 'three gates of liberation' are that the nature of mind lies beyond arising, dwelling, and ceasing. Within the state that is likened to space, we should place the watchman of mindfulness and conscientiousness on guard. In other words, we should be watchful and attentive in the correct way, which is not too tight or concentrated, and not too sloppy or relaxed either. The great master Brahman Saraha said:

> Just as when a Brahman spins his Brahman cord,
> Keep a balance between tight and loose.

When the cord or thread is spun, it does not turn out well if the strings are interwoven too tightly. On the other hand, if the weaving is too slack, it will not produce a nice cord either. A definite balance is needed between tight and loose. By sustaining the attention with the correct measure of balance between tight and relaxed, the multitude of very gross, tangible thoughts or very subtle thoughts will eventually utterly subside and be pacified.

The next section describes the result of the extraordinary way of practicing shamatha according to the Mahamudra system. We look into the nature of mind and rest in that unfabricated naturalness. Within the continuity of unfabricated naturalness of mind, all gross and subtle thoughts subside.

The four levels of experience arise in succession,

Through this, four stages of experience arise. The first stage is the experience likened to a mountain waterfall cascading from a steep cliff. This means that it will all of a sudden seem as though we have much more thought activity than usual. But this is not really the case. What has happened is that, for the first time, we are truly noticing how much thought activity is already present. It is like the rush of a violent mountain stream. Yet, with further practice, the experience becomes like a steady flow of a river. The third experience is like the gentle, placid surface of the ocean. The fourth experience is like an utterly clear sky. These are the four progressive experiences of shamatha.

> And the sun of luminosity continually dawns.

The 'sun of luminosity' is an example that means that the nature of mind is not like an expanse of pitch-black darkness. There is at the same time the presence of an incessantly occurring clarity. Recognizing this is what is called 'planting the root of Mahamudra realization.'

> The root of Mahamudra meditation is established.
> Without it, one's talk of higher realization
> Is like building a house without a foundation.
> However, excessive desire for this is the work of Mara.

This type of meditation experience is very important and is the foundation for further practice. But just to speak of higher realization without possessing the personal experience with both stability and clarity will not be of much benefit. It is like building a house without a foundation, which will not be stable at all. On the other hand, if we cling too much to the stability and clarity of general shamatha practice, this is the 'work of Mara,' who is a deceptive and seductive demon.

> Those who persevere, but have little knowing,
> Are deceived by superficial virtues
> And lead themselves and others along the way to the lower
>   realms.
> Even the good experiences of bliss, clarity, and nonthought
> Are the cause of samsara, if one fixates on them.

If we are extremely diligent in an ignorant attempt at meditation, without knowing much about genuine meditation practice, we can easily be deceived by Mara. We can be seduced by superficial virtues and various qualities that we feel are exceedingly great. We can lead both ourselves and others astray into the lower realms. How can this be? Through practicing shamatha, various excellent experiences arise, such as the experiences of bliss, clarity, and nonthought. Even though it is good that these experiences occur, if we cling to or fixate on them, this itself becomes a cause for further samsara.

This completes the section on shamatha. Now we have reached the section on vipashyana.

> When you intensify devotion in your heart,
> Rock meets bone in insight.
> And the ultimate lineage blessing is received.

'Devotion is the head of meditation, it is said.' To 'intensify' means to focus ardently on devotion. Through this, we will be able to receive the blessings of the true lineage — 'the ultimate lineage blessing is received.' 'Rock meets bone' is a phrase meaning 'authentic, genuine,' indicating the real state of Mahamudra is recognized through nondual awareness within our stream of being. However, this should be authentic, without any going astray or mistakeness.

> Not straying into the four strayings,
> Not falling into the three misunderstandings.
> Transcending the four joys, free from the three conditions.

'Not straying into the four strayings' means avoiding four pitfalls, which are:

— 'Misconstruing emptiness as a remedy' means that when a negative emotion arises, we extrapolate, "The essence of this emotion is emptiness," and use the thought of emptiness as an antidote.
— 'Straying as to the essence of emptiness,' means instead of seeing directly, we superimpose emptiness upon everything through deduction and reasoning.
— 'Straying as to generalized emptiness' means we plaster the label 'emptiness' on everything in a very general way.
— 'Straying on the path with regard to emptiness' means we form the thought, 'Since everything is empty, there is no result from engaging in virtue and no effect from negative deeds either.'

It is important that our experience of emptiness be free from the fault of the four strayings. Nor should we fall into the three misunderstandings or errors, which are:

— 'Emptiness arising as an enemy,' which is very similar to misconstruing the path concerning emptiness. In this case we form the strong thought that everything is empty, therefore there is no good, no evil, and no effect from practicing on the path.
— 'Compassion arising as an enemy' means we are overwhelmed by compassion for other beings, and convince ourselves that it is better to leave our practice and go out to help others, acting for the welfare of beings even though we are not really capable of doing so yet. As a result, we help neither ourselves nor others.
— 'Cause and effect arising as an enemy' means we become petrified by contemplating the result of karmic deeds, so that we are unable to do anything because we fear our actions will go wrong and the results will be terrible.

We should also transcend the four joys which refers to joy, supreme joy, special joy, and innate joy. All these result from the pranas moving through the different levels of the chakras while practicing the path of means, the Six Doctrines of Naropa. The ultimate, natural state of mind lies beyond any conditioned, temporary stage of the four joys.

We should also be free from the three conditions, which are the three experiences, mentioned above, of bliss, clarity, and nonthought. We should not defile or spoil the state of realization through attachment to those experiences.

> Realizing through the three stages of birth,
> Untouched by the mind of the three great ones.
> This is the self-existing nature, undefiled by experience.

'Realizing through the three stages of birth' means we realize or connect with the qualities through the three ways by which these qualities can take birth within our stream of being. The first is called the gradual type, meaning stage by stage from beginning to end in a progressive manner. The second is called sudden or instantaneous type, meaning all the qualities unfold at once. The third way is called the 'skipping-the-grades' type, meaning that without having to go through the steps successively, one jumps or skips to a higher level. Whichever of these three categories we may fall into, we should connect with or realize those qualities.

Realization should also be unspoiled or untouched by the mind, meaning the concepts, of the three great exaggerations. These are:

— 'Exaggeration of learning,' meaning just collecting information about the view of Mahamudra without genuinely connecting with the experience of samadhi within our stream of being. We nurture an intellectual understanding, our own version, of what the view is rather than experiencing the real thing.
— 'Exaggeration of reflection,' meaning too much reflection, speculation, and intellectualizing. We mistake our feeling of certainty about the view for the state of samadhi, itself. We develop certainty from our own speculation, which is not the true samadhi, the real introduction to the mind. We engender mistaken ideas about the pith instructions.
— 'Exaggeration of meditation,' meaning overemphasis on meditation experiences without true understanding of the view. In this, the dif-

ferent experiences that arise through meditation practice are mistaken as being the state of samadhi.

We should be free of all the above-mentioned faults, and instead experience the self-existing nature undefiled by temporary experiences.

Rather than discussing these faults, Jamgön Kongtrul describes the virtues or qualities of the state of genuine vipashyana:

> Like the center of a cloudless sky,
> The self-luminous mind is impossible to express.

'Like the center of a cloudless sky,' it is empty of any entity whatsoever: this describes the empty quality. The next line describes the luminous or cognizant quality. In the sutras there is a famous line: "It is within the domain of experience of individual self-cognizant wakefulness." This is what is meant here by 'self-luminous mind,' which cannot be expressed by any example whatsoever. Also, it lies beyond analogy.

> It is the wisdom of nonthought beyond analogy,
> Naked ordinary mind.
> Not clinging to dogmatism or arrogance,
> It is clearly seen as dharmakaya.

The 'wisdom of nonthought,' or 'nonconceptual wakefulness' is normally called 'ordinary mind' in meditators' terms. It is 'ordinary' in the sense of not being tampered with, improved or corrected in any way — just simply leaving it as it is. 'Naked' means not covered by any assumptions or temporary experiences that tend to fascinate us. Not covered by any of these, it is just the naked state of ordinary mind itself.

This is not an understanding that remains as a mere assumption. 'Dogmatism' here is our intellectualization of how the natural state is — not through actual direct experience but as the result of some information we have received or studied. We make up a version and assume that this is probably how it is. This is called 'dogmatism' or one's personal assumption of the view. Neither should it remain as 'arrogance,' a false pretense based on poorly founded experience. We just pretend to ourselves that 'this is how it is' in a rather arrogant manner.

Seeing simply and clearly as it is, is dharmakaya. Here, 'clearly seen' is a synonym for vipashyana.

> The appearance of the six sense objects, like the moon in water,
> Shines in the state of wisdom.

When directly experiencing the state of dharmakaya, clearly seeing ordinary mind, the appearances of the six sense objects occur vividly and clearly. Nothing is blocked or obstructed in any way whatsoever. Furthermore, the arising of various sense perceptions does not harm in any way whatsoever. This is what Tilopa meant when he said, 'Naropa, you are not fettered by appearances, you are fettered by attachment. So, cut your attachment!' This means that whatever appearances are perceived do not fetter, obscure or harm at all.

The problems we experience arise are due to our attachment. All the different sense perceptions are just like reflections of the moon in water. They 'shine,' or are vividly present, as the state of wisdom. When recognizing that they are nothing but empty reflections, they become the continuity of original wakefulness.

> Whatever arises is the unfabricated innate state.
> When not modified, this is the 'way things are.'
> Whatever appears is the nature of Mahamudra.
> The phenomenal world is dharmakaya great bliss.

All experience is Mahamudra. Whatever appears and exists — the phenomenal world — is dharmakaya, which refers to the empty aspect. At the same time, there is the quality of great bliss.

Within path Mahamudra, there were three points: shamatha, vipashyana, and the unity of the two. We have now covered the first two.

The Exhaustion of Conceptual Mind

We are now in the context of path Mahamudra. The two topics of shamatha and vipashyana have been covered, and we have arrived at the unity of shamatha and vipashyana. Jamgön Kongtrul says:

> Both shamatha meditation of natural resting
> And vipashyana, which sees the unseeable,
> Should not be separated but unified
> In stillness, occurrence, and awareness.

We can practice the unity of shamatha and vipashyana after we have been introduced to or had pointed-out the nature of vipashyana. Here, 'shamatha' refers to the time when we relax and rest loosely, free from involvement in thought activity. 'Seeing clearly the unseeable' means experiencing the nature of things, dharmata. This does not occur in the context of our normal mode of delineating material, concrete reality. It is seeing 'no' thing whatsoever. Shamatha and vipashyana meditation can be practiced together. In any situation, be it stillness, thought occurrence, or awareness, insight into the true nature of things, shamatha and vipashyana should be unified, not separated. This is very important.

First, we progress through the training in shamatha, then in vipashyana, and finally in the unity of the two. At that point, we are growing accustomed to the basic state of dharmata, the true nature of things. At this level, we are not enmeshed in any deluded thinking that must be abolished or abandoned.

> Beyond abandoning discursive confusion,
> Beyond applying antidotes,
> There will be a time when you spontaneously reach this.

It is beyond antidote, as we do not need to accomplish the basic state of Mahamudra by involving ourselves in some remedy of spiritual practice to counteract confusion. There will come a time when we will spontaneously arrive at or fully realize the natural state of dharmata, the nature of things.

We have now covered the topics of how to train in shamatha, vipashyana and the unity of the two. By applying path Mahamudra, we will obtain the fruition. According to the general system of Buddhadharma, fruition is reached by means of gradually progressing through the five paths and the ten bhumis, through the path of accumulation, the path of joining, the path of seeing, the path of cultivation, and finally through the final fruition, the path beyond training, also called the path of consummation. From the very first bhumi, which is the attainment of the 'path of seeing,' until the tenth bhumi, a progressive attainment of fruition occurs.

The extraordinary system of Mahamudra includes the Four Yogas of One-Pointedness, Simplicity, One Taste, and Nonmeditation. These are sometimes called 'the twelve segments of the path of Mahamudra,' or 'the twelve of the four times three,' meaning that each of the four yogas is divided into three steps, making twelve steps altogether. This is explained further on in the song. In terms of the practitioner, Mahamudra is explained first in a detailed way and is then summarized.

> When you have achieved realization,
> There is nothing other than the meditative state.
> At the threshold of freedom from loss and gain,
> Even meditation does not exist.

It is explained one way for the beginner approaching meditation, but there is also the basic state of the way it really is, the natural state. That is, once we have achieved realization, or stability in the unity of shamatha and vipashyana and Mahamudra, then everything becomes the meditation state. Having captured the freshness, the natural state of realization, there is nothing that is excluded from this state of meditation. At this point, we need not abandon one thing and achieve something other than realizing the natural state as it is. It can also be said that at this point there is no meditation whatsoever, because there is no meditation object and no act of holding any object in mind.

> But for those beginners, who are unable to dissolve the hairline of conceptualization,

Meditation is important.
When one practices meditation, there is experience.
This experience arises as the adornment of insight.

However, for a novice who still has the 'hairline of conceptualization' — referring to discursive thinking — conceptual thinking has not yet dissolved. In this case, training in meditation is extremely crucial. Why is this so important? Because when we engage in meditation training, it is possible to gain experience of the naked state of awareness, unadorned insight. Having experienced this, progress on the path is made possible. Progressing on the path, we will gradually journey through the four stages of Mahamudra called One-Pointedness, Simplicity, One Taste, and Nonmeditation. These four divisions of the path will be explained now.

This path is divided into the four yogas:
One-Pointedness means recognizing the nature of mind;

The first of these four, One-Pointedness, has a definite onset or dividing line by which we can say that now 'One-Pointedness' has begun. The boundary of One-Pointedness is when we recognize the 'natural face' or the nature of mind. The moment of recognizing the nature of mind marks the onset of One-Pointedness.

Divided into the lesser, medium, and greater stages:
One sees the alternation of bliss and luminosity,
One masters resting in samadhi,
And experience continuously appears as luminosity.

It is divided into three progressive stages, called the lesser, medium, and greater stages of One-Pointedness. The 'lesser stage' is described here as 'seeing the alternation of bliss and luminosity.' This means that sometimes there is the experience of bliss and sometimes there is not. Sometimes there is the experience of clarity, or luminosity, and sometimes not. It fluctuates, switching on and off. This characterizes the lesser stage of One-Pointedness.

The 'medium stage' is characterized by having gained some independent power over the state of samadhi. According to our choice, we can master resting or not resting in samadhi. The 'greater stage of One-Pointedness' occurs when experience continuously appears as luminosity.

> Simplicity means realizing the mind is without root;
> Divided into the lesser, medium, and greater stages:

After this is Simplicity, which literally means 'absence of thought constructs.' When do we arrive at Simplicity? At the time of realizing that mind is rootless, baseless, and empty. This yoga also has three levels: lesser, medium and greater Simplicity.

> One realizes that the arising, ceasing and dwelling are empty;
> One is free from the ground and root of fixating on appearance and emptiness;
> And one resolves the complexity of all dharmas.

In the 'lesser stage,' 'one realizes that the arising, ceasing, and dwelling are empty,' meaning that there is no self-entity and that the mind is utterly rootless and baseless. The 'medium stage' involves realizing that the notion of perceiving appearance, as well as the notion of perceiving emptiness, are both rootless and baseless. The 'greater stage of Simplicity' is 'to resolve the complexity of all dharmas,' to cut through erroneous notions about all phenomena.

> One Taste means dissolving appearance and mind into each other;
> Divided into the lesser, medium and greater stages:

After Simplicity is the stage of One Taste. The starting point of One Taste is 'dissolving appearance and mind into each other,' which means external appearance dissolves into the mind within. In other words, subject and object — the perceived and the perceiver — are no longer apprehended as being two different, distinct entities. Rather, they intermingle, being of one nature or 'One Taste.' That is the beginning of the experience of the samadhi called One Taste.

> All dharmas of samsara and nirvana are dissolved into equal
> taste.
> Appearance and mind become like water poured into water.
> And from one taste, the various wisdoms arise.

At the medium level, appearance and mind are no longer seen as distinct but intermingle like water poured into water. The greater level is that, although everything is one taste, the practitioner does not become stupid and unable to distinguish one thing from another. Rather, he or she possess discriminating wisdom, which is the wakefulness that sees all distinctions very clearly and individually. This arises in all kinds of different ways.

> Nonmeditation means the utter exhaustion of conceptual mind;
> Divided into the lesser, medium, and greater stages:

The fourth yoga is called Nonmeditation and it begins with the utter exhaustion of conceptual mind. Here, 'conceptual mind' means the unaware, ignorant aspect of consciousness which apprehends or experiences in terms of the duality of perceiver and perceived. When such grasping is utterly exhausted, this marks the onset of Nonmeditation. This also has the three stages of lesser, medium, and greater.

> One is free from meditator and meditation,
> The habitual pattern of primitive beliefs about reality are
> gradually cleared away,
> And the mother and son luminosity dissolve together.

At the lesser level, the practitioner is freed from meditation and meditator. The duality of training ceases. The medium level is that the tendency for the two obscurations, cognition and disturbing emotions, is gradually purified. When this happens, the mother and son luminosities dissolve together. These mother and son luminosities are also known as the luminosity of the ground and the luminosity of the path. Although the ground luminosity or mother luminosity is always present as our basic nature, it is not actualized or realized due to being veiled by the cognitive obscuration. But when the son luminosity or the luminosity of the path, which is our individual experience of the basic nature, is trained in through recognition, then the cognitive obscuration is purified. That is the intermingling of the mother and son luminosities. When this final stage is reached, it is said:

> The wisdom of dharmadhatu extends throughout space.

There is no longer any interruption or division in awareness: it is utterly unceasing.

This was a detailed explanation of the four yogas with their twelve aspects. What follows is a summary.

The great master Shang Tsalpa once said: "Mahamudra training is the sudden path, and it is delusion to divide it up into different stages." This is perfectly all right when speaking of the basic meditation state itself, which is indivisible. But when applying or describing our experience, all the great masters of the past have described it as a progressive path of individual stages, such as the twelve aspects of the four yogas. In *Moonlight of Mahamudra* by the great master Dakpo Tashi Namgyal, the path of Mahamudra is combined with the general system of the path and bhumis according to the general system. In this work, it is said the stage of One-Pointedness covers the path of accumulation up until the path of seeing. The song says:

> In short, in meditation:
> One-Pointedness means that the mind is still as long as one wishes.

The 'path of accumulation' is the stage of accumulating a vast amount of merit. The second of the five paths, the 'path of joining,' is what corresponds to One-Pointedness. The third path, the 'path of seeing,' corresponds to Simplicity. This is also the attainment of the first bhumi, called the Truly Joyous. This is the direct seeing of the true nature of mind and all phenomena. After this is the 'path of cultivation.' That which is experienced directly at the first bhumi is cultivated and trained in. Therefore, this is called the stage of One Taste. It covers from the second bhumi up to and including the seventh of the ten bhumis. These are called the 'seven impure levels.'

The song says:

> Seeing the very nature of ordinary mind,
> Simplicity means the realization of groundlessness.
> One Taste means liberating all possible dualistic fixations
> through insight.
> Nonmeditation means transcending all sophistries of meditation
> and nonmeditation,
> The exhaustion of habitual patterns.

The lesser and medium stages of Nonmeditation coincide with the final three of the ten bhumis, which are called the 'three pure levels.' The greater stage of Nonmeditation refers to complete enlightenment, the 'dharmakaya throne of nonmeditation.' At this point all notions or sophistries of meditation and nonmeditation, training or not training, are utterly transcended. This is the 'exhaustion of habitual patterns' in which the obscuration of disturbing emotions as well as the cognitive obscuration are entirely exhausted. This is called Nonmeditation.

> In this way, from the great lords of yogins,
> Naropa and Maitripa,
> Down to the lord guru, Padma Wangchen,
> The golden garland of the Kagyüs
> Reached the dharmakaya kingdom of nonmeditation …

All the lords of yogins, such as Naropa and Maitripa and so forth, down to and including Jamgön Kongtrül's own root guru, Padma Nyinche Wangchen, as well as all the 'golden garland of Kagyü gurus,' reached complete realization of Mahamudra, called the dharmakaya kingdom of nonmeditation, at the stage of Nonmeditation.

What are the qualities of realizing Mahamudra and reaching the stage of Nonmeditation? It is the same as the state of complete awakening to buddhahood that is described as endowed with the two qualities: abandonment and realization. With the quality of abandonment, the two obscurations are utterly cleared away: the obscuration of disturbing emotions and the cognitive obscuration. Here, the song says:

> Spontaneously cleared away the darkness of the two
>   obscurations
> Expanded the great power of the two knowledges,

The 'two knowledges' refer to the quality of realization in which the two knowledges fully unfold — the wisdom of seeing the nature as it is, and the wisdom that perceives all existing things.

> Opened the treasury of benefit for the sake of others pervading
>   space,
> And remained in the refuge of mind free from doubt.

'Free from doubt' means their disciples need not harbor any doubts about their spiritual level, the attainment of complete enlightenment.

> The Kagyü lineage is known to be passed from one to another.
> It is not known by words alone, but by their meaning.

This lineage has been transmitted from master to disciple uninterruptedly to the present time. Whether we call the lineage-holders who have secured realization of the awakened state buddhas or mahasiddhas, these are not just names. In actuality, they really achieved this, and it is 'known not by words alone, but by their meaning.'

> Please guide even such a lowborn savage as myself,
> Who possesses the merest mark of your noble lineage,
> Quickly to the kingdom of nonmeditation.

In these four lines Jamgön Kongtrül, describes himself as nothing but a savage, meaning someone full of disturbing emotions, completely lazy and so forth. He asks for blessings to be bestowed that he may progress through the four stages of Mahamudra and quickly reach the kingdom of nonmeditation. He says:

> Kind One, please utterly exhaust my conceptual mind.

Now, we have come to fruition Mahamudra. First, a summary is made in three lines mentioning the ground, path and fruition.

> The fruition Mahamudra is spoken of like this:
> The ground is receiving the transmission of the innate trikaya.

'Receiving the transmission' means in actuality recognizing our essence to be empty, its nature to be cognizant and its capacity to be the unobstructed play of experience. These are the dharmakaya, sambhogakaya, and nirmanakaya that are innate as the ground.

> The path is applying the key points of the view and meditation;
> The fruition is the actualization of the stainless trikaya.

Having recognized the view, to apply the key points in a correct and authentic way becomes the path. Fruition is the realization or actualization of the immaculate three kayas.

> Therefore, its essence is emptiness, simplicity, dharmakaya.
> Its manifestation is the luminous nature of sambhogakaya.
> Its strength, manifold and unceasing, is nirmanakaya.

Again, these three lines refer to what is in Tibetan, called *shi, dang,* and *tsal,* which correspond to the three kayas. The shi, essence, is empty, beyond constructs, simplicity, the dharmakaya itself. At the same time as being empty, it also has the quality of cognizance, here called 'manifestation.' The luminous nature, or dang, is the sambhogakaya.

How it expresses itself, its tsal, 'strength,' is unobstructed, manifold and unceasing. This is the nirmanakaya.

The next six lines describe the state of fruition as being the indivisible nature of space and wisdom. Space corresponds to dharmadhatu, which emphasizes the empty aspect, while wisdom emphasizes the quality of luminosity, or the cognizant capacity. These two are indivisible. The text says:

> This is the sovereign of all reality.
> The nature of Mahamudra is unity,
> The realm of dharmas free from accepting and rejecting.

The 'realm of dharmas' refers to the dharmadhatu, the empty quality. But, at the same time as being utterly empty, meaning devoid of any entity whatsoever, it is not completely nonexistent, like the hair on a tortoise or the son of a barren woman, but possesses the quality of wisdom, or cognizance. It is also described as:

> Possessing the beauty of unconditioned bliss,
> It is the great and vast wealth of wisdom.
> It is the natural form of kindness transcending thought.

This undefiled bliss or tranquillity is present as well as the great wealth of wisdom. This unity is what expresses itself naturally in inconceivable forms of compassion.

The nature of mind is not something that needs to be affirmed or denied. In the context of the progressive stages of meditation of the Mahamudra system it is taught that the nature of mind, which is spontaneously present is naturally liberated. It does not matter whether or not we emphasize the empty aspect according to Rangtong or the wisdom aspect according to Shentong: space and wisdom are indivisible in essence. The indivisibility of space and wisdom cannot be indicated by any example and cannot be described by any words. The nature of mind, the truth of dharmata, is realized by means of the individual's naturally cognizant wakefulness. If we try to establish it through the power of mind, saying 'the nature of mind is this, it is emptiness,' we miss the point. If by using conceptual mind we say 'it isn't such-and-such,' that is also incorrect and we will not be able to realize the nature of mind. Intellectual mind is ignorant in nature; it cannot investigate or fathom the inconceivable beyond concepts that is dharmata. The state of fruition Mahamudra, or the complete and perfect awakened state of buddhahood, is described as transcending both existence and peace, meaning samsaric existence and nirvanic peace. There is no dwelling in the three realms of samsaric existence, nor is there any abiding in the passive peace of nirvana.

In the general Buddhadharma system we must gather a tremendous accumulation of merit through three incalculable aeons in order to awaken to true and perfect buddhahood. But by means of the path of Mahamudra, it is possible to accomplish this in one body and one lifetime. So, what is the quality of this twofold nondwelling that was just mentioned? The song says:

> Through prajna, it does not dwell in samsara.
> Through karuna, it does not dwell in nirvana.
> Through effortlessness, buddha activity is spontaneously accomplished.

'Through prajna' means 'by knowing or realizing' the natural state of Mahamudra, the nature of things as they are, there is no basis for dwelling in samsaric existence. The basis is utterly eliminated. On the other hand, we do not, as in the case of a shravaka or pratyekabuddha, dwell in the passive state of nirvanic peace either. Out of great compassion for all sentient beings who have not realized the natural state of Mahamudra, we do not linger in the state of peace. Through the unity of prajna and karuna, meaning knowledge and compassion, we effortlessly act for the welfare of all sentient beings in a way that is utterly spontaneous.

> The luminosity of ground and path, mother and son, dissolve together.

The state of ground luminosity, which is the basic nature of luminosity, is of course always present as the very nature of things. However, by means of path luminosity, meaning the experience of shamatha, vipashyana, and their unity, ground luminosity is actualized. At the point of fruition, the luminosities of ground and path, mother and son, dissolve together and become an indivisible unity. Moreover:

> The ground and fruition embrace one another.

This means there is no longer any dividing-line between how things are and the realization of such, which is fruition. In this way, there is no expectation of finding the Buddha, meaning the awakened state, elsewhere than in our own mind.

> Buddha is discovered in one's mind
> The wish-fulfilling treasure overflows within.
> E ma! How wonderful and marvelous!

In this way, whatever we might wish for and require, here likened to a treasure mine, is not found outside but overflows from within. This is most wonderful and marvelous. This completes the description of fruition Mahamudra.

Now we have arrived at a summary of view, meditation, action, and fruition. The first line of this verse says:

> Since in the view of Mahamudra
> Analysis does not apply,

The 'view of Mahamudra' means we simply recognize the nature of things as it is, rather than forming our own speculative opinion or assumption about 'how it is' or 'how it isn't.' As this kind of thinking does not really apply, Jamgön Kongtrül says:

> Cast mind-made knowledge far away.
> Any self-made version of how the view of the natural state is should be thrown away.

Regarding the meditation, the song says:

> Since in the meditation of Mahamudra,
> There is no way of fixating on a thought,

This means we should not hold onto our own fixed idea about how the natural state is. The term 'natural state' implies 'as it is,' by itself. We should simply rest in how it is, without fabricating some intellectual understanding or conviction about it. The song goes on to say:

> Abandon deliberate meditation.
> Since in the action of Mahamudra,
> There is no reference point for any action,

This means we do not need to perform any particular action in order to achieve or realize the natural state of Mahamudra, such as avoiding one thing and adopting something else. Rather:

Be free from the intention to act or not.

> Since in the fruition of Mahamudra
> There is no attainment to newly acquire,
> Cast hopes, fears and desires far away.

'Fruition of Mahamudra' is the realization of the basic state that is already present. It is not some achievement that is new or unprecedented. Therefore, there is no need for any fear of not accomplishing, nor any desire, ambition or expectation to achieve something. Simply cast all this away.

Now, Jamgön Kongtrül describes the special, unique quality of the Kagyü Lineage. This is the ground, path, and fruition of Mahamudra, or alternately stated, the view, meditation, action, and fruition of Mahamudra. Referring to the realization of all the Kagyü masters, he says:

This is the depth of the mind of all Kagyüs.
It is the only path on which the victorious ones and their sons journey.

Traveling this path leads away from samsaric existence to the fully awakened state. This path is exactly the path of Mahamudra.

Theirs is the upaya that reverses the vicious circle of existence
And the Dharma that brings enlightenment in one life.
Here is the essence of all the teachings, sutras, and tantras.

By cutting the very root of samsara, it is also the method, or upaya that destroys the magical machinery of samsaric existence. It is the teaching through which we can attain buddhahood in this very lifetime. It is the quintessence of all the Words of the Buddha, including the extensive sutras and the profound tantras.

Jamgön Kongtrül concludes with the wish:

May I and all sentient beings pervading space
Together attain the simultaneity of realization and liberation,
And attain supreme Mahamudra.

This completes the explanation on *The Song of Lodrö Thaye.*

Are there any questions?

STUDENT: Yesterday you spoke about blessings. I don't understand how blessings seem to come in so many unexpected forms. Would you talk about the various ways in which the guru blesses the disciple?

RINPOCHE: Because of our faith and devotion, it is possible for blessings to appear in different forms. Unusual experiences such as an appearance of light are probably also blessings, but let's ask ourselves, "What are true, genuine blessings?" True blessings are realization, the genuine insight that takes birth within our personal experience of the correct meditation state itself. When our ability to correctly train in meditation becomes familiar and stable, we personally experience the insight of realization that is called the 'authentic blessings.' Other experiences, like lights and different visions and so forth, are called 'blessings,' but are more ordinary, common blessings.

It is often said that the sign of learning and studying is to be gentle and disciplined, while the sign of meditation practice is to have fewer disturbing emotions. Here, 'learning' or 'studying' does not refer to accumulating trivial, mundane information. It is 'learning' in the sense of absorbing the meaning of the words of the Buddha and of the explanations of what the Buddha said. All these Dharma teachings are really concerned with just one thing — how to eliminate our faults and how to realize virtue. Studying how to do that will ensure a thorough understanding of the negative characteristics of pride, jealousy, anger, desire, and stupidity. When we become less and less involved in these and grow more and more gentle and disciplined, this is the sign of learning.

Here, 'meditation' means 'training.' When meditating, what is it that we train in? We train in the natural state of all things, in the natural state of mind. Why do we do this? Because we want to eliminate the negative effect of disturbing emotions. By training in the natural state, we are able to uproot disturbing emotions. That is why it is said that the sign of practice, meaning meditation, is to have fewer disturbing emotions.

On the other hand, disturbing emotions cannot be kicked out all at once so that presto, we are free of them. We have been wandering throughout samsaric existence for countless lifetimes — since time without beginning. Therefore, disturbing emotions and their shortcomings cannot just be switched off and done away with. If we try our best and are not instantaneously successful in being free of all disturbing emotions forever, there is no reason why we should become completely depressed and frustrated. Whatever energy we put into practice is never wasted. Even if we are not 100 percent successful, still, the practice we do and the opportunity to be able to practice and know how to practice is in itself an incredibly great fortune and is not wasted at all.

STUDENT: You mentioned the Six Doctrines of Naropa. Maybe I have a misunderstanding but I thought a person needed to practice the Six Doctrines a little bit before he or she could be introduced to Mahamudra. Perhaps that is incorrect?

Rinpoche: In the Kagyü lineage, there are two great teachings passed down through the tradition. One is called the path of means, which is the Six Doctrines of Naropa; the other is called the path of liberation, which is Mahamudra.

There are some people who are unable to simply recognize the state of simplicity. Even if they do recognize the nature of mind, or the view of Mahamudra, they are not able to progress in this. Such people practice the 'path of means,' which in terms of the development stage, involves the preliminaries and the yidam practices. In terms of the completion stage, it involves the Six Doctrines of Naropa. This path of means greatly helps the practitioner to recognize the nature of mind and stabilize the recognition. If one has already achieved recognition, these practices nurture the progress and enhance the insight of realization.

On the other hand, there are some people who are unable to practice the Six Doctrines of Naropa or may not be very interested in pursuing them. At the same time, they are able to recognize the view of Mahamudra. By means of shamatha and vipashyana, they are able to recognize the correct view within their meditation training and progress, even without having to engage in the completion stage practices with characteristics of the path of means, such as the Six Doctrines. Nevertheless, in order to progress further, they can be benefited by engaging in the practices of the Six Doctrines later on.

Sometimes people begin by practicing the Six Doctrines and then enhance that with Mahamudra. Sometimes people will start out with the view of Mahamudra and enhance that by means of the Six Doctrines. Either is fine. There is no fixed, categorical way of proceeding. What is indispensable is to give rise to the unique, genuine realization within our stream of being. Exactly how we proceed to attain this is of lesser importance.

Student: Here in this song, Jamgön Kongtrül describes the recognition of one's own nature, and later the progression to 'seeing dharmakaya.' What is the difference between recognizing one's nature and the 'seeing of dharmakaya?'

Rinpoche: According to the general system of teachings, it is impossible to immediately realize the true nature of things. It is said that there are five stages of path. The first is called the path of accumulation, because, in order to approach realization of the nature of things, we need to gather a tremendous accumulation of merit. We then try to meditate and gain some experience. Whether or not we are successful, we at least try to practice meditation in order to come closer to realization. This period is called the path of joining. When we directly see the nature of things, or dharmata, the nature of mind, this is called the path of seeing, which is traditionally the attainment of the first bhumi. In terms of Mahamudra, this is called 'recognizing the nature of mind,' or 'recognizing the natural state of Mahamudra.' Often, you hear people say they have had a flash or glimpse of Mahamudra, like the sun shining through a gap in the clouds. Having a glimpse of or recognizing the correct view of the natural state of Mahamudra is not itself sufficient. The mere glimpse or short moment of Mahamudra must become continuous and complete. We must arrive at the stage where there is no distraction or straying from this state. It must be totally unceasing and all-encompassing.

Having recognized the nature of mind, we need to train in this. This training is called the path of cultivation. We train again and again, progressing further and further, so that the meditation state becomes clearer and clearer and more and more stable. Finally, we arrive at the stage where realization is uninterrupted and has become continuous and all-encompassing. This is called the path beyond training, and at this point there is no more straying. It is the complete and perfect realization of dharmakaya, also called the dharmakaya throne of nonmeditation.

STUDENT: Rinpoche, could you talk a little bit about the relationship between the four empowerments of Vajrayana? In particular, could you say something more about the wisdom of example empowerment in its relationship to ultimate Mahamudra, the fourth empowerment?

RINPOCHE: The four empowerments are known as the vase empowerment, secret empowerment, wisdom-knowledge empowerment, and precious word empowerment. The first, the vase empowerment, usually has five aspects called the five knowledge empowerments, meaning the empowerments for the buddhas of the five families — one each for

Vairochana, Akshobhya, Ratnasambhava, Amitabha, and Amoghasiddhi. By receiving these five knowledge empowerments, we are authorized to practice the development stage. It also serves as an aid to realizing the pure nature of the five disturbing emotions as being the five wisdoms, the five aspects of original wakefulness. This is called the 'body empowerment of the vase' by which we are bequeathed with the legacy to realize the nirmanakaya, the enlightened Body.

Next is the empowerment of speech, the secret empowerment. This second empowerment is given in order to realize sambhogakaya. Just as the voice is more subtle than the physical body, this second empowerment is more subtle than the first. When we receive the consecrated nectar on our tongue, we are empowered by means of its taste to realize the pure nature of the nadis, pranas, and bindus, meaning the channels, energies, and essences. We are empowered to realize the sambhogakaya state.

Next is the empowerment of mind, which is the wisdom-knowledge empowerment. The 'example wisdom' is pointed out, and often given by means of the symbolic smear of sindhura powder on a mirror. The 'wisdom of example' is almost the direct realization of the innate nature of things, of dharmata. However, it is more the flavor of it. We are given the taste of the ultimate state of wisdom, experienced by means of an intellectual deduction, so that we get an approximate though clear feeling of what the ultimate state really is. This is called the 'example wisdom.'

When the ultimate natural state of Mahamudra is pointed out by means of the fourth, or 'precious word,' empowerment, this is the introduction to the unchanging nature itself — the ultimate state of Mahamudra.

STUDENT: I have heard about 'nonthought in the midst of discursive thought.' Could Rinpoche clarify this? Are they like the two sides of a hand or the two sides of the same coin? Can they happen simultaneously, or is there a break?

RINPOCHE: 'Simultaneous' can be understood in two different ways: either on a very subtle level or in a more general way. If we speak in terms of a series of moments or instances of fractions of time — the subtle impermanence of things — then, in the context of discursive thought and nonthought, the word 'simultaneous' should not be applied in this way. When we are involved in thinking of something, this does not occur in a single instant, but takes place in a series of instances that we group together as the arising and disappearing of a single thought. A thought is not just one single moment. During that stretch of time that we call one thought, it is possible to realize nonthought. It does not usually happen in the beginning of thinking of something, but closer to the end of thinking about it. At that instant it is possible to realize the nature and then rest in that. Hence, the statement 'within discursive thought, I discovered nonthought.' They are not really simultaneous.

STUDENT: Is prajnaparamita the same as the nature of mind? Is it the basis of both samsara and nirvana?

RINPOCHE: Prajnaparamita, transcendent knowledge, is identical with the essence of mind. However, it is not the basis or source of samsara because samsara is formed out of unknowing, out of ignorance. Transcendent knowledge is not the cause of unknowing. At the same time, we can say that samsara takes place within the expanse, or space, of the innate nature of dharmata, because samsaric states of experience do not exist anywhere other than or apart from the expanse of the nature of things.

For example, based on the 'ground' of knowing the alphabet, we can acquire knowledge of a tremendous number of topics. If we do not know the alphabet, it is extremely difficult to become learned or truly educated. On the other hand, is the alphabet the cause of our being uneducated? No, it is not. It is the not knowing of the alphabet that is the basis for being uneducated, not the alphabet itself.

STUDENT: If we recognize innate wakefulness, do we still have to travel the path of the ten bhumis? If so, must we do that in one lifetime?

RINPOCHE: Do we have to? (Laughter) Yes, to arrive at complete enlightenment we need to go through the path, which in the general system of Dharma, is divided into five paths and ten bhumis. We do indeed need to cover that mileage in order to arrive at buddhahood, there is no way around that. But if you possess the extraordinary methods and have great diligence, then definitely this can occur in a single lifetime. Still, you would need to traverse the path very quickly. Take the analogy of traveling home: You can go by boat, which maybe takes a couple of months, or you can fly in a few hours. However, you will not just spontaneously arrive there without covering the full distance. You have to journey over that distance. Whether you do it slowly or quickly is up to you, right?

STUDENT: Since Tibetan Buddhism has spread to the West, do you have a rough idea, very, very rough, whether or not any — and if so how many — Westerners have attained enlightenment? (Laughter)

RINPOCHE: (Laughing) On one hand, it is only a very short time since Buddhism went to the West. On the other hand, quite a number of years have gone by now since the Dharma became accessible, so why not? But I don't personally know how many there are or if there are any. Why? Because I am not clairvoyant.

STUDENT: At the time of practicing the yoga of One-Pointedness, especially at the time of practicing directly cutting sudden arising, what approach should one take to appearances of the five sense objects?

RINPOCHE: We need not do anything about the five sense consciousnesses or sense perceptions. In and of themselves, they are nonconceptual, meaning the arising of hearing, seeing, smelling, tasting, and touching are just like reflections in a mirror, without any accompanying concepts or intrinsic value whatsoever. Therefore, they can be left just as they are. As Tilopa said, "You are not fettered by the way you experience, but by your attachment to it."

We as practitioners practice the direct cutting of sudden arising at the time of One-Pointedness. This occurs at the level of the sixth consciousness, or mental consciousness, which is conceptual. It forms all notions, such as conceptualizing 'this is good, that is bad,' or 'this should be accepted, that should be rejected,' and so forth. This is what must be cut. Based upon the concepts of this sixth mental consciousness, we become entangled within disturbing emotions and distraction.

Let us conclude with dedicating the merit of my teaching Naropa's and Jamgön Kongtrül's *Songs of True Accomplishment* as well as your listening and practicing, towards the happiness and well-being of all sentient beings, towards peace and prosperity in the world, and towards pacifying the causes of war, disease, and hunger, represented by desire, aggression and stupidity.

Acknowledgements

Songs of True Accomplishment is a reconfiguring of two former books, *Songs of Naropa* and *The King of Samadhi.* The previous books came about due to our gracious and skilled, Dharma friends. Without them, it could not have come into existence. We are indebted to S. Lhamo, Michael Tweed, Ian Saude, and Marilyn Jones for the time and energy they donated to transcribing, to Patrick Sweeney for sponsorship, to Kerry Moran for editing, to Michael Tweed for editing the initial versions of Naropa's songs, to the earlier proofreaders Shirley Blair and Gloria Jones. Always gratitude goes to Gloria for her continued support.

Many thanks to Shambhala Publications for permission to use *The Song of Lodrö Thaye,* which is from *The Rain of Wisdom,* translated by The Nalanda Translation Committee under the direction of Chögyam Trungpa.

This new incarnation of *Songs of True Acomplishment* was proofread by Peter Sage and Deidre Goldberg and typeset by Joan Olson.

May this effort hasten the swift rebirth of Khenchen Thrangu Rinpoche and help immeasurable beings reach fruition on the path of Mahamudra.

www.ingramcontent.com/pod-product-compliance
Lightning Source LLC
Jackson TN
JSHW020302160625
85831JS00001B/1

* 9 7 9 8 9 9 1 7 2 5 0 0 2 *